EVERYTHING YOU KNOW
IS
WRONG

EVERYTHING YOU KNOW
IS
WRONG

BOOK ONE: HUMAN ORIGINS

▼

Lloyd Pye

▲

Authors Choice Press

San Jose New York Lincoln Shanghai

Everything You Know is Wrong
Book One: Human Origins

Authors Choice Press
an imprint of iUniverse.com, Inc.

For information address:
iUniverse.com, Inc.
620 North 48th Street, Suite 201
Lincoln, NE 68504-3467
www.iuniverse.com

Originally published by Adamu Press

ISBN: 0-595-12749-5

Printed in the United States of America

DEDICATION

To my parents, of course;

and to all members of
the Invisible College

ACKNOWLEDGMENTS

No project of this size and duration can be completed without a great deal of help along the way. Therefore, I must sincerely thank the following people, all of whom have provided me with either technical advice, critical feedback, emotional support, or financial assistance: Dr. Lloyd A. Pye, Sr. and Nina Pye, Jonathan Pye, Evie L. Pye, Thomas Wilfred Pye, Susan (Pye) Stone, Bob and Susan Dawson, Col. Jim Spring, Weldon Russell, Carolyn Mistoler, Joe Eddy Anzalone, Paul Arnold, Robert Aulicino, Karren Baugh, Joanna Broussard, Coach Dale Brown, William E. (Bill) Brown, David Carter, Fred Carpenter, John Cogswell, Teresa Campos-Coelho, Charles Cabler, Dr. Larry Fambrough, Don Galias, Germaine Galjour, Debbie (Westall) Garcia, John Graham, Logan Guess, Harvey Hagman, Dr. Madelaine Hedgepeth, Mark and Debbie Herlyn, Cynthia Hutchinson, Larry Jacobson, Bud Johnson, Shirley Leong, Mike MacNees, Ron and Marion Marcotte, Mary Mocsary, Melissa Moore, David de Neufville, Susan Norris, Greg Purdy, Ken Redler, William T. "Boogie" Roberts, Bob Roesler, Bob Rue, Zecharia Sitchin, Bruce Stewart, Mike Sharp, Marie Sheffield, Phyllis Simpson, Dr. Butch Sonnier, Carmen Sunda, Nat and Francis Toulon, Bob Vickrey, Katie Wainwright, Jim Williams, Bruce Young, Kay Young, and those who prefer to remain anonymous. You know who you are.

PREFACE

This book consists of four Parts, I and II of which are relatively short, while III and IV are both twice the length of I and II combined. If you have heard about the sensational aspects of the latter two parts, do not succumb to the temptation to go straight to them. If ever a book was constructed to be read from first page to last, this is it. Though the latter parts are indeed sensational, they are much more so if read after absorbing the basic information provided in Parts I and II.

***

As for the "Invisible College" mentioned in the dedication, its original "student body" was comprised of the first (1950's) UFO researchers, who labored in quiet obscurity for nearly two decades before gathering enough evidence to override constant official denials and make UFO's understandable and acceptable to a majority of people worldwide.

Now a similarly controversial subject—how humans came to be on Earth—is being studied by a scattered group of iconoclasts quietly pursuing their "post-graduate" work in a different part of the Invisible College. This book is designed to be a basic text for that unsanctioned course of study, and to help current "students" enroll their friends and acquaintances.

INTRODUCTION

This book is about life on Earth, how it came to be here and how it has progressed from that point forward. On opposite sides of the issue are two main groups: Darwinists and Creationists. Darwinists believe life is explainable as an ongoing process that began in utter simplicity and steadily proceeds toward increasing complexity. Creationists believe a Supreme Being was divinely inspired to create all life whole and complete, with no alterations or addendums since the original effort brought it all forth. Naturally, Darwinists are quick to point out that alterations and addendums are an easily detectable fact of life, while Creationists are equally quick to note that evidence for a gradual progression of life forms from simple to complex is dubious at best. This leaves the two sides at loggerheads, fueled with enough facts to prove their opponent is at least partially wrong, but not possessing enough proof to establish their own case beyond doubt.

Accepting that both sides have serious holes in their arguments, it seems logical to seek a better understanding of life's processes somewhere in the large swath of middle ground between the current entrenched positions. That is what this book attempts to accomplish, the staking out of a defensible position in the terra incognita beween the Darwinists and Creationists. Of course, such a contentious objective will strike many as hopelessly quixotic because to question Darwinism is to doubt the collective wisdom of the entire scientific community, while to question Creationism is to defy the teachings of every major organized religion. To dispute both groups simultaneously is even more quixotic, and will strike others as a senseless act of deranged lunacy.

Deranged or not, lunacy or not, this book is filled with fact-based propositions and logical suppositions that will convince many readers of its veracity, while others will disagree, some quite strongly. That is usually the case when radical ideas are presented for public examination. But no matter how you have come to this book, whether as a Darwinist, a Creationist, or an "agnostic" without a firm opinion, it will forever change how you view the origin and progression of life on Earth. You may even end up reevaluating your own place in that grand, glorious scheme.

TABLE OF CONTENTS

PART III: HOMINOIDS

PART IV: THE TRUTH?

PART I

LIFE ON EARTH

INTRODUCTION

This book's title is clearly a misnomer because certain facts are undeniable: 2 + 2 = 4, the sky is blue, etc. However, in a universe filled with dark matter and black holes, event horizons and parallel dimensions, singularity and relative time, it is hard to know what is real, much less true beyond doubt. So *Everything You Know Is Wrong* might well be more to the point than *Many Important Things You Think You Know About The World Are Serious Misconceptions*.

Title aside, this book deals with some of the most fundamental issues of human concern: What is life? How did it come to be on Earth? What is humanity? How did we become such an unusual species, so incredibly different from everything else? And underlying all that: *Why* are we here? This cartoon expresses it perfectly:

1

Fig. 1. (© Patrick Hardin)

Many people (especially scientists) believe life on Earth has been well accounted for since 1859, when Charles Darwin's *The Origin Of Species* suggested it was the result of gradual transitions among and between species. Darwin's theory postulated that simple forms developed into more complex forms by incremental, ever-ascending spirals of improvement generated by survival pressures inherent in any environment. That concept hit like a bombshell in a world that until then had looked only to religion for secular guidance and wisdom.

Until the mid-1800's ignorance and superstition had been the bedrock of cultures around the world, so it was relatively easy for the abstract mysticism of religion to hold sway. But education of the masses was making inroads everywhere, replacing ignorance and superstition with knowledge and rationalism. Enlightened individuals were coming to realize that life's profound questions were being plausibly answered by the naturalism of science, which made religion's entrenched orthodoxy ripe for overthrow. Darwin's theory of "natural selection" provided the means to supplant it.

Inevitably, such a profound societal power shift will cause hard feelings. Darwin's supporters and detractors battled toe-to-toe until 1925, when a Tennessee teacher named John Scopes agreed to be the point man for an attempt to settle the debate once and for all. In defiance of his state's laws against teaching "evolution"—as natural selection came to be known—he admitted doing so and was arrested.

The subsequent trial created a riveting battle between science and fundamentalist Christians, who represented all religions confronting erosion of their influence by the worldwide proliferation of education. However, the tide had irrevocably turned. *The Origin of Species* had struck religion a crippling blow, then its humiliation at the Scopes Trial seemed to knock it out of contention. Now, seven decades later, we know it went down but not out.

***

The Scopes Trial was a watershed for Darwinists because it legitimized propagating evolutionary theory. They did it so thoroughly that today children everywhere are taught life began in ancient seas filled with countless complex but inanimate (non-living) molecules whose presence turned the seawater into a "prebiotic soup." Those isolated molecules somehow came together (with the possible influence of lightning) to link themselves into ever more complex chains. At some point a critical mass was reached and voila! Life spontaneously began, transforming those previously dead clumps of molecules into creatures that could somehow (to this day no one can say exactly how) utilize other molecules in the soup to perform the miracle of reproduction.

After reproduction, of course, came growth into ever more complex forms: algae and bacteria became early sea plants and worms, worms became fish, fish became amphibians, amphibians became reptiles, reptiles became birds and mammals, mammals became humans, and humans became scientists, who assure us that wherever they look they find Darwin was correct, evolution *is* how life works, and nothing is left to proving his theory except dotting a few i's and crossing a few t's. Well, there is a bit more to it than that.

MISSING LINKS

In *The Origin Of Species* Darwin never used "evolution" to describe the process underlying his theory. He called it "natural selection," while today we use the more cryptic "descent with modification" or "gradualism." Whatever it is called, it expresses the idea that all life forms continually upgrade themselves into more complex (higher) forms by very slight genetic changes multiplied and/or combined over vast periods of time. Favorable changes remain in a species' growth pattern, adding to the abilities of higher incarnations in an unbroken chain of increasing sophistication. Unfavorable changes are eliminated by not being passed on.

The most pivotal aspect of the theory is that it calls for "innumerable intermediate forms" (Darwin's own words) to appear in the fossil record, where life's myriad species are frozen for eternity. In 1859 there was a complete absence of transitional forms, but this did not greatly concern Darwin because he knew his era's fossil record was woefully inadequate. He was confident that once his theory caused his colleagues to begin intensive searching, they would find many so-called "missing links." Unfortunately, that bold prediction has left his followers continually chasing their tails in frantic efforts to explain why no matter where they look they cannot find any, not in 1860 and not now, nearly 140 years later. In fact, what today's much more complete fossil record reveals is that life forms have never—*never*—existed the way Darwin predicted they would.

In geological terms every life form appears virtually overnight, with both sexes fully developed and functioning, in the physical state they maintain until they go extinct, which on average requires about a million years, and which has happened to as many as 99% of all species that have ever lived. There can be certain degrees of physical change (size, weight, etc.) during a species' lifecycle—sometimes profound changes—but never transformation into another genus (the biological classification above a species). In other words, small sharks may have "evolved" into larger sharks, and vice versa, but no shark ever evolved into an amphibian.

By 1882, when Charles Darwin died, the "missing links" hole in his theory had seriously widened. Today all Darwinists know (but rarely admit) that the doctrine undergirding their entire ideology is fatally flawed. Some have even constructed modifications to it

4

(such as "punctuated equilibrium," to be discussed later), trying to plug the holes without admitting the basic concept is in doubt. That distortion of reality is embarrassing but necessary because Creationists are not content to hold contrary opinions about evolution solely as a matter of faith. They insist everyone else should see the matter only as they do, so they have to be met head-on and defeated in open intellectual debate, which by default has become the responsibility of the Darwinists.

* * *

Throughout human history the most powerful group of individuals has been the equivalent of today's Creationists. (Don't think of spit-shined beggars like Jimmy Swaggart and Jim Bakker, who are aberrations.) For much of the human epoch "holy" men of most cultures have been able to execute—often without question—anyone who challenged, offended, or otherwise confounded them. (Sadly, echoes of those days remain; just ask Salman Rushdie.) Consider the Crusades, the Inquisition, or Galileo, forced to recant his "heresy" that Earth was not the center of the universe. Religious dogmatists had the upper hand then and wore an iron glove when they used it—especially against scientists, who were a small minority of the populace and were considered "wicked" and/or "evil" because they did not blindly accept "God's word" in the Bible.

Whether openly or surreptitiously, questioning the Bible's veracity put early scientists on a par with the small mammals scurrying underfoot when dinosaurs ruled the Earth. Then came the miles-wide asteroid that wiped out the dinosaurs and lifted the scurrying mammals from obscure bit players to stars at center stage. Similarly, Darwin's theory of natural selection was an intellectual asteroid that in one brilliant stroke unseated the religious hierarchy that had ruled society until then. It gave science and scientists the upper hand, and they have clung to their newfound power as fanatically as the ecclesiastics ever did. In fact, Darwinism itself has become a kind of religion to them, to be taken on faith no matter how the evidence stacks up against it.

IN THE BEGINNING

In the beginning Earth coalesced from a primordial cloud of dust and gas to become a protoplanet with the viscosity of thick soup. By dating cratonal rocks (remnants of the original crust), geologists have determined this occurred around 4.5 billion years ago. For the next half-billion (500 million) years the seething ball cooled, forming a thin crust of silicates the way a cooling milk-based soup forms a "skin." As the crust grew thicker, it added a pressure-cooker effect to the ball it encased, which—as any cook might anticipate—thickened the soup's consistency while accelerating gas venting (primarily as steam) and the formation of more crust.

By 4.0 billion years ago rock was present all over the ball, pebbling its new surface like chunks of meat and vegetables in a stew. It was not land as we know it because there was still far more stew than rock at the surface, but the stew continued to cool, which kept forming more rocks and venting more gases—still mostly steam that would condense into water. That process continued until the surface had hardened into true land and sea, around 2.5 billion years ago. Not until that "continental threshold" was reached, providing a foothold of sorts for subsequent generation and proliferation, does it seem life would have the necessary environment to kickstart itself and then gradually flourish, as—according to all Darwinist tenets—it so obviously did.

In their view the only questions remaining are "How?" and, perhaps peripherally, "Why?" Life would start small, no doubt, with molecules having a chemical affinity somehow managing to clump themselves together in the prebiotic soup. Then, somehow, someway (no one is quite sure how), they would cross the line from inanimate molecule clumps to animated life force. However, if it did happen that way it was nothing less than a divine miracle, because the absolute simplest form of animated life has hundreds of genes (humans have 100,000), and that complexity compares to the largest inanimate molecules the way a metropolis like New York City compares to a rustic village.

***

Darwin's theory of gradualism would be in perfect harmony with the above scenario, but what actually happened was nothing like it. The planet was still a seething cauldron when life first appeared, suddenly and without precedent at around 4.0 billion years ago. And it didn't come in one form, it came in *two*; both quite different, and complex rather than simple. Yet despite their obvious differences, they had equally obvious similarities in their genetic make-ups, which could only mean they shared a common ancestor of greatly reduced complexity.

That common ancestor is another serious problem for Darwinists because it had to exist much further back in time than when its two progeny appeared on the early Earth. That, in turn, means Earth could not have been its spawning ground because not enough time was available for evolution to work its magic. Consider the time-frame: about 4.0 billion years ago, only 500 million since Earth's timeline began (11% of 4.5 billion), with only thin, steam-drenched crust floating on viscous, scalding magma, two kinds of single-cell bacteria left indirect traces in the earliest rocks. Then, at 3.8 billion years ago, they left bodies as fossils. Thus, by at least 4.0 billion years ago (if not earlier) life was here on the protoplanet, fully formed and with no apparent predecessor.

The first single-cell bacteria were called prokaryotes (pro-carry-oats), and originally it was thought there was only one kind. But in the late 1970's bacteriologist Carl Woese studied prokaryotic RNA and—to his own astonishment and the even greater astonishment of scientists everywhere—discovered there were two separate, distinct types. The predominant ones he named "eubacteria," which have come to be known simply as bacteria. The new group he called "archaebacteria" (archae means "ancient") because they seemed more primitive in function than the apparently adaptive bacteria. They have since come to be known as archaea (ar-kay-uh).

Woese's discovery was the bacteriological equivalent of finding two distinct types of human beings, each with roughly half the same genetic sequences and half completely different. Yet the two prokaryotes were clearly related because, in addition to sharing genetic sequences, neither had a cell nucleus, leaving their genes to float freely within their body membranes.

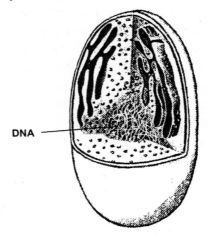

Fig. 2. Prokaryotic cell

That dramatically separated them from the next life form to come along (about 2.0 billion years ago), the eukaryotes (you-carry-oats), a much more sophisticated form of bacteria whose unicellular bodies held their genes in a nucleus enclosed by an inner membrane.

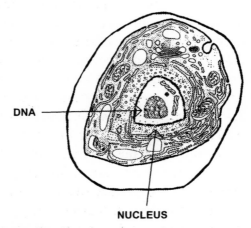

Fig. 3. Eukaryotic cell

Scientists contend that the enclosed nuclei of eukaryotes makes them the obvious precursor of all subsequent "higher" plant and animal life forms, all of which have similarly enclosed nuclei, and all of which—including humans—are technically classified as eukaryotes. However, the following chart clearly shows that from day one of its presence on Earth, life did not follow Darwin's scenario of initial simplicity leading to increasing complexity in gradual stages.

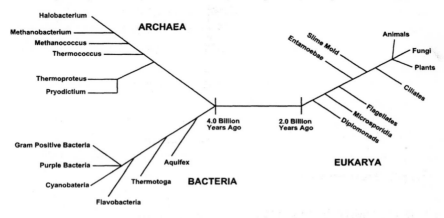

Fig. 4. Archaea, bacteria, and eukarya

Faced with such an unexpected, inexplicable "tree" of earliest life forms, biologists have diligently searched for Darwinian links between them (such as one bacteria "blending" into another), but thus far they have found none. In fact, when the entire genome (1.7 million genetic letters) of *Methanococcus jannaschii*, a methane producing "extremophile" (archaebacteria living in the most hellish environments on Earth, which resemble their original homes on the cooling protoplanet), was completely sequenced, it was found that 44% of *M. jannaschii's* genes were similar to those in bacteria or eukarya, while 56% were completely different from any genes yet sequenced in other unicellular organisms. This suggests that all three types of early life forms are indeed related to some common distant ancestor, but as stated earlier, there is simply not enough time available for that ancestor to have evolved on Earth.

Naturally, all this is a severe embarrassment to Darwinists, driving many of them to begin seriously considering the once-preposterous notion that life may not have originated on Earth, but instead was "seeded" from beyond by the blizzard of comets and asteroids that crater evidence on the Moon indicates bombarded the cooling protoplanet from 4.5 billion years ago to around 4.0 billion years ago, when everything seemed to stabilize (more about this in Part IV). That such a profound change of philosophical tack is being contemplated, much less openly discussed, is testament to the squeeze of the rock and the hard place the Darwinists find themselves stuck between.

Another of their difficulties is trying to explain how one or both prokaryotes might have evolved into early eukaryotes. Here they suggest that during the 2.0 billion year gap between their appearances, small prokaryotes "invaded" the bodies of large ones, established symbiotic (mutually beneficial) relationships, and thus evolved into eukaryotes. Others from the fang-and-claw school contend that small prokaryotes were "eaten" by larger ones, then turned into nuclei by some inexplicable osmotic (equalization of pressure on both sides of a membrane) process. While superficially satisfying, these explanations do little to account for the vast increase in complexity found in eukaryotes. In fact, the jump from prokaryotes to eukaryotes is equal to the jump from inanimate molecules to animate life: both are like comparing a rustic village to New York City.

Apart from strong overtones of implausibility and desperation, those "explanations" fail to address the bottom-line question: How did prokaryotes and eukaryotes gain life in the first place?

WHAT IS LIFE?

The standard Darwinist answer to that is built around the famous Harold Urey and Stanley Miller experiment of 1953. As a graduate student of Urey's at the University of Chicago, Miller approximated in a glass flask what was then thought to be the forming Earth's earliest atmosphere (mostly methane and ammonia), then he sent sparks through the mixture to approximate lightning (which is assumed—but not proven—to have been a constant in Earth's history). That ingenious experiment produced tiny amounts of two amino acids, the essential ingredients of proteins, which made Darwinists everywhere giddy with delight because amino acids could legitimately be publicized as "the building blocks of life." Similar experiments using different assumed atmospheres produced other amino acids and compounds involved in the processes of life, so it was easy to suggest a rain of such materials filled Earth's earliest seas and turned them into the original prebiotic soup, in which inorganic molecules somehow came together and lived.

The public and media (which readily exploits such simplified imagery) needed only a small leap of imagination to equate the Miller-Urey experiment with Victor Frankenstein's electrical creation of life. They jumped on the Darwinist bandwagon and resolutely disregarded several troubling facts that subsequently came to light regarding the prebiotic soup theory:

(1) No one can be certain what the early Earth's atmosphere was actually like. Even now, guesses are the best anyone can manage, although today's atmospheric chemists believe carbon dioxide was the main constituent. (Ironically, if they are right, then the whole range of molecules needed to construct a living organism would have been virtually impossible to synthesize.)

(2) No matter what combinations of gases were tried, the most any experiment ever produced was a handful of amino acids, life's most primitive "building blocks," which were not even close to organic. In addition, equally essential components of life, like proteins, nucleic acids, polysaccharides, lipids, etc., were nowhere in sight, so where might they have come from?

(3) The intense temperatures of the volatile early Earth would rapidly reduce any organic compounds to their constituent elements. This makes it doubtful the prebiotic soup ever existed.

(4) If life could spontaneously generate itself anywhere on primordial Earth, shouldn't it have done so in different ways in different

11

places? That would give us multiple genetic codes.

These are vexing conundrums for Darwinists, and here is another: assume everything on primordial Earth was just as they claim, and life could spontaneously create itself in seas clogged with amino acids, sugars, and all the other necessary building blocks. How were those disparate components brought together to create functioning units when, even today, with all the high technology available to our best biochemists, they cannot approach the first stages of actually creating life? Its simplest form—the multigened prokaryote bacteria—is so mind-bogglingly complex that none of its internal components can be assembled, much less the entire organism.

So even if the prebiotic soup did exist and teemed with all the necessary building blocks of life, how could they have been correctly assembled into an actual living prokaryote? The task has been wonderfully analogized by astronomer Fred Hoyle, the man who first proposed the notion that life did not evolve on Earth but was seeded from outside by comets and/or asteroids. He calculated the likelihood of any living organism—even one as simple as an (assumed) prokaryote ancestor—emerging naturally from a prebiotic soup is equal to "a tornado sweeping through a junkyard and assembling a Boeing 747 from the materials therein."

Another conundrum for Darwinists is that the biochemistry of life on Earth is not quite right. Logic tells us the ratios of elements in organic molecules should bear a strong resemblance to the ratios of elements on their home planet, but on Earth there are odd exceptions. For example, hydrogen and oxygen are abundant and combine as water to dominate both the planet itself and all of its life forms. Chromium and nickel also abound, yet they are relatively unimportant in biochemistry. On the other hand, elemental molybdenum is scarce, yet it plays a significant role in many crucial enzymatic reactions. Darwinists resolve these mysteries with a blunt syllogism:

(Major Premise)—Life obviously exists.

(Minor Premise)—It can only exist by "natural" means explainable in "scientific" terms, which requires a mechanism like the prebiotic soup theory.

(Conclusion)—Therefore, the fact that all available evidence makes such a theory *seem* impossible in naturalistic, scientific terms does not necessarily mean it *is* impossible. It could mean we simply have not reached a point yet where we can fully comprehend it.

Such reasoning is as difficult to refute as the idea it defends is to prove.

***

The next conundrum bacteria and archaea present for Darwinists is that after appearing at 4.0 billion years ago, most stay virtually unchanged to this day (which is how Carl Woese's RNA analyses of them and the eukaryotes were possible). Yes, there have been dramatic changes of lifestyle among certain extremophiles (archaea)—some methanogens learned to utilize oxygen instead of methane; some halophiles learned to live without salt; some thermophiles learned to survive without boiling heat—which makes them seem more flexible than bacteria. However, such changes are nowhere near the wholesale transformation called for by descent with modification to a higher form.

On the other hand, the nuclei of the eukaryotes seem to grant certain of them the possibility of transforming themselves into more complex forms, so Darwinists accept eukaryotes as the seeds from which all subsequent life on Earth evolved. This is despite the fact there are *no* intermediate forms that indicate connections between any of the eukaryotes (say, an organism that is part diplomonad and part microsporidia, or part flagellate and part ciliate). Thus, with no visible links between species in the earliest fossil record, Darwinists must rely on another syllogism:

(1) All eukaryotes have nuclei in their cells.

(2) All plants and animals have nuclei in their cells.

(3) Therefore, while there is no discernable evidence for links between eukaryotes and plants and animals, such links *must* exist. We humans have just not managed to find them—yet.

What the above establishes is the complete muddle at the beginning of Charles Darwin's work, the flawed foundation on which his theory's complex superstructure rests. So if natural selection cannot plausibly account for even the rudiments of what happened "in the beginning," what can it ever hope to explain? How about when higher, multicellular life forms first appear?

THE CAMBRIAN

At about 1.0 billion years ago multicellular algae (a plant type) appears, still remarkably simple but definitely multicellular. At 600 million years ago soft-bodied corals and tiny worm-like creatures appear. All come suddenly and—like prokaryotes and eukaryotes—with no precursors. Then, within only a few million years of those, something else suddenly appears: ediacaran fauna, which are exceedingly bizarre creatures that have always befuddled the scientists who try to characterize them. They were not definitively plants nor animals; they had no heads, no tails, no outsides, no insides, no fronts, no backs. Nobody knows exactly what they were, but they left fossils that resemble small, extremely thin seaweeds, and they lasted until a mass extinction wiped out most of them and cleared the way for the next major step in the ascent toward complex life.

It is now approximately 4.0 billion years since Earth coalesced, and 3.5 billion since life first appeared. During those 3.5 billion years trillions of microscopic creatures have permeated the planet's water, air, and land with free forms of the element oxygen, making our world ripe for exploitation by any creatures that could utilize it in their metabolism. Sure enough, at around 530 million years ago, the start of the geological epoch known as the Cambrian, with free oxygen available throughout the biosphere, there was a literal explosion of animal forms in the oceans, rivers, and seas. This event was so unlikely in its occurrence, so comprehensive in its scope, and so unbelievable in its consequences, most attempts to explain it fail to do it justice.

Within 5 to 10 million years (.002% of the 3.47 billion years of bacterial life preceding it), all major groups of complex animal life—the phyla (body design) subgroupings within the animal kingdom—appeared in large numbers. Imagine it: all twenty-six animal phyla, including the entire spectrum of invertebrate life—sponges, brachiopods, arthropods (trilobites, chelicerates, crustaceans), mollusks—along with the spineless chordates in the same phylum as vertebrates . . . all of it came in that nuclear-level explosion of life forms. Here is how it looks as a timeline:

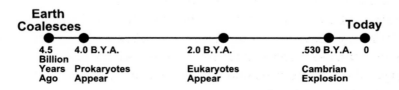

Fig. 5. Earth's timeline

Not surprisingly, the Cambrian Explosion (its acquired name) is the greatest obstacle presented to Darwinists by the entire fossil record. Its comprehensive suddenness has been verified by modern genetic analysis of living phyla, which strongly indicates they all did, in fact, come into existence at about the same time. So to explain it solely within the parameters of what the facts indicate, the most likely scenario requires a stretch of imagination few Darwinists are willing or able to make. They would have to suppose something like "cosmic dumptrucks" teeming with life forms are cruising the universe looking for planets to "accept" their loads. One or more finds Earth a likely "landfill" capable of supporting their cargo, so they lift the bed and dump it out. But even disregarding all such explanations as preposterous, the Cambrian Explosion nonetheless defies classic Darwinism.

Another defiance of Darwinism is the intriguing fact that no new phyla have developed on Earth since the original twenty-six appeared during the Cambrian Explosion. Darwinists logically anticipate countless examples of altered body structures in the subsequent 500 million years, yet the actual history of life on Earth shows nothing like that. After 3.0 billion years of unicellular life forms (both prokaryote types and the early eukaryotes), and 500

15

million years of exceedingly simple multicellular life (the ediacarans), there is 5 to 10 million years of intense creativity followed by another 500 million years of variation on the anatomical themes established during the 5 to 10 million years. This is hardly the steady progression called for by the tenets of classic Darwinism.

Darwin, of course, had no idea anything had lived before the Cambrian because the bacterial evidence had not been found, and the bizarre ediacaran fauna would not be discovered until the mid-1860's, a few years after *The Origin of Species* was published (and then they would be misinterpreted as gas bubbles that had percolated up through ocean sediments and been trapped and fossilized). That led him to concede that any absence of intermediate forms preceding the Cambrian would be potentially fatal to his theory. "The case [for no predecessors] at present must remain inexplicable," he wrote in *The Origin of Species*, "and [it] may be urged as a valid argument against the views here entertained." In other words, if his theory was correct, then the Pre-Cambrian eras must have swarmed with intermediate forms evolving toward the known phyla. If not, his theory could only be judged wrong—no ifs, ands, or buts.

After nearly 140 years of diligent searching by every Darwinist worthy of the name, none has yet discovered a legitimate precursor to even one creature that appeared in the Cambrian Explosion. In most areas of inquiry, 140 years would be long enough to indicate a wrong approach has been taken. However, because evolution plays such a dominant role in the ideological war between Darwinists and Creationists, the Darwinists cannot afford to acknowledge Darwin's own admission of worst-case fallibility. So how do they handle it? They deftly work around it.

***

Because the lack of Cambrian predecessors is such a backbreaker for Darwinists, they have devised two exculpatory brainstorms to try to explain it away. The first is called the artifact theory, which says missing links did exist but for unknown reasons—possibly bodies too soft or too light to imprint on ancient seabeds—the fossil record failed to preserve them. This is in spite of microscopic, virtually weightless bacterium fossilizing for millennia prior to the Cambrian Explosion, and the exceptionally flimsy ediacaran fauna also fossilizing with astonishing clarity.

The second theory, called fast transition, says Cambrian precursors either did not exist or were not identifiable as such, and the process by which all the phyla appeared was simply Darwinian evolution inexplicably but temporarily jammed into a fast-forward mode. In other words, somehow the accelerator got floored for a brief evolutionary joyride, then everything returned to its usual gradual pace. Unfortunately for Darwinists, they must stand by one or the other of those options with nothing in between. Either all of the "innumerable"—remember, Darwin's own word—predecessors called for by the theory of natural selection were somehow able to disobey the usual rules of fossilization; or evolution as Darwin described it was not really evolution as he described it.

Despite the difficulties posed by both theories, most Darwinists support the fast-transition scenario because the evidence against precursors is so overwhelming. Also, it is obvious to all but the most hidebound diehards that strict Darwinian evolution (gradualism) bears little relation to reality. In fact, it might never have gained such a firm grip on the public's imagination if it had not been put forth precisely when it was: in an era of burgeoning social enlightenment when millions were looking for ways to break the stranglehold religion had on intellectual freedom.

DARWIN

The 19th century's greatest scientific quest was trying to explain how and why all forms of life on Earth were so clearly related at the most basic levels. It was obvious that: (1) everything shared a few common body designs (external skeletons, internal skeletons, etc.); (2) everything could be loosely grouped into categories (mollusks, conifers, vertebrates, etc.); and (3) everything showed lesser or greater similarities within those categories. So the question was, how were they linked to each other, and to the vast interlocking web of every species, both living and extinct?

Trying to answer that question was equal to today's search for a Unified Field Theory to explain how all matter and energy interrelate. After thirty years of research and analysis, Charles Darwin supplied an answer that, like all great ideas, was appealing because of deceptive simplicity. Its essentials could be reduced to one easily understandable sentence: Life started billions of years ago and very slowly became more complex as simple forms improved themselves and grew into higher forms, the ultimate result of which is humanity. Better yet, such an upward spiral of slow, steady improvement reflected what all of history seemed to demonstrate, which was that everything stayed in flux and nothing ever seemed to regress.

Despite being apparently true and demonstrable in the 1800's, Darwin's theory of natural selection has not been well-served by time and the fossil record. Genetic research has proved him right about the biological interconnectedness of all living things, which is enough to justify much of his reputation. But a fairer assessment is that he deserves only about half of what he has.

***

The correct part of Darwin's theory was the concept of microevolution, a breakthrough insight generated by his studies of animals on the Galapagos Islands, a chain of 16 isles (Darwin visited only 4) dated at 3.0 to 5.0 million years ago and located 650 miles off the coast of Ecuador. Each species he studied had developed physical adaptations to the various environmental niches found throughout the island chain. The widest range of modifications had been developed by ordinary, garden-variety finches that had somehow (perhaps propelled by a storm) managed to wing their way from the South American mainland out to the Galapagos. The largest aspect of change was in beak modifications. There were long beaks, short beaks, thin beaks, thick beaks—whatever was needed to exploit the environmental niche any finch found itself in, whether for seed eating, insect eating, or fruit eating.

18

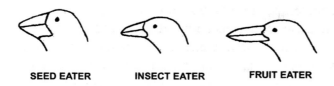

Fig. 6. Darwin's finches

Notice every finch was still a finch; that genus of birds had not turned into another. But because adaptive modification was and is so patently visible at the micro level, Darwin and his later supporters made the unfortunate assumption that—given the enormity of historical time (500 million years for complex life)—change could likewise occur at the larger macro, species-into-a-higher-genus-into-a-higher-family (etc.) level. However, going strictly by the evidence, there is no such thing as macroevolution. There is no trace of it in the fossil record, nor in the world around us. Sea worms did not and do not become fishes, fishes did not and do not become amphibians, amphibians did not and do not become mammals. In every case the differences between critical body parts and functions (internal organs, digestive tracts, reproductive systems, etc.) are so vast, transition from one to another would require dramatic changes that would be easily discernable in the fossil record.

What the fossil record actually reveals is that every class, order, family, genus, or species simply *appears,* fully formed and ready to "eat, survive, reproduce." And they all exhibit a certain range of physical variation that is sometimes wide and sometimes narrow. For instance, one buffalo looks like any other (narrow), while Shetland ponies are nothing like Clydesdales (wide). Giraffes are giraffes (narrow), while dogs range from palm sized to Shepherd sized (wide). Those limits on size and shape—which seem to be guided by laws of genetic inheritance—force all plants and animals to remain essentially what they are throughout their lifecycles on Earth.

A convincing proof of this is a series of experiments done with fruit flies. Some were bred with severe genetic mutations like mul-

19

tiple sets of wings, grotesque eye malformations, even legs growing where antennas should be—the more monstrous the better.
However, if those "monsters" were then allowed to breed normally,
in only a few generations their offspring reverted to typical fruit
flies showing no traces of their aberrant ancestors. This demonstrates that not only is there the famous "wisdom" in all genetic
codes, there is great tenacity and resistance to change.

THE HORSE CHARADE/INSECTS

Darwinists often promote horses as proof of evolution in the fossil record. Most people have probably seen one form or another of
the pictograph shown below, in which the collie-sized Eohippus of
the Eocene era of 60 million years ago is sequentially "transformed" into today's large, streamlined Equus.

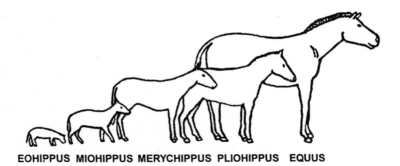

EOHIPPUS MIOHIPPUS MERYCHIPPUS PLIOHIPPUS EQUUS

Fig. 7. Horse sequence

Despite its apparent congruity, this series of "steps" up an evolutionary "ladder" does not represent a true interspecies transition.
All it really illustrates is that every aspect of change in, say, Eohippus to Miohippus is no more than the changes in beaks among
Galapagos finches. But the key to this pictograph has more to do
with what is left out than what is shown. In reality, many other creatures are considered "proto"-horses. Some are: Orohippus, Haplo-

hippus, Epihippus, Mesohippus, Parahippus, Archaeohippus, and Hypohippus. And these only lead up to the Miocene era of 20 million years ago. From there more than a dozen appear and disappear in the fossil record, some being successful in one area while going extinct in others.

The truth is that the transition from Eohippus to Equus is blatantly misrepresented by the famous pictograph above, yet we cannot be certain Eohippus did not, in fact, "evolve" into Equus by continuous microevolution on an extended scale. After all, Eohippus did exist 60 million years ago, and numerous protohorses existed during the intervening eras; so if viewed in a plausible sequence, their body changes were never more dramatic than those in the beaks of Darwin's finches. In fact, a veterinarian today could probably autopsy an Eohippus and recognize everything in it.

**

Apart from telling us to what lengths the scientific establishment will go to keep the public ignorant of Darwinism's shortcomings, the horse charade illustrates how badly Charles Darwin skewed off-course when he assumed macroevolution was a logical extension of the microevolution he had observed on the Galapagos Islands. Like Einstein's relativity, microevolution is an unquestioned rule of life, and its means of expression does seem to be that superior or necessary traits are selected for replication as species proliferate. The selection process, however, remains quite unclear (though indications are strong that it, too, will prove to be gene-based).

This bears repeating: the fossil evidence clearly indicates that all basic forms of life simply *appear* on Earth, and after arriving and settling in they definitely do not evolve into higher, more complex forms the way Charles Darwin proposed. No doubt there *is* a mechanism that dictates how they behave, but thus far that mechanism has eluded everyone's grasp—including Darwin's.

**

Another good example of scientific truth-twisting is insects, of which there are millions in existence today, about 5/6 of all animal species. However, that ratio is fairly recent, coming only after the advent of flowering plants (angiosperms) at 110 million years ago. For the preceding 250 million years there were relatively few insect species spending their lives foraging in detritus. But as flowering plants multiplied and spread across the planet, insects multiplied and spread with them, forming the symbiotic relationships that define their existences today.

With so much going on so recently, it would seem that hundreds and thousands of intermediate forms would be easily detectable in the fossil record or—more convincingly—among and between living species. Yet to the great frustration of scientists everywhere, there is no discernable evidence of "upward" evolution among or between the flowering plants and/or insects. With what would seem to be literally millions of opportunities to find any kind of transitional forms—say, a housefly becoming a firefly—scientists remain embarrassingly empty-handed.

NEO-DARWINISTS

Even the most diehard Darwinists know their icon's theory is seriously flawed; so flawed, in fact, that some of the bolder ones have suggested modifications to make its most spurious aspects conform more closely to the real world. However, they are careful to retain enough of gradualism's basic precepts to keep the ever-pressing Creationists at bay. (In any discipline this would be a fine line to walk, but that it is being done by "objective" scientists makes it all the more interesting.) Chief among the "neo"(new)-Darwinists is Harvard biologist/essayist Stephen J. Gould, who, with Niles Eldredge, coauthored an alternate evolutionary theory called punctuated equilibrium (punk eek to its fans). Both insist their revision is merely an "enhancement" of classic Darwinism needed to address three intransigent problems spawned by the modern fossil record:

(1) The "sudden appearance" of all life forms. This continues unabated for 4.0 billion years, with not a single contradictory example. As we have noted, nothing transforms into anything "higher;" it all simply appears, somehow, as fully functioning units—

preformed, in numbers, ready to live and procreate. As renowned biologist Richard Dawkins has uneasily conceded: "It is as though they were just *planted here* [emphasis added], without any evolutionary history."

(2) Stasis. This is the general stability of structure that all life forms exhibit while living on Earth. After a typical sudden appearance, neither plants nor animals will show significant morphological (fundamental physical) changes until they go extinct (after lasting on average about a million years). Changes that are detectable invariably occur at the micro level, such as beak alterations, height and weight alterations, etc. (Two familiar examples of stasis are cockroaches and sharks, which have remained essentially unchanged for more than 100 million years.)

(3) Catastrophism. Darwinism predicts continuous extinctions of species caused by being outcompeted for resources by better-adapted newcomers to their habitats. However, this is seldom observed in the fossil record. While as many as 99% of all species that have ever lived are now extinct, the vast majority of those resulted from cataclysmic events that created "overnight" global-wide extinctions. Such catastrophes are caused by collisions with large asteroids and/or comets, or periodic rounds of massive volcanic activity, all of which destroy ecological and biological niches, cause drastic changes to weather patterns, and remove key links from the food chain.

Of the five major worldwide extinctions catalogued by paleontologists, two are especially noteworthy. The Permian extinction of about 245 million years ago wiped out half of all marine invertebrates and 90% of all species. At 65 million years ago the famous Cretaceous extinction caused a similarly extensive range of damage, wiping out the dinosaurs and almost everything else alive at the time. Of course, a few species always manage to survive every major extinction, but the usual pattern is a global annihilation followed by a relatively rapid refilling of the freshly vacated environmental niches with entirely new species ready to proliferate.

(This is where the idea of a cosmic dumptruck originated. In real-world terms what seems to happen is that following any extinction

23

event the Earth is first allowed to restabilize, then a life-carrying, cosmos-cruising dumptruck comes along to unload itself and re-populate the planet. And for as preposterous as that sounds, it suits the facts much better than any Darwinist explanation.)

The overriding problem for Darwinists in all this is that each extinction event is a fresh "wipe of the slate" that should give gradualism a chance to express itself in clear, unambiguous ways. Yet what the fossils reveal is the same old record playing the same old tune: sudden appearances, stasis for a million years or so, then extinction by natural means (such as over-specialization in an altered habitat) or a sudden die-off caused by a global-wide catastrophe.

To account for the huge holes those facts knock in Darwin's theory, Gould and Eldredge formed punctuated equilibrium by blending the fast-transition theory used to explain the Cambrian Explosion, and the unproven but widely-believed notion that Nature abhors a vacuum. Thus, they postulate, after each extinction event evolution somehow shifts its own gears into fast-forward to rapidly fill the newly vacated ecological niches; but as soon as they are refilled, things slow back down to normal. While this scenario flatly ignores Darwinism's basic tenet of gradualism (not to mention stark reality), punk eek support-ers insist their theory validates its fundamental message:

(1) Life first appeared by natural means.

(2) Life exists in its entirety by natural means.

(3) Life invariably expires by natural means.

That the details of these processes are still unclear to us in no way means they are inherently flawed. It only means *we* are flawed for not being able to discover and explain the naturalistic design that has to be lurking at the heart of everything. In other words, some of Darwin's details may be wrong, but the core of his theory remains solid: Nature, not the supernatural, is the unexplained mechanism that drives the engine of life on Earth.

***

From punk-eekers to classic diehards, all Darwinists support the notion that evolution mainly occurs slowly-but-steadily as species accumulate small, discrete improvements in various aspects of their anatomy. This is Darwinism's proverbial "bottom line." However, the reality is that most new classes of animals stopped appearing in the fossil record 300 to 400 million years ago. The last vertebrate class was Aves (birds) at roughly 170 million years ago. Most placental mammals appeared after the Cretaceous extinction of 65 million years ago. And while some classes and many orders have become extinct in the intervening years, no new orders have appeared for millions of years. Consequently, today there are more species in the groups that have survived, whereas in prior eras there were fewer species in more groups.

If that sounds as if it actually verifies evolution, please understand the difference between evolution and speciation. Evolution calls for new, improved species to evolve from current ones; speciation is simply variations on a species resulting from inbreeding within isolated populations. Darwin's finches are examples of speciation, as are eight genetically distinct rats living in a confined area of the Amazon. Several million years ago there was only one species of that rat. However, unlike Darwin's finches, the eight rats are outwardly identical; only their genes differentiate them. On the other hand, a 30 million-year-old extinct termite recovered from a piece of amber had enough of its genes intact to allow them to be sequenced. They turned out to be almost identical to a living descendant with only eight (8!) base-pair changes out of several million (over 30 million years!). Such infinitesimal change screams "Stasis!" rather than speciation *or* evolution.

In none of these examples—which are not atypical—does classic Darwinism work. It unequivocally predicts new orders, classes, and even phyla appearing as natural selection causes species to continually upgrade and improve themselves. However, what actually occurs—more species in fewer groups or infinitesimal change—could not be more opposite. So we are left with one inescapable conclusion: in the real world, Charles Darwin's revered model is turned on its head.

A final nail in Darwinism's coffin is the recently mentioned flowering plants, which appeared on Earth 110 million years ago with structures and lifestyles utterly unlike any plants that had existed before. There was no known catastrophe at 110 million years ago, no major upheaval. Like everything else, flowering plants simply appeared, in numbers, with no evidence of evolution—gradual or otherwise—from anything prior. However, their history was known to Darwin, who grudgingly admitted they were "an abominable mystery." And so they remain.

***

The above is a simplistic analysis of an enormously complex, bitterly contested ideological dispute with much more to it than can be mentioned here. Countless volumes pro and con have been produced by both sides, several of which are listed in this book's bibliography. Also numerous are magazines dealing with evolution from a scientific viewpoint (*Nature, Discover, Scientific American, Archeology*, etc.) Be aware, however, that magazine articles supporting Darwinism tend to analyze isolated examples of microevolution in mind-numbing detail, then announce yet another proof has been found for the efficacy and total accuracy of Darwinian macroevolution.

Despite their highbrow tone, these articles are merely a sophisticated version of supermarket tabloids. If they were actually proving evolution is real—proving it beyond doubt—the news coverage of such a landmark event would rival a Presidential election. So while it is extremely erudite, extremely technical smoke those articles blow our way, it is nonetheless smoke.

CAREER SUICIDE

Whenever any major scientific breakthrough occurs—viruses and bacteria cause disease; space and time are not what they seem; etc.—it impacts on a well-entrenched cadre of "experts" who control the relevant discipline's power structure. Those experts have a deeply vested interest in preventing changes to the status quos on which their careers have been built, so whenever they are openly challenged, they mobilize to close ranks and stave off the threat. However obvious a new reality is to the public or the media, it is not obvious to them. However much evidence is offered in support, they are not satisfied. If they cannot dismiss such evidence outright, then the way it was secured or those who secured it will be ridiculed. No proof will be enough to convince the old guard, who will insist that only their "properly credentialed" judgements should be heeded.

For as absurd as this might sound to the uninitiated, it is repeated with every major breakthrough. There are countless examples to illustrate it, but a personal favorite exemplifies the many things that can and do go wrong when scientific egos and reputations are challenged.

***

In 1915 a 35-year-old German meteorologist and explorer named Alfred Wegener published *The Origin of Continents and Oceans*, which produced detailed geodetic, geophysical, geological, anthropological, botanical, paleontological, and paleoclimatological arguments supporting the "radical" notion that at some time in the remote past North and South America had been connected to Europe and Africa. It was a work of impeccable scholarship and stunning audacity that was—and should have been recognized as—the geological equivalent of Darwin's *Origin of Species*. Unfortunately, it served no larger societal need like wresting power from religious fundamentalists, so Wegener and his brilliant theory were left to the judgement of status quo "experts" whose acceptance of him would seriously embarrass them at both professional and private levels.

Not surprisingly, many geologists had long known South America's "nipple" (its eastward bulge) fit nicely into the bight of middle-western Africa; and there were interesting links between North America's Appalachian Mountains and North Africa's Atlas Mountains. Botanists understood Wegener's comparisons of flora on the opposite coastlines, where many "native" plants had identical examples on both shores, begging the question of how and when they could have crossed the Atlantic. Biologists understood his comparisons of native animals, which revealed identical examples of several, including monkeys and—most irrefutable of all—freshwater fish! How, Wegener demanded, could identical species of freshwater fish have crossed the vast, salty Atlantic?

His proofs seemed—and literally were—overwhelming.

Fig. 8. Wegener's Pangea

Despite the blatant obviousness of numerous connections between the three continents, no experts had ever looked for—much less found—ways to demonstrate them because they *knew* such connections were impossible. And if Alfred Wegener had been one of them, he would have believed as they did. Only his outsider status as "An unqualified, know-nothing weatherman!" gave him the clarity of vision to see facts as they were, not as they were supposed to be.

***

28

Though Wegener's research was meticulous and his results undeniable, his conclusion—that all land on Earth had once been fused together into a supercontinent he called Pangea, and that since then it had broken into gigantic moveable pieces—was beyond outrageous, it was flatly intolerable to the scientific establishment of his day. In addition, the era's conservative media and religious commentators were still licking the wounds Darwin inflicted on them, so they were in no mood to even consider that God might have created an unstable planet.

Rather than seeing his theory of Continental Drift hailed as the brilliant stroke of genius it so clearly was, or at minimum granted the further analysis it cried out for, Wegener was buried under an avalanche of criticism from all sides. He was lampooned and ridiculed as a man who should stick to meteorology and leave the subjects of his "reckless, irresponsible theorizing" to their recognized experts, all of whom insisted it was beyond absurd to doubt that the Earth was—apart from occasional earthquakes or volcanos—absolutely immutable.

By the 1920's Wegener and Continental Drift were forgotten. In the 1930's and 1940's they were a footnote to a bygone era. But by the 1950's a new establishment was in charge, and they were faced with mounting evidence that Earth *was* constructed the way Wegener had proposed. What they needed, they realized, was means of proof that were more direct and concrete than the "reason" Wegener was forced to appeal to. Not until the early 1960's did they secure enough evidence to tentatively conclude that Earth's crust did indeed seem composed of a collection of irregular, gigantic plates that slowly slid around like a jam-up of bumper cars at a state fair. And not until the late 1960's did the Glomar Explorer secure proof not even stable-crust diehards could deny: varying magnetic alignments in core samples from the Mid-Atlantic Ridge.

***

This example typifies the resistance to change within any status quo. Truth has nothing to do with it; proof has less to do with it; and forget logic—logic is wasted. What counts in such disputes is about 50 years, two generations, which is what has to die out before a controversial new reality will be fully accepted. First is the status quo at the time of discovery. They reject it because it means three very bad things: being wrong on a major issue; having to rewrite a large portion of their purview; and a ripple effect of doubt cast on everything else they profess to know.

The next generation spawns two groups: those who cling to the old status quo, and those who accept the new reality. As a whole they never fully embrace it, but they produce enough converts to grant it limited acceptance, allowing it to be openly supported without committing career suicide. The converts then teach their views to the next generation, and when they take over they see to it the old heresy is accepted. It always requires time, but time and truth invariably win out.

BACK POCKET EVIDENCE

For as harsh as criticism can be toward dissent from outside the scientific establishment, dissent from within is often worse. There are countless examples of this, too, but another personal favorite occurred in the 1800's, when there was no proof of when Paleolithic Indians first came to the New World. Rather than admit, "We just don't know that yet," the era's scientists felt it was logical to assume Indians could not have come until sometime after the last Ice Age, 10,000 years ago. That logical assumption gradually evolved into a baseline fact called the "postglacial theory."

As Wegener's case illustrated, baselines are believed and protected with the same fervor Creationists believe and protect scripture. Never mind that on a regular basis scientists somewhere are eating rations of crow—small or large—because one of their baselines has been overturned by new data. They insist such mistakes are aberrations, and that all of their *other* baselines are solid and correct—until proved wrong. That insistence on their own infallibility means scientists must maintain strict discipline and cohesion within their ranks. But how can they do that when freedom of expression and the search for truth are supposedly at the heart of everything they do?

They mimic their rivals by using the trappings of religion.

***

Once the postglacial theory was *invested* as official *doctrine*, the new *gospel* was preached from *pulpits* in classrooms everywhere, and soon developed a dedicated following of *priests* and *acolytes*. Then, disturbingly, in the mid-1800's the *gospel* began being plagued by *heretical* evidence. In 1846 a human pelvis was found with some extinct ground-sloth skeletons in Natchez, Mississippi. There was no question the pelvis was found with the ground sloths, which dated to well before the last Ice Age, but the *high priests* of the postglacial *gospel* refused to consider the new evidence. Instead of going to Natchez to examine the site, they used old reliable ridicule to professionally *excommunicate* the *heathens* who had discovered and interpreted the bones.

"Obvious incompetents!" they howled. "Backwoods buffoons!"

Everybody *worshiping* at the postglacial *altar* received the church's message loud and clear: this baseline *gospel* was not to be questioned. So nobody dared. No more preglacial *testimony* was offered (which is not to say none was found) until the turn of the century, when a *heretical* young *priest* used a new method of dating archeological finds—fluorine testing—on the disgraced Mississippi pelvis and sloth bones. Those fluorine tests proved the pelvis and sloths were indeed in the New World prior to the last Ice Age, which was *altar*-shaking news to the scientific *priesthood* of that era. Remember, those people were several generations removed from the forgotten souls who formulated the postglacial theory, so they might be expected to gladly welcome the dating news and get busy looking for more evidence to verify it. Right?

Not quite. Whenever a baseline *gospel* is challenged, the reigning *priesthood* cannot accept it without admitting they—and their predecessors—have been wrong. So, they continued to disregard the Natchez pelvis and sloth bones, which were unaccountably "lost" by the curators of a well-respected museum; and the whole incident was so thoroughly mocked by the usual ridicule, it was once again ignored by the entire *church*.

* * *

As time passed, archeologists who discovered preglacial artifacts did not bother putting them forth. Slowly, though, the volume of such "back pocket" (where it was metaphorically kept) evidence mounted. Eventually the younger generation of archeologists knew beyond doubt that the postglacial theory was wrong. They began privately sharing information at official symposiums and conferences, waiting for a chance to mobilize against the status quo's dogma. It came in 1926—80 years after the Natchez find—at a dig near Folsom, New Mexico, where a hand-made stone spearpoint was found lodged *between the ribs* of an extinct, preglacial Bison Antiquus.

After that, not even the highest high priests could deny humans were in the New World prior to the end of the last Ice Age. And with archeologists finally free to look for preglacial evidence, it popped up everywhere. By 1930, 19 more Folsom spearpoints were found in direct association with 23 more extinct bison. That fueled even closer examination of preglacial strata in North and South America, and in ten years Paleo-Indian sites were found throughout both continents, from Alaska to Patagonia. All those sites and all that evidence had always been available, but because archeologists were trained from their earliest classroom experiences not to expect it, they were consistently unable—or unwilling—to see it staring out at them.

* * *

This story has four important lessons: (1) People must believe in something before they will make a serious effort to look for it. (2) They have to make such a serious effort before they can ever hope to find it. (3) Establishments are in business to resist change to their status quos every way they can. (4) Every significant increase in the world's accumulated body of knowledge has come from an individual (Wegener) or a group (the Folsom point gang) that found ways to overturn some long-lived baseline's "canon."

That is how, in the fullness of time, all current theories about Darwinian evolution as the mechanism behind life on Earth—particularly human evolution—will ultimately be revised.

SUMMATION

We now have a general overview of how life actually came to be on Earth. We have examined the ongoing power struggle between orthodox science and religious fundamentalism, neither of which can possibly be correct about the basic tenets of its doctrine. Creationists who insist Earth was created in six literal days approximately 6,000 years ago (a date based on 17th century cleric James Ussher's calculation of the accounts of who begat whom listed in the Bible) automatically exclude themselves from serious consideration, while those willing to grant that the Bible's six days may instead have meant six eras of unspecified length still spit into the wind of reality. Similarly, nothing in the fossil record has ever verified any portion of the macroevolution called for by the Darwinian theory that primitive species gradually evolve into complex ones. The only reason it has not been jettisoned as an obvious mistake is because the scientists stuck with it have no acceptable substitute.

"Acceptable" is the key word. They would love to have an alternate theory that believably explained the mysteries of life, but it must have one overriding characteristic to remain effective against the Creationists: it must function by *natural* means. Anything that smacks of the *un*natural or—worse—the *super*natural is totally unacceptable. But whether natural, unnatural, or supernatural, the truth will eventually be discovered, and everyone then alive will look back on our superstitious, close-minded ignorance the same way we look back on the superstitious, close-minded ignorance of generations past. The more things change, the more they stay the same.

PART II

THE FOSSIL RECORD

INTRODUCTION

The fossil record of supposedly "pre"-humans is so pitifully incomplete, if every fragment of prehuman fossil ever found was laid out together, they would not cover half a tennis court. Entire species are often projected from scraps of jawbones and pieces of skulls, and full skeletons are not found until 50,000 years ago, when a few Neanderthals inexplicably buried some of their dead. That paucity of data allows its interpretation to be blatantly subjective and therefore highly controversial, which means only a fraction of our knowledge about prehumans can be considered true beyond doubt. Everything else is merely the opinion of "experts" and "specialists" doing their best to shoehorn into place a great deal of evidence that simply does not fit the Darwinian model.

Another way of saying this is that anthropologists and paleo-anthropologists spend a great deal of time trying to pound square pegs into round holes. By far the biggest round hole confronting them is the so-called "missing link" between prehumans and humans, which is every bit as elusive and legendary as UFO's, Nessie, or Bigfoot. Every discoverer of every new fossil hominid does all the shoehorning they can get away with to try to position their find as close as possible to the presumed direct "line" leading from prehumans to humanity.

Unfortunately, the vast majority of what they have to work with is clearly square pegs, so a great deal of hedging, fudging, and out-right deception goes into their efforts to portray humanity as evolving toward its high state of consciousness and self-awareness from a single type of primitive creature that also produced our closest genetic relatives—apes, monkeys, baboons, and orangutans.

Notice this is not the 19th century misconception which lingers to this day: Humans did not descend *from* our hairy kin, we descended with and alongside them. That misconception began soon after *The Origin of Species* appeared, in the first salvos of the war between the Creationists and the Darwinists. In 1860 the mass media consisted of newspapers, which the Creationists of that era dominated. Many used their power by making all-out assaults on Charles Darwin and his abhorrent theory, most often by cartooning his head grafted onto an ape's body.

Fig. 9.

These created a lasting impression of humans evolving from apes, which is not what Darwin postulated. He said humans and apes shared a common ancestor that lived somewhere in the depths of prehistory, but they did not precede us on the lower rungs of our evolutionary ladder.

* * *

Fossil bones are so rare because it takes a highly unique set of circumstances to create them. First, death must occur in such a way that the corpse can be covered by sediment before it is consumed by scavengers. The preferred methods are burial and—before burials were routine—death in, or near, shallow water. In those cases the flesh beneath the sediment would quickly rot away, then minerals in the muck would gradually leach into the bones left behind. Over hundreds of years the minerals would replace the bones with exact stone replicas of themselves.

As fossilization occurs, more sediment piles on top of the fossil while the land it has become a part of shifts, twists, buckles, or folds as plate tectonics constantly reshapes the planet's crust. Those movements—along with weathering or mining or other excavations—occasionally expose fossils to view, sometimes after a few thousand years, sometimes after millions. So any fossil's discovery is the end result of improbabilities stacked upon improbabilities. They must not only appear in a position to be found, they must be found by someone who can recognize them for what they are. That makes each one's detection a near miracle.

For obvious reasons fossilization occurs most frequently among aquatic (water-dwelling) animals. The rate drops significantly among terrestrial (land-dwelling) animals, but there are still decent amounts because they tend to visit water holes daily, and water holes are where a great deal of hunting is done by natural predators. However, fossilization is extremely rare among arboreal (forest dwelling) animals because they normally obtain their liquids within the habitat, relieving them of the need to routinely risk their lives at water holes.

Because of the rarity of fossilization among arboreal animals, the fossil record of all apes and monkeys is in as much dispute as the purported prehuman record. There are, in fact, *no* fossilized bones of early chimpanzees, and the few supposedly of ancient gorillas and baboons and monkeys are riddled with many more speculations than hard facts. It could well be that nothing currently "known" about the ape and/or monkey record will turn out to be true. And, believe it or not, the same can be said about humanity.

***

Technically, humans are in the class of mammals and the order of primates, along with lemurs, tarsiers, marmosets, monkeys and apes. We are further distinguished as a family called hominids because we habitually move upright on our hind limbs. Our family includes all the so-called "prehumans." That distinction aside, from now on this book will refer to gorillas, chimpanzees, baboons, orangutans, and monkeys as primates, and all human types as hominids.

Darwinism says all hominids and primates descended from a common ancestor that lived 20 million years ago in the Miocene era. The Miocene was verdant and produced a surprising number of mammals called Miocene Apes, ranging from small, cat-like creatures up to an 8- to 9-foot tall, 700 pound ground-ape known as Gigantopithecus. Debates swirl around which Miocene ape might be the common ancestor because—as is typical for such old fossils—evidence about them is primarily shards of skulls and jawbones, and several isolated teeth and body bones; nothing approaching a full skeleton. However, despite severe limitations imposed by a lack of evidence and a wealth of confusion and speculation, there is no shortage of experts willing to construct and advertise models of how and when apes and prehumans diverged.

The current model (which, as usual, will be altered after the next major find) says the common ancestors of early apes and prehumans lived as Miocene apes until about 8.0 million years ago, when plate tectonics rapidly (in geologic terms) began to widen Africa's Rift Valley, tearing the eastern horn away from the continent. That profound change in geography caused a dramatic change in climate, leaving the western areas moist and tree-filled while starting a dry-out of the eastern horn. In the wet west the common ancestor apes continued to evolve, turning themselves into the arboreal chimps, baboons, and gorillas. Meanwhile, the common ancestors stranded in the desiccating east had no choice but to move onto the new savanna as upright gatherers/scavengers who radically diverged from their parent stock and cousins on the other side of the valley.

Like its many predecessors, that theory sounds logical and reasonable in light of the best current evidence. The problem with it—as with the others—is that it is total speculation.

***

The most recent Miocene ape fossil has been dated at 8.5 million years ago. The first fully upright hominids appear by 3.5 million years ago. Between those two seminal events stretches 5.0 million years that provide us with virtually no prehuman or pre-ape fossils in the record. A recent find considered hominid—Ardipithecus Ramidus—has been dated at 4.4 million years ago, though its discoverers refuse to release much information about it until they are ready to make a formal presentation. All they have been willing to say up to this point is that its remains are "comprehensive and compelling," and it "had a type of locomotion unlike any (hominid) living today." That may be somewhat of an exaggeration, but it certainly whets the appetite of those concerned.

Since the Ramidus data is currently unavailable, the gap that must presently be dealt with is 5.0 million years, and it reveals almost nothing about how early apes and/or prehumans might have evolved from presumably down-on-all-fours, ground-dwelling Miocene apes. (If they were exclusively tree-dwellers we would not have nearly as many fossils of them as we do.) But then, at around 3.2 million years ago, we supposedly find incontrovertible evidence that mankind was on its evolutionary way. Lucy and the First Family appear on the scene.

LUCY AND THE FIRST FAMILY

Lucy and the First Family are a group of fossils found in Ethiopia's parched wastelands in 1974 and 1975, during expeditions led by American paleontologist Donald Johanson. He officially classified them as Australopithecus Afarensis because Australopithecus had long since been designated as the earliest genus of hominids, and the species Lucy represented was found in the Afar region. When revealed for public display she created a sensation, being by far the most complete hominid specimen found up to that point. By mirror imaging her bones (assuming a missing bone on one side is the same as its counterpart), it was possible to obtain a nearly 50% image of her.

Fig. 10. "Lucy"

Paleoanthropologists usually must work with only scraps of jaws and skulls because those are the body's strongest bones and better withstand destruction by predators, time, and tectonics. Lucy gave them vastly more, then was soon followed by a dozen partial skeletons found at a separate site and known collectively as the "First Family." The First Family appears to be an extended family or tribal group killed by some natural disaster that left their bodies clumped together (flash flooding through a dry gully seems the likeliest explanation). Taken together, they supplied bones from nearly every part of their bodies, so their picture was even more complete than Lucy's.

Johanson and his team originally contended that Lucy and the First Family were the same kind of creature. However, it did not take long for independent researchers to realize that every First Family member was physically similar, while little about Lucy aligned her with them. Lucy's height was about 3.5 feet, while First Family members were in the 4.0 to 5.0 foot range, or taller. Even allowing for sexual dimorphism in a species (the tendency of males to be substantially larger than females), Lucy was still outside a reasonably acceptable range. Also, Lucy's jaw had a "V" shape that is closer to the parallel row of teeth possessed by modern apes than to the parabola of modern humans. First Family members had a "U" shape, still not the human parabola, but much closer to it than Lucy. The cusp patterns in Lucy's teeth were more primitive and ape-like than the First Family's, especially her first premolar, which had the single cusp of a chimpanzee. First Family premolars had the unmistakable double cusp of modern humans.

This is not to suggest the First Family's mouth and teeth were human: they were not even close. Their lower jaws had a strong thickening behind the back of the bottom teeth, similar to any ape's simian shelf, which compensates for their lack of a chin. The First Family's thickening was halfway between apes and humans, who have chins rather than a thickened shelf. Also, the First Family's upper teeth had an opening between the incisors and canines called a diastema, needed to accommodate the large lower canine teeth of most primates. Humans have lost all signs of a diastema. Therefore, to judge solely by teeth and jawlines, the First Family was much closer to apes than humans; but Lucy was even farther away from humans than they were.

Further separating Lucy from the First Family was the subsequent discovery of an even more primitive Australopithecine called Anamensis, dating to 4.0 million years ago. Its remains are typically scarce, only a few skull parts, and a few teeth and body parts; but enough is there to tentatively cast Lucy as perhaps a late version of Anamensis rather than an early Afarensis, which can and probably should be left to the larger and clearly more sophisticated First Family types.

***

Despite differences in each, the early Australopithecines were alike in many ways. They were bipedal, meaning they habitually walked upright in a manner similar to (but not exactly like) modern humans. They had what amounted to ape-like heads on upright bodies. Their average cranial capacity was around 400 cc (compared to modern humans' 1400 cc). Their bones were much more robust than ours, which tells us they were extremely strong and/or heavily muscled to have developed (or needed) such a skeleton. Of course, vigorous activity can somewhat thicken human bones (a la champion bodybuilders), but nothing the early Australopithecines would have been doing on a daily basis could account for the head-to-toe thickness of theirs.

Their arms were markedly longer than human arms, which at rest put their hands down around their knees. This set them well apart from humans, and even from Miocene apes (some of whose arms were more like hominids than primates). Many Darwinists say it was not that their arms were too long, but that their legs were too short. This obscures the main point, which is that either option—legs too short or arms too long—means they did not have typical hominid limbs.

Their finger bones were a bit longer than human and curved slightly, indicating they may have maintained a partially arboreal existence (swinging limb-to-limb). Their thumbs also fit a partially arboreal pattern, being not as well-developed as human thumbs, nor quite as opposed. That means their fine grip (for picking berries or body lice) would be excellent, but their power grip (for making and grasping tools or weapons) would be poor.

Like their fingers, their toes were a bit longer than human toes and had the same slight curves, which would give them an arching—and perhaps even a slight grasping—capacity ours do not have. This indicates they had feet substantially different from those utilized by humans, and having feet so different has to mean they had a substantially different kind of walk. As it turns out, we have astonishing evidence of exactly such a situation.

LAETOLI

In 1978, near a place called Laetoli in northern Tanzania, East Africa, paleoanthropologist Mary Leakey led a team that discovered a long trail of fossilized hominid footprints that date to 3.5 million years ago, making them contemporaneous with A. Anamensis and A. Afarensis. Those tracks were laid down on a plain near a volcano regularly spewing out layers of ash. After one eruption deposited a pristine layer, at least two early hominids—one smaller than the other—strolled across the ashfall. Shortly thereafter a sprinkle of rain came to "set" the prints like concrete, then more ashfalls covered them, perfectly preserving them until they were discovered.

Consistent smudging inside the larger of the two prints indicates there were perhaps three individuals on the plain that day rather than two, with the third walking in the tracks of the larger print maker. It cannot be determined if the third was walking with the pair or came along later; but whether two or three, their sizes (6″ and 8″ long) are what would be expected from First Family (4 to 5 feet tall) types. And, fortunately, the smaller of the two left several excellent prints.

Though obviously bipedal in gait and stride, and possessing a barely discernable arch, these prints reveal feet that in no other meaningful way can be considered human. They have a significantly different length-to-width ratio; different shapes, alignments, and functions in their small toes; an even greater difference in the shape, alignment, and function of their big toes (an inward, "pigeon-toed" slant); and the mechanics of their movement seem to be completely different.

Slow-motion films of humans walking reveal a distinctive, discombobulated, up-and-down gait. At the start of every step we lock our knee joint, which lets it act as a conduit for the transfer of our body weight into our heel (the heel strike). As a step proceeds, our momentum carries our weight forward, moving it up slightly to carry it through our hip joint while transferring it along the outer edge of our foot sole, skirting the arch area until our weight is directly over it. At that point our hips rotate slightly as we "fall" forward and sideways into our next step, a maneuver that creates small bumps and bobbles as we move.

Once the midpoint of a stride has been reached and our weight passes beyond the arch area, it does a sharp crossover into the ball of the foot. The ball—like the heel—gathers, holds, and then transfers our body weight forward, simultaneously generating energy, which is necessary to pass our weight out to the big toe and, to a much lesser extent, to the small toes, which act as balancers for the thrust generated by the big toe. Here is how it looks:

Fig. 11.

As a result, we walk in a surprisingly inefficient way that—if it could be redesigned or reformatted—could be greatly improved upon. But guess what? We can find exactly such improvements in the footprints at Laetoli! How? By photogrammetric analysis, which reveals fine subtleties of pressure in a given print by analyzing it with the techniques of spy-satellite photography.

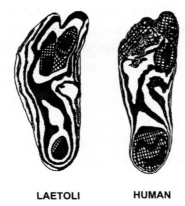

Fig. 12.   **LAETOLI**   **HUMAN**

This shows the Laetoli feet work in a much flatter plane than humans, impacting the heels, a flattened arch, and forefeet about equally, giving them a more balanced weight distribution than we have. They glide the entire surface of their feet to a landing, then shift their weight forward along the foot's midline, which means no locked knees and a smoother "carry" through each step. That smooth shift of weight follows a gentle "S" along the foot's midline, rather than a human's sharp crossover from the outer edge to the ball, which eliminates more of the human's jerky motion. From that point the push-off comes from the forefoot area just behind their toes—the big toe and the smaller ones—rather than pushing off from the end of the big toe as humans do.

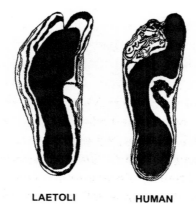

Fig. 13.   **LAETOLI**   **HUMAN**

Such a smooth, gliding walk could only come from a creature keeping its knees semi-bent with each step, never fully locking at any point, and using the thigh bones and muscles as shock absorbers and weight carriers rather than—as in humans—letting the knee joints and hip joints absorb the stresses of each step. So this bent-kneed, even-keeled, well-balanced gait tells us that the two or three hominids walking across a stretch of African savanna 3.5 million years ago were utilizing bipedality in its most efficient form.

The amazing truth is that the ancient Laetoli track makers, though clearly not human, had already perfected upright walking to a degree humans have not yet mastered—and never will.

UGLY BRUTES AND UGLIER FISH

The human family tree is a subject of strenuous ongoing debate among anthropologists because each major fossil find causes it to be redrawn. Lucy and the First Family were no exceptions. Once discovered, their ancient age and bipedality spliced them solidly onto the main trunk and drove a stake through the hearts of Creationists everywhere. Since that initial euphoric assessment, however, careful analysis has necessitated recasting them as merely another of the several lines of prehumans that have become evolutionary "dead-ends."

Joining them on that dead-end branch of our family tree are three super-primitive, super-robust creatures and one most anthropologists feel is on a direct line toward humans. The three biggest "losers" in this scheme are called Australopithecus Aethiopicus, Australopithecus Boisei, and Australopithecus Robustus. They are out-and-out brutes, no other word for them, with heads that are even more apelike than Lucy's, including a thin ridge of bone across the tops of their skulls to anchor huge chewing muscles. Such "sagittal crests" are seen in modern gorillas, which indicates how close Aethiopicus (a thus-far "minor" species not well-represented in the fossil record), Boisei, and Robustus must have been to their ape "relatives."

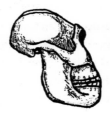

AUSTRALOPITHECUS BOISEI   **AUSTRALOPITHECUS ROBUSTUS**

Fig. 14. (A & B)

The Australopithecine considered the most likely candidate to form the trunk line of the human family tree is called A. Africanus. Africanus is portrayed as a slightly larger form of Afarensis with a slightly larger brain (which, of course, follows a Darwinian progression). Such judgements are highly subjective because Africanus fossils are nowhere near as complete as Afarensis. Nonetheless, Africanus clearly looks more like Afarensis and Anamensis (another minor species like Aethiopicus) than any of their more "primitive" Australopithecine cousins.

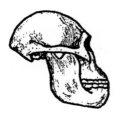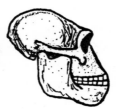

AUSTRALOPITHECUS AFRICANUS   **AUSTRALOPITHECUS AFARENSIS**

Fig. 15. (A & B)

Some anthropologists argue that Robustus and Boisei, and Afarensis and Africanus, represent only two species rather than four because of marked sexual dimorphism (a strong tendency in all primate species, including our own). So perhaps Boisei and Robustus are the male and female version of a single "primitive"

Australopithecine. (Don't let their names mislead you: Boisei is larger than Robustus and might have the larger sounding name if its discovery had not been financed by a man named Boisei.) Similarly, Africanus and Afarensis could be male and female versions of a single "advanced" Australopithecine. (Don't let "primitive" and "advanced" confuse you, either; the "advanced" Australos appear at 4.0 million years ago, 1.5 million earlier than the "primitives" at 2.5 million. This demonstrates how early the Australos' Darwinian progression went haywire.) At any rate, combining the advanced and primitives into pairs leaves Aethiopicus and Anamensis as wallflowers at the dance; but since their lack of remains makes each a marginal species at best, we can speculate that they, too, might eventually become blended into just two dominant groups.

The final (for now) confusion to warn you against is the above speculations. No matter if there were six, four, or only two Australopithecines, they clearly deserve a genus category of their own. Apart from the glaring physical differences between them (Aethiopicus, Robustus, and Boisei compare to Anamensis, Afarensis, and Africanus like sumo wrestlers compare to ballerinas), they shared several similarities, starting with looking like upright, bipedal apes. They all had the same backward sloping foreheads, heavy browridges, large, round eyesockets holding nocturnal (night vision) eyes, broad nasal passages, and prognathous (projecting outward) upper and lower jaws containing large teeth, which meant heavy chewing and possible vegetarianism.

Judging by their skulls, which carry brains ranging from around 400 cc for Afarensis to 500 cc for Boisei (compared to humanity's 1400 cc), and the extraordinary thickness of every bone in their bodies, it is not hard to imagine them all being rather dimwitted brutes with exceptional physical bulk and power relative to their stature. (And despite a 1.0 million year age differential, this should also hold true for the yet-to-be-detailed Ardipithecus Ramidus.)

***

While it is logical and plausible to assume the Australopithecines microevolved from at least two substantially different Miocene apes, it must be said that once each species appeared in the fossil record (like everything else, seemingly "out of nowhere"), it remained morphologically stable (looked the same) and coexisted with its peers for the 1.0 to 2.0 million years of its currently accepted timeline (any new example of any one of them could easily expand that). Such long-term stability (stasis) indicates that very little physical change occurred among them—certainly not presumed Darwinian macroevolution, nor even much microevolution—until 1.0 million years ago, when all six have dropped from the fossil record and are assumed to have gone extinct.

In this context "extinct" is a rather arbitrary designation. If any creature's bones disappear from the fossil record during a certain period of time, that does not necessarily mean it is extinct. Maybe its lifestyle changed, keeping it from areas where fossilization is likely. Maybe its bones were still fossilized, but not where field researchers are looking. Maybe researchers simply have not gotten lucky when looking for it. These common-sense possibilities are every bit as plausible as assuming a creature with a multimillion-year lifecycle at or near the top of the planet's food chain suddenly goes extinct because its fossilized bones have not been found in recent strata.

One good case proves the point.

***

An extremely primitive fish called the coelacanth (see-la-canth) is found in Devonian era fossils of 400 million years ago. That was only 130 million years after the Cambrian Explosion of marine invertebrates, and only 30 million years after the first true fish appeared, which means coelacanths helped to raise the curtain on every subsequent advanced form of life in the seas. They were also quite bizarre. Rather than a segmented backbone, they had an elastic, unsegmented notochord—an unprotected spinal cord. Unlike most fish, they were ovoviviparous, which meant that rather than lay eggs that hatched later, they carried offspring in their bodies until ready to bear them (like mammals but without a placenta). They could survive in fresh or salt water; came in a range of sizes; had thick, stalk-like fins; and had large, thick, oily scales.

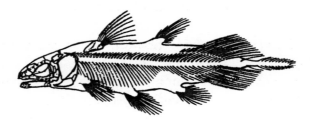

Fig. 16. Coelacanth

Because of their many oddities, coelacanths seemed an ideal candidate for extinction in the massive die-out at the end of the Cretaceous era, 65 million years ago (which eliminated the dinosaurs). Sure enough, after producing unchanging fossils for one of the longest streaks in the primitive animal kingdom (335 million years), at 65 million years ago coelacanths disappeared from the fossil record along with nearly everything else alive, causing archeologists to make the logical assumption they had gone extinct with all the others. Logical, but wrong.

In 1938 a coelacanth was netted by a fishing trawler in the Indian Ocean. Where one was there had to be others, so an all-out hunt was mounted. Despite everyone's best efforts, it took an improbable *15 years* to obtain a second one. Since then scientists have had their hands and cameras on enough coelacanths to learn a great deal about them, including that they drastically reduced their habitat from the entire globe—literally every sea and ocean, and even freshwater rivers—to their current range in and around the Indian Ocean (so far as we know). How long that habitat reduction required is a matter of speculation, as is whether they left any undiscovered fossils along the way. But the Indian Ocean is not conducive to forming fossils, so at least we have a hint as to how they wiped themselves from history and embarrassed so many scientists.

The point is, it makes no sense to automatically assume a creature has gone extinct simply because it produces fossils for a certain period of time and then disappears. Things change, just as they did with the coelacanth, and there might be another, equally valid explanation.

"REAL" HUMAN FOSSILS

Following the supposedly extinction-bound Australopithecines was the hominid line that supposedly led to humans—Homo ("man"). Disregarding the shovel-faced Australo "primitives," which no one considers even remotely prehuman, the Homos were clearly a giant step away from the "advanced" Australos, having a significantly different cast to their faces (sharp reduction in the zygomatic arches and jawline) and skulls (a distinct "rounding" of the braincase).

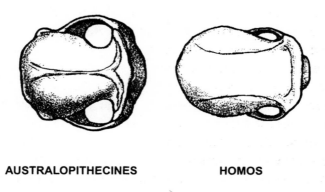

AUSTRALOPITHECINES   **HOMOS**

Fig. 17.

Most importantly, however, they underwent a 50% increase in brainpower (500 cc to 750 cc) literally overnight! This is more "improvement" than any Darwinian mumbo jumbo could ever plausibly account for; it is, in fact, an outright *transformation*.

The three earliest members of the Homo line are: Homo Rudolfensis (yet another minor player with scant remains in the fossil record), Homo Habilis, and Homo Ergaster. H. Rudolfensis resembles a larger bodied, larger brained version of H. Habilis, so again we have the possibility of sexual dimorphism creating two species where there should be only one. But whether there were three or only two, the faces of early Homos retain strong morphological kinship to apes, with sloping foreheads (not as sharp as Australos), thick browridges (not as thick as Australos), large nocturnal eye-

51

sockets (like Australos and quite unlike the smaller rectangular shape of humans), prognathous faces with heavy jaws and teeth, plenty of room beside their eyesockets for large chewing muscles, and no chins. This makes them "prehuman" in name only.

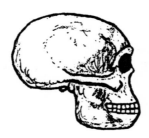

Fig. 18. Homo Habilis

Homo Habilis ("handy man") is the best known of the trio because it was the first hominid to be discovered in association with what can loosely be called stone "tools." Their bodies show little downsizing from A. Afarensis and A. Africanus, with bones that are only marginally thinner and more gracile (human-like) than either Australopithecine, and much thicker and sturdier than all modern humans. Their height falls somewhere between the "primitive" and "advanced" Australo trios, with males in the 5.0 to 5.5 foot range and females up to a foot less. They, too, apparently expressed significant sexual dimorphism.

(If a disputed 1986 specimen is indeed an Habilis, they had Australo-length arms that hung down around their knees. This is disconcerting to paleoanthropologists because any creature supposedly initiating the human line should not have arms the same length as the Australopithecines. Different should be different in more ways than just a change in skull shape and brain size.)

**

Tool use makes Homo Habilis potentially a direct ancestor of humans because no Australopithecines appear to have attempted it. Debate swirls around this, however, because the "tools" in question (called Oldowan) are simply rocks with chips flaked off in the most rudimentary way possible, with no attempt made to shape the remainder into anything useful. In fact, the same effect is produced when gorillas and chimps have access to similar stones. They bang them together out of apparent boredom and create virtually identical "tools."

Fig. 19. Oldowan "tools"

Interestingly, apes in the wild often make and use real tools to accomplish goals. For example, they strip twigs or grass stems, lick them to make them sticky, then thread them into holes in ant and termite hills, and trails in rotten logs, to snare the denizens therein. And it is no simple matter. The right kind of material must be chosen and correctly prepared, and often many tries are necessary before a useful implement is fashioned. This means it is impossible to say if Homo Habilis made "tools" for a similar purpose, such as cracking bones to extract marrow, or if they were merely a product of idle amusement. Both theories are equally plausible.

Because anthropologists found Homo Habilis "tools" decades before they discovered the footprints at Laetoli, they convinced themselves that tools and brains were locked in an upward spiral leading to humanity, with improvements in one inexorably leading to refinements in the other. Likewise, as tools were gradually transformed into weapons, hands had to be free to carry them, which led to ever more upright posture and then to full bipedality.

For years those anthropologists loudly proclaimed (and taught) that the "tool/brain—weapon/bipedality" scenario was the only logical way humans could have evolved, so they were quite embarrassed when—like the "impossible" spearpoint stuck in the bison's ribs— Lucy demolished their theory at a stroke. She proved bipedality appeared long before hominid brains even thought about expanding, and then stem-using apes proved tools were not dependent on bipedality.

This is similar to the Australo/Homo situation, in which Darwinists insist all of the latter *had* to have evolved from one or more of the former, even though—apart from their huge brain increase—the early Homos were only marginally more "human" looking than the apish Australos, and in no way should be considered on a direct line moving toward humans (i.e. a "missing link").

Reality aside, however, most anthropologists feel quite comfortable starting the human line with Australopithecus Africanus, carrying it through to Homo Habilis, then on to Homo Ergaster and beyond (despite the timelines of the last two overlapping for about half a million years!).

HOMO ERGASTER

As stated above, Homo Ergaster is considered the next step after Homo Habilis on the Darwinian ladder of evolution leading to humans, even though their timelines (2.5 to 1.5 million years ago for Habilis and 2.0 to 1.0 for Ergaster) overlap by 500,000 years. One reason is that Ergaster is so clearly a physical upgrade from Habilis, being a much larger species, with long, robust bones and a brain boosted up to 850 cc. Covering that increased brain capacity was a skull with a fuller, rounder shape than any Habilis, though it had the usual sharply slanting forehead; thick, heavy browridges; and large, round, nocturnal eyes. However, the eyesockets had noticeably less concavity beside them, indicating their chewing muscles had been proportionately reduced. Also, their jaws and teeth were somewhat reduced relative to their cousins.

In 1984 an extraordinarily complete Homo Ergaster skeleton was recovered near Kenya's Lake Turkana by members of an expedition led by Richard Leakey. Well-dated at 1.5 million years ago, it is much more complete than Lucy. The Turkana Ergaster produced parts of every bit of anatomy except feet, and mirror imaging provides a comprehensive picture of how it looked.

Fig. 20. Homo Ergaster

The skeleton was that of a boy about 12 years old. He was 5.5 feet tall at his death, which is tall for a human that age. He would have reached 6.0 feet or more at maturity. His bones were thick and sturdy, and his arms had the distinctive extra length of every other pre-human, with fingertips that brushed near the tops of his knees as he walked. His jawbone and teeth were, relative to Habilis, somewhat reduced but which, relative to humans, were huge. His nasal cavity was high and wide, his eyesockets large and round, and his browridges prominent and extended across his forehead. (Modern humans have slight browridges that do not extend fully across the forehead.) His forehead went straight back from his browridges, as in everything else that preceded him.

Superficially, then, Homo Ergaster seems little more than an enlarged Homo Habilis.

***

As is typical in this discipline, analysis of the Lake Turkana boy (as it is called) presented Darwinists with another vexing conundrum, because every step up any evolutionary ladder should represent a distinct improvement. H. Ergaster was obviously not that, and considering the timeline overlap with the more svelte H. Habilis, they could be considered something of a backslide. Some paleoanthropologists answer that contradiction by saying Ergaster was, like the Australos, a dead-end on the ladder to humanity. Others insist such concerns are mere quibbles, and that a direct line can and should be drawn from Habilis to Ergaster to humans. (To true Darwinists, of course, details of the climb are not nearly as important as keeping the concept of the ladder solidly in place.)

As the last paragraph indicates, anthropologists do not always see eye-to-eye regarding all aspects of human evolution. In fact, most are split into two markedly different camps centering on the men who have most recently dominated the fields of hominid discovery and research. Intense professional rivals, they are American Donald Johanson, discoverer of Lucy and the First Family; and Richard Leakey, a son of paleoanthropology's "first family," Louis and Mary Leakey of South Africa, and a researcher and discoverer in his own right (the Lake Turkana boy and two other famous prehuman fossils—KNM 1470 and the "Black Skull"—are his).

A good example of the results of this conflict—and the difficulties such results create for researchers—is the following pair of quotes about the Lake Turkana boy. Reading each one, keep in mind they are direct quotes published by two of the leading lights in all of paleoanthropology.

Richard Leakey first unveiled Ergaster in 1985, in the pages of *National Geographic* magazine. In the article that accompanied it he described it as follows: "This spectacular find dramatically confirms the antiquity of the human form. In its parts and proportion only the skull of the Lake Turkana boy would look odd to someone untrained in anatomy. The rest of his skeleton, essentially human, differs only subtly from that of a modern boy. Suitably clothed and with a cap to obscure his low forehead and beetle brow, he would probably go unnoticed in a crowd today."

Contrast that with what Don Johanson says about Homo Ergaster in 1989, four years later (plenty of time for a thorough, factual analysis), in *Blueprints: Solving the Mystery of Evolution*, written with his literary collaborator, Maitland Edey: "Their bones were uniformly heavier and more massive than those of modern man. This was particularly true of their skulls, which also had pronounced eyebrow ridges. Clearly these were extremely powerful people, if indeed they were people. They made the brutish Neanderthalers seem positively effete by comparison."

As stated above, these men are professional rivals and intellectual opponents. Leakey prefers a narrow interpretation of human evolution that says we arose from the early Homo line discovered by his late father, Louis. Johanson prefers a broader canvas to include his own discoveries, Lucy and the First Family types, one of whose subgroups must somehow have evolved into the Homo line. So rest assured, Richard Leakey knows no cap on Earth could pass off his Lake Turkana boy as a human, and Donald Johanson knows Homo Ergaster does not make Neanderthals look like sissies. Both men are simply slanting the evidence to support their own position.

Remember: Nearly every "fact" provided by the scientific establishment for popular consumption will first have been filtered through a need to support classic Darwinian evolution, then further filtered through a need to support the viewpoint of the individual supplying the fact. Consequently, very little reaches the general public undistorted by bias, prejudice, or agenda.

THE ERECTUS DISPUTE

The Erectus dispute is this: many anthropologists consider the next rung on the Darwinian ladder after Homo Ergaster—Homo Erectus—to be the true root stock of all humanity (dismissing everything prior as evolutionary dead-ends that for unknown reasons went extinct), and they believe H. Ergaster is nothing more than a crass pretender, a creature that does not deserve its separate species designation. However, others just as fervently believe early Ergaster was totally distinct from Homo Erectus; so distinct, in fact, that it may well have evolved *into* Erectus as it (Ergaster) undertook to leave its home base in Africa to explore and settle the rest of the world.

Fig. 21. Homo Erectus

Whether or not Erectus got its start from the loins of Ergaster, it ended up on at least four continents (and possibly six), stopping at all points in between. Beginning at 1.8 million years ago and carrying on for 1.5 million (to about 300,000 years ago), Erectus carried its wanderlust (and other lusts) out of Africa to populate from western Europe to eastern China, and the South Sea island chains to Australia. (Reports from Indonesia claim they might have lived there as late as 30,000 years ago, but evidence for that astounding claim is at present sketchy and unconfirmed.)

Despite the dispute about whether Ergaster or Erectus actually started the great migration of hominids out of Africa, anthropologists do accept that their worldwide walkabout ultimately led to the development of all subsequent prehuman species, and finally to humans. That occurred, of course, as isolated populations began to interbreed, thereby accelerating genetic diversity away from their parent stock, much the way Darwin's finches microevolved on the Galapagos Islands as distinct entities from their parent stock back on the South American mainland.

Once the dispersal took place, Asian Erectus came to be distinct from European Erectus, which is not surprising considering the vast distances separating them. In fact, if we say "Erectus" now, the meaning more specifically applies to Asian Erectus than to European Erectus, which has come to be better known by later incarnations (to be discussed next). But whether Asian or European, Homo Erectus was as clearly distinct from its predecessors as it was similar to them.

Most noticeably, their travels expanded more than their personal horizons, giving them a brain increase over Ergaster of more than 100 cc (up to around 1000 cc). Physically, however, they changed relatively little, keeping their thick-boned, robust bodies in the 6.0 foot range while still retaining ape-like faces dominated by the usual slanting forehead; thick browridges; large, round, nocturnal eyes; wide cheeks and nasal passages; heavy jaws and teeth; and no chin.

Surprisingly, their increased brain capacity did not do much for their tool making ability. Before the dispersal, in Africa, Ergaster had developed a tool style called Acheulean (Ah-cue-le-an), which entailed flaking a stone on both sides to make an edge that could be used as a cutter, a scraper, or a chopper, as needed. After the dispersion, Asian Erectus continued making their stone tools just as they did in Africa, mostly using them as choppers. European Erectus, however, managed a slight upgrade to hand axes, which had edges and points that could be used in a wider variety of ways.

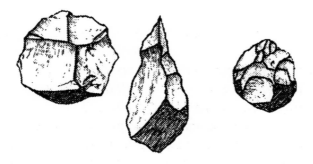

Fig. 22. Acheulean tools

This is not to imply that European Erectus generated some kind of technological breakthrough; the tools they were making were still basically rocks with pieces chipped off. But it was definitely more chips than Homo Habilis ever managed. To put it in proper perspective, consider this quote from paleoanthropologist Mary Leakey (the late wife of Louis and mother of Richard, considered by many anthropological insiders to be the true genius in the Leakey family). Regarding the simplicity and boring sameness of Homo Erectus hand-axes (which Mary Leakey spent a large part of her career studying) throughout their 1.5 million year timeline, she summed them up with this pithy phrase: "They must have been *very* dimwitted fellows."

Another intriguing aspect of Homo Erectus in Asia (particularly in China) is that many of their skulls there are found shattered and piled into scrap heaps along with the shattered bones of other animals. This indicates they were the victims of cannibals, either by their own kind or by some other, as-yet-to-be-determined hominid type, because no terrestrial predators except hominids routinely smash bones to extract marrow and/or skulls to extract brains to eat.

Whatever else can be said about Homo Erectus ("dimwit" and "cannibal" are only two of numerous criticisms and speculations that have been leveled against them), they stand alone in the history of hominid development on Earth because they were the ones who planted the flag for all those who followed. Dimwit or not, cannibal or not, that surely counts for something.

ODD "MEN" OUT

Following European Homo Erectus on the supposed ladder to humanity is a relatively new species (thus far found only in Spain) called Homo Antecessor. Its date of 800,000 years ago and its purported mixture of Erectus and Neanderthal traits make it seem a logical "transition" species from one to the other and then, by extrapolation, to modern Homo Sapiens. However, there is another, markedly younger (500,000 years ago) species called Homo Heidelbergensis, which is much better represented in the fossil record than H. Antecessor, and which the early betting says might also prove, ultimately, to be a descendant of Antecessor. Homo Heidelbergensis is based on several skeletal remains, several partial skulls, and one unbroken beauty from Petralona, Greece, reliably dated at 300,000 years ago, 100,000 years earlier than classic Neanderthals appear.

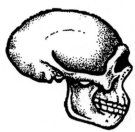

Fig. 23. Homo Heildelbergensis

The Petralona skull lies at the heart of the Homo Heidelbergensis designation because its date so clearly precedes classic Neanderthals (by half of their accepted timeline), and because, like Antecessor, it has traits of both Erectus and Neanderthal, as well as traits of neither. It also shows a substantial increase in brain size over Erectus, from 1000 cc to 1200 cc. Its skull is bigger and rounder and in most other measures shows growth toward modern humans. Once again, however, such "growth" is only in relation to Erectus. Compared to true modern humans there is literally no resemblance. Heidelbergensis remains extremely primitive looking, even more than Neanderthals.

Its browridges have grown thicker than Erectus and extend across the forehead in that distinctly nonhuman pattern. The eyesockets are less wide and less round than Erectus, but remain larger and rounder than humans (which means they still cling to night vision). Its nasal passages remain quite large, twice as large as humans. Its upper jaw is ponderously heavy, with large teeth and a still-quite-massive lower jaw. Its skull bones are much thicker and heavier than Erectus, and its body was in all likelihood proportionately larger and more heavily muscled. Its forehead still moves back sharply from its eyebrows, but not quite as sharply as Erectus and perhaps a bit more than Neanderthal. Its cheekbones are about the same size as both Erectus and Neanderthal.

Like Erectus and Neanderthal (and probably Homo Antecessor), Heidelbergensis seems to have been a wide-ranging species. Its few remains have been found sprinkled throughout the Old World (leading to some anthropologists' desire for an Africa-Old World split). Leaving aside the lightly supported Antecessor of 800,000 years ago, Heidelbergensis appears as early as 500,000 years ago (based on debatable skull fragments), but surely by 300,000 years ago (the Petralona skull's date) and lasting to about 200,000 years ago, when Neanderthals began appearing in relatively large numbers. Based on that timeline (which, it must be said, could easily be a structure of convenience more than an accurate accounting), one could speculate that Heidelbergensis microevolved into Neanderthal, which is what will be accepted until more complete fossils are available.

NEANDERTHAL

The next rung on the Darwinian ladder of evolution is Homo Neanderthalensis, or as they are universally known, the Neanderthals, in homage to Germany's Neander Valley, where the first one was found. They officially appear 200,000 years ago and move forward virtually unchanged until 30,000 years ago, when they too disappear from the fossil record.

Fig. 24. Homo Sapiens Neanderthalensis

As noted earlier, Neanderthals are distinctive because in a few isolated cases they seem to have buried their dead. However, some anthropologists feel they were much too primitive to have originated such a huge cultural leap. They point out that the first burials don't appear until 50,000 years ago, 150,000 years after the Neanderthals appear and 50,000 years after the infinitely more sophisticated Cro-Magnons arrive. Why a few scattered Neanderthal groups near the end of their timeline on Earth would suddenly develop an urge to bury their dead clearly defies logic. It can be explained, though, by simple learning: the few who performed burials may have seen Cro-Magnons (who unquestionably buried their dead) do it and copied them. Or, for reasons we can only guess at, Cro-Magnons might have buried isolated Neanderthals. Either case seems more likely than that the extremely primitive Neanderthals developed the moral sensitivity to originate it.

Another trace of "culture" apparently developed by the Neanderthals was stone "tools" (Mousterian) that were markedly better than those of Homo Erectus, being a genuine upgrade of the Erectus hand axe. However, as with Erectus, once the Mousterian technique was established throughout the Neanderthal species, it remained static for their entire 170,000 year timeline. Also as with Erectus, such creative stasis is difficult for Darwinists to explain in creatures supposedly locked into an upward spiral of self-improvement directed at becoming ever more "human."

Fig. 25. Mousterian tools

There is no question Neanderthal brains are significantly larger than all that have come before them. Their 1500 cc average is a

63

large step up from Homo Heidelbergensis' 1200 cc, and ironically is even more than our own 1400 cc. We do not know how the internal structure of their brains might have compared to ours (their extra mass might have been used to manage the extra mass of their bodies), but the shape differences are obvious. The upper rear and rear base of their skulls were expanded to hold their extra volume, while we carry our extra brains in our foreheads.

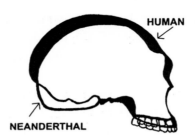

Fig. 26.

One reason Neanderthals might have had to carry their extra brains away from the upper front of their faces is that their large nasal passages and huge sinus cavities were in near-constant use, warming and humidifying the cold, dry air of Ice Age Europe. Having your extra brains resting atop sinus cavities regularly being filled with barely warmed frigid air might be inviting non-stop "popsicle" headaches, so a better idea would be to keep all brains away from those sinuses. Supporting that notion are several Neanderthal skulls well-enough preserved to show they had triangular flanges of bone jutting into their nasal passages in a way utterly unlike modern humans.

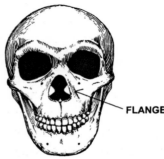

Fig. 27.

It is assumed those flanges helped Neanderthals breathe easier by providing additional surface area for mucous membranes that help warm and moisturize cold, dry air before it passes into the sinus cavities, throat, and lungs. Another assumption is that the expanded nasal passages of prehumans in general means they—like apes and monkeys—breathed more through their noses than modern humans do. If so, the Neanderthals' extra mucosal area (which no other primates possess) would have made it difficult for them to breathe warm, humid air; at least until—like humans who must quickly shift from a cold to a warm climate—their nasal passages had time to adjust or adapt to the change. (This will be important in several instances in Part III.)

Neanderthals match humans in average height (5.5 to 6.0 feet), but otherwise are clearly non-human. They have the big, heavy faces of their predecessors, with thick browridges extending across their entire foreheads. Under those eyebrows are the same large, circular, night-visioned eyes. Above their just-discussed nasal passages they have no hint of an arch in the upper bone bridge that supports humanity's off-the-face nose. As mentioned, they have the typical forehead sloping sharply back from the eyebrows; the same protruding jaws and teeth that bear no resemblance to humans in size, shape, or positioning; and there is an obvious lack of the human chin.

Neanderthal remains have been found at 100 sites around the world, some of which provided complete skeletons, so by a wide margin they are the most thoroughly analyzed prehuman hominids. What those analyses tell us is that Neanderthals had the same extraordinarily thick bones that began appearing back with the Australopithecines and the early Homos. That means heavy, robust bones are genetically dominant among prehumans from Lucy, at 3.5 million years ago, to the Neanderthals' assumed extinction around 30,000 years ago.

Another genetic trait the Neanderthals carry from their predecessors is extra-long arms (which, remember, are equally dominant since Lucy). They also provide the prehuman fossil record's first complete feet, and those feet are starkly different from human feet.

They have thickened bones, no arches, a greatly reduced length-to-width ratio, a much broadened forefoot, and an ankle placed well forward of the human ankle. (This, too, will be important in Part III.)

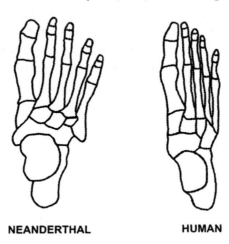

Fig. 28. **NEANDERTHAL**   **HUMAN**

As with the 3.5 million-year-old Laetoli tracks, several well-preserved imprints of Neanderthal feet have been found in petrified clay from caves they inhabited. Those imprints mirror what the bones indicate: their feet were built much more like the Laetoli track makers than anything resembling human feet. (Another key element in sections of Part III.)

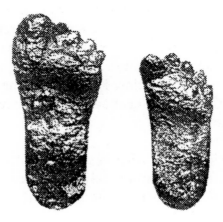

Fig. 29.

What all of the above means—and this is crucial to understand—
is that the Neanderthals represent no significant increase in anything
except brain and body size and "tool" sophistication since the first
appearance of bipedal hominids! This is one of the most important
facts—and it *is* a fact in every sense of the word—within the entire
hominid/prehuman record. Take a look at a cross-section of one of
their thigh bones compared to one of ours:

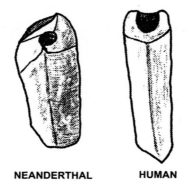

Fig. 30.   **NEANDERTHAL**   **HUMAN**

This should disabuse anyone of the fantasy that Neanderthals are
in any way related to humans. It is like looking at a shovel handle
alongside a mop handle. And understand that in all species, bones
and muscles have a closely interdependent relationship. If bones are
thick, the muscles attached to them are correspondingly powerful.
If muscles are powerful, the bones they attach to must be able to
withstand the stresses such muscles generate. So the muscles
attached to bones the size of those Neanderthals carried must have
been a sight to behold. If you need more proof, look at this comparison of two index finger tips. Their little fingers were as large as
our thumbs, with everything about them sized proportionately.

Fig. 31.

Another proof of the dichotomy between humans and Neanderthals comes from Israel. A modern skull (Cro-Magnon) from a cave there is dated at 90,000 years ago, while a Neanderthal skull from a cave sixty miles away is dated at 30,000 years ago. Weather records indicate that in those intervening 60,000 years Israel's climate changed from warm and lush at 90,000 to cold and damp at 30,000, which suggests the Neanderthals followed the cold south as the modern people there retreated to warmer regions. (Remember, the Neanderthals' large, bone-flanged, mucous-membrane-filled nasal passages are optimized breathing cold Ice Age air, while the narrow passages and thin membranes inside human noses are best suited for milder climates.)

Another problem Neanderthals present to scientists committed to maintaining Darwin's gradual linear progression is this: They are obviously the penultimate (next-to-last) distillation of hominid "development" on Earth. ("Development" is less precise than "evolution" and leaves room for the eventual clarification of the actual mechanism that drives all of life's processes.) Furthermore, it is equally obvious that Neanderthals bear no meaningful relationship to the supposedly ultimate distillation of hominids—modern humankind.

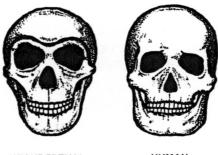

Fig. 32.   **NEANDERTHAL**   **HUMAN**

Those physical distinctions have recently been bolstered by the remarkable recovery and analysis of a minute sample of actual Neanderthal DNA (recovered from the aforementioned first specimen found). 378 genetic base pairs of that ancient individual were compared with humans, and 28 mismatches were found. Among humans, that stretch of base pairs normally contains only 7 or 8 such mismatches, while chimpanzees have around 55. This places Neanderthals near the genetic midpoint between chimps and humans, which will be important in Part IV so keep it in mind.

For now we can leave the Darwinists scrambling to plausibly explain how 4.0 million years of supposed "evolutionary" progress could so clearly point to the development of a robustly built, massively muscled, rather dimwitted brute; then suddenly, at only 120,000 years ago, modern humans appear—as if by magic!—to live alongside their "cousins" while looking almost nothing like them?

Above all others, that question lies at the heart of this book, and it is what we will be trying to answer as we move along from here.

CRO-MAGNON

The official Neanderthal timeframe is that they appeared around 200,000 years ago and slowly built to a peak at around 75,000, then at 35,000 they began a rapid decline and by 30,000 they were completely gone. They were followed (actually "joined" is a more accurate term) on the ladder of Darwinian evolution by their supposed successor, Homo Sapiens (Modern)—universally known as Cro-Magnons. (As occurred with the Neanderthals, the Cro-Magnon moniker comes from the region where the first one was discovered, in France rather than Germany.) They are unquestionably modern humankind's physical and genetic predecessor.

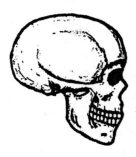

Fig. 33. Cro-Magnon

With the same suddenness as everything else in the fossil record, Cro-Magnons began to appear around 120,000 years ago, as the Neanderthals were building toward their peak at 75,000. The Cro-Magnons slowly expanded to their own peak at 35,000 years ago, just as the Neanderthals began their slide to extinction at 30,000 years ago. Those overlaps so convincingly (and so conveniently!) enhance the Darwinist scenario, one can legitimately wonder if the dates are as accurate as possible. Only the scientists who determine them know for sure.

What *we* know for sure is that those alleged overlaps have led to a widely-held belief that Cro-Magnons eliminated Neanderthals as they took over. However, the evidence from the Israeli caves indicates it was a climate-driven exchange of habitats rather than a systematic elimination, and in that case the Cro-Magnons were "driven" out. This is not to state flatly that the Cro-Magnons did not eliminate the Neanderthals; it *is* possible. However, given that both groups coexisted for at least 60,000 years, the changing climate and habitat swap seems a more likely scenario.

The Neanderthals probably went where the Cro-Magnons were not.

***

[An issue that must be addressed, but only in passing, is how, when, and why the different races of humanity came to be. Some anthropologists think the answer lies as far back as 500,000 years ago, when Homo Erectus was supposedly evolving into Homo Heidelbergensis. Supporters of that idea feel there are enough distinctions between the far-flung Erectus groups to substantiate their claim. Others point out that all aspects of race—particularly skin color—are superficial traits that can be bred in or out in only a few generations. Thus, they suggest, the separation into races was probably a result of regionally dictated micromutations which only developed within, say, the last 50,000 years (making this, from a timing standpoint, the appropriate place to mention it). In effect, they contend, race is one of humanity's variations on Darwin's multiple finch beaks.]

***

70

Though considered fully modern, Cro-Magnons were not exactly humans. They were near to us, but not actually us. For example, they still had slightly heavier bones than we have (though nothing like Neanderthals), which indicates they were much better muscled than we are. Their arm length was often a bit longer than ours, but not with the uniformity of everything prior. They were also taller than we are, averaging over six feet, which puts them on a par with Homo Erectus. But where it counts most, in skull shape, Cro-Magnons were remarkably like us.

They had our high foreheads in front of nicely domed crowns holding our brain capacity of 1400 cc. They had our faint brow-ridges that did not go across their foreheads. Their eyesockets were as small as ours and had our distinctive rectangular shape, which indicates they—like us—had lost all but rudimentary night vision. Their sinuses and nasal passages were as reduced as ours and but-tressed by the bridge of bone that lifted their noses off their faces like ours. Their teeth and jaws were like ours, as were their chins and necks. In addition to looking like us, their intelligence prob-ably equalled ours. Without doubt their tools and weapons—made of stone, bone, and wood—were marvels of engineering. And their cave art shows that by 20,000 years ago they were only inches away from being fully human, if not already there.

As for the final transition from Cro-Magnons into modern humans, most anthropologists think that occurred around 12,000 years ago (10,000 B.C.), once again precisely when needed to support Darwin's concept of gradual linear "improvement" in all plant and animal species. Certainly the convenient overlap of their decline and our rise leaves plenty of room to wonder how that transition might have occurred. Did we "eliminate" them the way they supposedly elimi-nated the Neanderthals? Did an upsurge in interbreeding between isolated populations produce slimmer and weaker, shorter and smarter hybrids? Did some unknown technological advances propel them headlong from the heart of the Stone Age into farming, metals, and credit cards? Or was it a combination of those possibilities and others? We will address all of these questions in Part IV.

SUMMATION

In Part II we have learned that after 4.0 million years of supposed evolution, the ultimate distillation of prehuman development was the heavy-boned, massively muscled, rather dimwitted brutes called Neanderthals, who—apart from upright posture—bear no physical relationship to modern humans. That means there is no legitimate way to connect humanity to Earth's remote past, which means Darwinism does not, can not, and never will explain how mankind got here.

That is a powerful statement most scientists would prefer the general public never hear, much less understand. Also realize that it opens some unusual avenues of inquiry along very non-traditional lines. For example, if humanity did not evolve here on Earth, how on Earth did we *get* here? And if Neanderthals and other early hominid types are the true native population of planet Earth, why and how and when did all of them go extinct? Better yet, *did* all of them go extinct? This is where the hominoids come in.

***

Funk & Wagnalls defines "hominoid" as: "Like or related to man; an animal resembling man." The term is meant to signify creatures clearly not human but with enough of our characteristics to warrant some kind of close association. And while clearly not us, neither are they the early homin*ids* discussed up to this point—at least, not exactly. They are homin*oids*—living, breathing, procreating creatures alive and well and living on Earth now, today, sharing it right along with us. They just do it in their own way, at their own pace, in their own isolated habitats.

In the next Part (III), you will be thoroughly, intimately introduced to hominoids. Much of what you will discover about them will at first seem improbable (if not impossible), which is as it should be. How can ordinary people be expected to have access to even a sliver of the truth about such matters if both the scientific establishment and religious fundamentalists link arms against it? Nonetheless, what you will learn next *is* the truth, and we all might as well start dealing with it.

PART III

HOMINOIDS

INTRODUCTION

In keeping with this book's title, most if not all of what you think you might know about hominoids is wrong. You probably know that in the West we call the one from the Himalayas "The Abominable Snowman" and/or "Yeti;" the one in the U.S., "Bigfoot;" and the same one in Canada, "Sasquatch." You also probably know they are labeled "fantasy" creatures by scientists, religious leaders, and mainstream media. However, you probably do not know they have dozens of other names in places around the world where they live and are well-known. To show how widespread this "fantasy" is, here are some of those names: Alma, Sedapa, Kaptar, Agogwe, Oh-Mah, Mapinguary, Wauk-Wauk, Hsueh-Jen, Meh-Teh, Gin-Sung, Apamandi, Teh-Lma, Muhala, Toki-Mussi, Dwendi, Kang-Mi,

Orang Pendek, Golub Yavan, Jez-Termak, Kish-Kiik, etc., etc.

Because the world's scientific and religious establishments would be devastated if hominoids were recognized as real, they insist such creatures are the figments of overactive imaginations. They turn encounter reports into bouts with bogeymen, which makes those who submit the reports seem like frightened children; and it turns into gullible dupes those who dare to believe them enough to examine the details of their stories. That strategy succeeds despite many of us being intrigued (if not fascinated) by the possibilities inherent in phenomena like hominoids, UFO's, alien abductions, crop circles, cattle mutilations, reincarnation, etc. But we also feel threatened by what the reality of those things might mean to the world as we know it. So we assume a look-but-don't-touch attitude, a kind of intellectual window shopping that lets us peruse what is on display without making a commitment to buy (i.e., accept).

What most of us—including many scientists and all clergy—prefer to believe is the comforting notion that we humans are divine creatures put on Earth by a divine Supreme Being who, for His/Her own divine reasons, made us in His/Her own image for the divine purpose of having dominion over everything here and managing it in the continual physical absence of our (and its) Creator. The more pragmatic and literal among us—which includes some scientists but few if any clergy—choose to think we have earned our place at the head of the food chain by battling our way up through Darwin's evolutionary ranks, taking "survival of the fittest" to its ultimate end in order to claim our just rewards. As for everything we have managed to eliminate on our ruthless rise to the top . . . Well, all of that is just too damn bad.

***

Unlike Parts I and II, this section requires substantial detail because there are not many sources of reliable information about hominoids, and much of what is available is old and difficult to access. Adding to the difficulty is the fact that hominoids have largely been relegated to the tabloids, putting them on an equal reality footing with Elvis sightings and celebrity fad diets. But despite the taint of tabloid buffoonery, a fact-filled body of data has been produced by serious, credible researchers, which this book's bibliography illustrates.

There are few recent titles because nobody likes to publish books that come off the press tainted by fraud. However, before hominoids were exiled to tabloid limbo, research and publications about them were as respectable as UFO research and publications are today. (Though every bit as anathema to science and religion as hominoids, UFO's are more acceptable to the public because they don't cut as close to our bones. We feel that if UFO aliens do exist, they won't be a part of us. They may be *like* us in certain ways, but they won't actually *be* us. But if hominoids turn out to be real, they will probably be connected to us in some direct, physical way, which will force us to decide whether to put them in zoos or treat them like embarrassing relatives.)

This is a subjective opinion, but I think the best hominoid book is, ironically, the oldest: *Abominable Snowmen, Legend Come To Life*, by Ivan T. Sanderson, first published by The Chilton Company in 1961 and reprinted by Jove/HBJ in New York in 1977. The late Dr. Sanderson, the godfather of serious hominoid research, was a highly qualified member of his era's scientific establishment, a zoologist and botanist who authored a dozen scholarly books. He also dabbled in offbeat disciplines like hominoids and other aspects of cryptozoology (officially unaccepted phenomena, particularly "unnatural" phenomena), which placed him well beyond the limits of formal scientific tolerance. But despite how he was regarded by his colleagues in academia, Ivan Sanderson was a true genius who deserves—and one day should receive—a much higher niche among the pantheon of visionaries who have helped us all find our way to our ultimate destiny.

In my opinion a close second-best to Sanderson is John Green's *Sasquatch: The Apes Among Us*, Hancock House, 1978. John Green is a meticulous, hard-nosed journalist with a no-nonsense approach to his subject. He never pulls punches or slants material, and is totally dedicated and totally credible—a true pro who digs for his facts and presents them thoroughly and objectively. And last but not least is *The Search For Big Foot: Monster, Myth or Man?*, by Peter Byrne, Acropolis Books, 1975, and Pocket Books, 1976. Though several steps past his prime, Peter Byrne remains the most famous and most dedicated of the top hominoid researchers. His book is notable for containing detailed official reports about several key hominoid encounters.

Snowmen and *Sasquatch* are both thick tomes crammed with facts and lore and encounter stories and analyses. *Snowmen* covers hominoids on a worldwide basis, while *Sasquatch* focuses on North America and Canada. And, as stated, *Big Foot* mostly deals with full official reports. Together they contain enough valid information to impress any open-minded skeptic.

***

When discussing hominoids, the same questions inevitably arise: If they are real, why don't we have proof by now? Where do they live? How do they subsist? How do they manage to stay so well hidden? What are they? Where did they come from? Why can't we capture or kill at least one? For as obvious as those questions are, they are only asked by people not familiar with the evidence. Anyone aware of it knows there is plenty of data to answer those and more. Unfortunately, one bottom-line question must be confronted before any others can be addressed. It exists at the heart of the entire hominoid debate (and all fringe subjects like UFO's, ET aliens, the Loch Ness monster, etc.). It is this: Can the individuals who report them be trusted not to lie?

As you read the following material you must ask yourself whether you can believe an astonishing number of ordinary people would willingly accept public ridicule and private censure to draw attention to testimony they know is flatly unacceptable to the mainstream. If you can answer that question to your own satisfaction, you should know what to believe. In the meantime we will begin at the beginning, and in the seldom-seen world of hominoids, everything begins with tracks.

TRACKS

Tracks have always been the most compelling evidence in support of hominoids. If not a shred of other evidence was on hand—no sightings, no spoor, no hairs, no film—we could still make an airtight case for their existence by their tracks alone! That shocking statement is true. In any court in America—indeed, in much of the world—such evidence is admissible and used to gain convictions. In fact, apart from one recent notable exception, many prisoners in the world's jails are there because they left tracks at a crime scene.

But that is getting ahead of ourselves.

***

The heavy jaws, grinding teeth, and thick chewing muscles of the early "prehuman" hominids indicate they were primarily plant gatherers/eaters rather than hunters. Understand that this does not rule out occasional opportunistic scavenging of kills by animals more naturally equipped as predators. But for bare-handed hominids like, say, Homo Erectus, even rabbits would be difficult to prey upon and kill for food. Evidence of active, large-animal hunting by hominids does not appear in the fossil record until Cro-Magnons begin leaving their well-crafted spearpoints behind.

This means that for at least 120,000 years (the Cro-Magnon timeline) the most important survival skill for early hominid groups had to be the ability to track the animals in their environment. It had to be more important than how to secure water or shelter, both of which were vital. But tracking was even more vital for two crucial reasons: it was essential for securing food, and equally essential to avoid becoming something *else's* food. Thus, recognizing lion or tiger or bear tracks in your immediate area would be every bit as valuable as recognizing bison or antelope.

Prior to Cro-Magnons, defensive tracking skills would be the most critical aspect of living that any early hominid group could pass to succeeding generations. After Cro-Magnons, both defense and offense would be needed, which would be the largest body of accumulated wisdom they passed to their progeny. And that pattern has prevailed up to our own era. Recall the legendary tracking feats American Indians accomplished; or mountain men; or fur trappers. Now, of course, modern people seldom need to track, but most primitive societies still do it every day. To those untrained in it, practitioners can seem like sorcerers. A skilled tracker can pinpoint the animal that made a set of tracks, approximate its size and weight, distinguish male or female (if there is sexual dimorphism in the species), even gauge when the set was laid down. But sorcery doesn't tell them that, it is experience, like a good mechanic diagnosing a car ailment from a faint engine rattle.

Keep this in mind: Tracking is one of the oldest, most thoroughly developed "sciences" practiced by humans on Earth. If every scrap of knowledge ever known about it had been written down and saved, an entire library might not hold all the necessary volumes.

***

Apart from practical, in-the-field, kill-or-be-killed survival, tracking has other valuable applications, most notably in police work. (Who will ever forget O.J.'s bloodstained Bruno Magli shoeprints?) In addition to footprints, fingerprints, and tire tracks left at the scenes of crimes, criminals leave spoor like blood, hair, fibers, and semen that can be used in court.

Another valuable use of tracking occurs in the science of ichnology. Ichnologists study tracks left in fossils, whether those fossils are microscopic chains of ancient prokaryotes, or trilobite trails from the Cambrian Explosion, or giant pelmatograms (impressions of the soles of feet) from the age of dinosaurs. In fact, in their own ways ichnologists are every bit as skilled at tracking as the best Cro-Magnon hunters. They can tell remarkable things about the creatures that leave fossilized tracks behind. If it is only feet, then size, weight, and educated guesses about carriage are possible. If a crawling creature leaves a track that is clear enough, its size and the texture of its body surface can be speculated about. The point is, in the science of ichnology the body that made a fossilized track is not required to prove the body existed—the track itself is enough. This is because humans were not around when most fossils were created, so there is no way they could be faked. As we shall see, that is a convenient cover for hominoid skeptics.

OUTLINING THE PROBLEM

Tracking game, criminals, and fossils are accepted applications of the undeniable fact that a readable track can tell a great deal about whatever made it. This is due to some very basic rules of physical reality, namely: When any object—organic or inorganic—has enough mass (physical density) and weight to impress a mirror image of itself—or some part of itself—into a suitable medium of less density, the impressing object leaves a track. The impressed medium can be either dry—dirt or sand—or damp—mud or snow—but it must have enough cohesion to preserve the impressing object's image. When those few conditions are met and someone knows enough about what they are seeing to interpret it "competently," they can tell what made a specific track.

I stress "competently" because that is one way skeptics dismiss hominoid tracks. They will readily consider people who live and work in wilderness areas as trappers, hunters, guides, etc., experts at interpreting tracks in their environment. However, if one interprets a set of hominoid tracks in exactly the same manner, using exactly the same principles and criteria, the skeptics suddenly consider them no longer competent to make such an assessment. The same ichnologists who can study the track of a worm on a piece of 500 million-year-old shale and gather a remarkable amount of information from it, and who know perfectly well the irrefutable proof supplied by any bona fide tracks, will nevertheless insist that tracks made by hominoids are not real, never have been real, and never will be real . . . and anyone saying differently is a liar or a fool.

***

Scientists must condemn *all* hominoid tracks because to accept even one as real would turn a major portion of their world upside down, creating professional turmoil and personal embarrassment that is not hard to imagine. With such ugly prospects looming, they are only acting responsibly by doing what they do. But despite rejection by officials worldwide, hominoid tracks are reported from every continent except Antarctica. They have been appearing for centuries (along with much less frequent encounter reports), but only for a century-and-a-half have photographs and/or plaster casts been able to provide a permanent record of them.

A clear photo or plaster cast is every bit as reliable as a fossilized imprint. That is regularly proved in courts worldwide when photos and/or casts of footprints and tire tracks at crime scenes are considered reliable and acceptable as evidence. Yet when it comes to hominoids, scientists refuse to accept the exact same kind of evidence. Their unwavering position is that the worldwide, centuries-long, multicultural "hoaxing" of hominoid tracks can be satisfactorily explained (away) with another of their elliptic syllogisms:

(1) Humans exist and can fake tracks.

(2) Hominoids cannot and do not exist.

(3) Therefore, humans must be faking all hominoid tracks.

***

In source after source the total number of hominoid tracks preserved worldwide is reported as a ballpark estimate of 10,000. Since there is no coordinated effort to collect them, the actual number could be more or less, but it is surely between 1,000 and 50,000, so we can use the absurdly conservative figure of 100. Understanding that all we need to make our case is *one* authentic track, we will begin by saying with a high degree of confidence that throughout the world there are at least 100 well-preserved (by photo and/or cast) hominoid tracks that by any reasonable standard can be considered authentic.

As with the best human footprints, our 100 hominoid tracks were made in fine-grained mediums—powdery dirt or sand, or viscous mud or clay—which show intimate details of foot morphology (structure) that human feet have, like nicks and scars on the soles, and—the clincher—dermal ridges, the faint lines (as in fingerprints) that whirl and swirl across human hands and feet in unique, never-repeated patterns. (In that regard hominoids and humans have the same kind of feet.) While they indent mediums the same way, they are clearly not human. They have different sizes and shapes, sink into mediums to different depths, exhibit substantially different length-to-width ratios, and have thicker-than-human sole pads (firm flesh more than callouses).

To be fair, before we begin to analyze our 100 tracks we should explore the scientific contention that because any hominoid track *can* be faked, every single one *must* be faked. Certainly it is true that fake hominoid tracks exist, as do fake crop circles, fake UFO photographs, etc. However, in each discipline the number of fakes is small relative to bona fides, and few fakes ever withstand close scrutiny by experts in the field. Thus, for someone truly knowledgeable about tracks, any phony is ridiculously easy to spot. With ten minutes of instruction the average first-grader would be as hard to fool with a fake track as any ichnologist.

MAKING A FAKE

When any living fleshy foot comes down on a suitable medium, its padded, segmented structure displaces the medium outward from midline to edge, distributing its force sequentially (as in humans) or radially (as in camel pads). Each method produces a similar pattern of tiny parallel cracks along the print's outside edge, running down-and-into the print's trough. Those downward-running cracks—called compression lines—are unmistakable, and no one with a magnifying glass—not even a first grader—could misinterpret them.

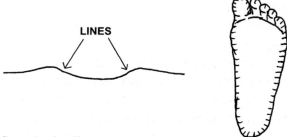

Fig. 34. Compression lines

Conversely, no matter what a phony foot is made of—wood, plastic, rubber, etc.—it must be pressed or stamped into a medium as one solid unit rather than laid down in subtly segmented parts. No matter how that pressing or stamping is done, it delivers a uniform force across the surface of the print, all at once, which squeezes rather than eases the medium out and away from where it was. That raises a small uplift—called an impact ridge—of the medium's material along the print's outside perimeter. A distinctive feature of the impact ridge will be tiny cracks running through and beyond it, with none inside the print (as there is with a bona fide).

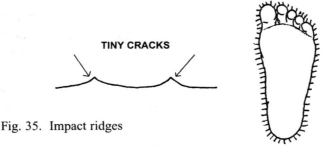

TINY CRACKS

Fig. 35. Impact ridges

This is not meant to oversimplify a comprehensive, highly analytical discipline like ichnology. Nonetheless, those are two of its most basic aspects, and by utilizing them no one of normal intelligence should be fooled by fake tracks of any kind. (In this context "tracks" does not mean two or three isolated prints, which are nearly always fakes. To make our Top 100 they must be part of a string that extends for a considerable distance, which the best ones invariably do.)

All of that being the case, let's put our first-grader with a magnifying glass to a real test by creating a convincing string of fake Bigfoot/Sasquatch tracks. The best Bigfoot tracks among the best 100 hominoid tracks resemble barefoot human prints in dirt, clay, loam, mud, or snow. They reveal nicks, scars, creases, dermal ridges, and noticeable differences in shape, size, and depths sunk into mediums. In short, Bigfoot tracks are made by outsized versions of the widely varied feet owned by all Earth primates—humans, apes, and monkeys.

When moving over natural terrain, the best Bigfoot tracks show the expected variations: different heel strikes and toe pushes walking upgrade or downgrade; different toe placements, toe-grip forces, pressure ridges, lateral breaks, weight shifts; and different depths of compression in varying mediums. Such complex subtleties of motion will be extremely difficult to duplicate.

***

Our first visits are to prosthetic makers to secure a pair of artificial foot cores that can articulate like the tightly interconnected mesh created by the dozens of muscles, ligaments, and tendons attached to the twenty-six bones and thirty-three joints that comprise primate feet. Unfortunately, every prosthetic maker tells us nothing like what we require is available, nor is it on the horizon. For as advanced as many prosthetic devices are, living feet are far too intricate to even approximate, much less duplicate. That means we have to make our own, which we initiate by acquiring a pair of casts from a Bigfoot's left foot and right foot that are exact external replicas of a pair of the best authentic casts. Luckily, any number of Bigfoot researchers can supply what we need.

We choose a pair that show the typical wear-and-tear (scars, nicks, etc.) that comes from years of walking on difficult terrain, along with visible dermal ridges under the toes and in the forefoot and heel and edge areas of the fleshy foot pads. Once we have a pair of superior casts, we put them in plaster and let it harden to make our molds. Then, since we copied prints already on record, we must make sure our fakes cannot be linked to them. That means carving a new, realistic pattern of nicks and scars and—especially tedious—dermal ridges, which requires the patience of Job and the precision of a hundred watchmakers.

To speed things up, let's make money no object and acquire laser cutting devices to incise our copied molds. Once they are convincingly altered, they must then be lined with the best faux-skin available, something to duplicate the texture and firmness of flesh that has never been shod. The best will be the latex compounds Hollywood makeup artists use to create realistic face masks and body parts. It will be expensive and we will need expert help to utilize it, but we have made money no object and can afford to hire the best in the business. They soon produce faux-skin covers for our fakes that are indistinguishable from real skin.

Next we need cores to go in our covers, cores that flex and articulate like real feet. Prosthetic makers have already told us such things do not currently exist, so now we must bend reality a bit. Let's assume we briefly visit another dimension in the space-time continuum, where we acquire fully segmented, fully articulating, spring-wire-and-fiberglass cores to go inside our Hollywood latex feet. Our fakes are now the equal of real feet with a full range of movement.

Because we are faking Bigfoot tracks, we have to take them where Bigfoot sightings most often occur—in America's Pacific Northwest. Once there, we have to go waaaay out in the boondocks where most Bigfoot tracks are found. But wait. If we do that, people are not likely to see them, and the whole point is to have them found so they can get in the tabloids and dupe the gullible public. That means when we arrange to lay our tracks out in the middle of nowhere, we also must arrange to have some unsuspecting hikers find them not long after we make them.

Now we are ready to get to work. Step one: We need a medium to match the ones where the clearest tracks are found, so we choose a stretch of soft loamy soil that will copy prints like a 3-D Xerox. Step two: The terrain has to be irregular, with flats that give perfect prints, and ups-and-downs that show the subtle foot movements—toes digging in harder going uphill, heels digging in deeper going down—that real tracks exhibit. Step three: We have to lay our tracks from where the stretch of loamy soil begins to where it ends because genuine tracks never start and stop like magic. They come *from* some place and go *to* some other place.

Okay, we have a nice stretch of varied terrain overlaid by loamy soil. What now? Well, we can't leave human tracks anywhere near our phonies or the jig is up before it begins, so we have to attach our fake feet to our own feet. Unfortunately, that creates two more serious problems: we must stretch our normal stride into "giant" steps to match a typical Bigfoot's stride; and we will not sink to anywhere near the depth a typical Bigfoot would. Let's tackle stride-length first.

Adult Bigfeet average 7 to 9 feet tall, which produces an average stride of 40 to 50 inches, heel to toe. Humans average only half as long, 20 to 25 inches. Sounds easy enough to solve: we hire a 7-foot-plus basketball player (remember, money is no object) to take steps equal to a small Bigfoot. Are we set now? Not quite. A 7-foot-plus basketball player would weigh in at around 300 pounds (think of Shaquille O'Neil), while adult Bigfeet average 600 to 900 pounds, which has to be matched by our faker because ichnologists can easily calculate how much weight is needed to sink to any depth in any given medium. So let's say we find a 7-foot-plus, 300 pound basketball player who can and will carry a barbell with 300 more pounds on it.

Now are we ready? Nope, sorry—two more major problems. We still must get our mechanical cores to move in perfect unison with our faker's feet; and we must somehow relocate his ankles forward to nearer the center of the weight-bearing areas, which is a distinctive feature of all legitimate Bigfoot tracks. Rather than tackle the incredible complexities involved in solving these last two problems, let's just call a halt and hope that by now everyone can see how ludicrous it is to contend that anyone anywhere could make a "fool-the-experts" string of fake hominoid tracks. It just cannot be done, not by anybody, not now or in the past, never—period.

***

Hopefully the preceding has eased any doubts about the reality of hominoid tracks. There are literally thousands of them from all around the world, in every shape and size, and even if hoaxers could match our impossible fakes, it is absurd to suggest they would make new models each time they wanted to have fun at the public's expense. It is absurdity piled upon absurdity.

Remember: In any court in the world the evidence now on hand would be enough to convict any other unknown creatures of first-degree reality. However, because these would cause scientists and religious leaders such colossal inconvenience and painful self-evaluation, all evidence supporting them is inadmissable. Now, let's discuss the feet that make those tracks.

HOMINOID FEET

As we found in Part II, there is a wide range of difference in human feet, from 7-foot-plus basketball players (Shaq wears a 20 EEEE) to African pygmies whose average adult size equals a typical ten-year-old. From length and width, to toe shape and size, to arch depth (if any), human feet run an astonishing gamut of variability. However, despite those variations human feet have certain commonalities: a length-to-width ratio in the 3:1 range; a big toe larger than the others, which usually curve down and away from it in a smooth arc; and an expanded basal joint behind the big toe to provide the rounded "ball" used as a forward thrust generator (see Fig. 11).

Hominoid feet are radically different from our feet because hominoid body structure is radically different from ours. That is to be expected. However, the real mind-boggler is that hominoid feet are also radically different from each other! They have structural variations that demolish the rules of species identity as we now understand them. It is as if horses had different kinds of hooves, or lions had different sets of paws. In fact, hominoid foot morphology is so far beyond human parameters that, in relative terms, it is as if we could look at any human footprint and tell the race of whoever made it. It simply isn't done.

***

Before we analyze feet any further, you need to know that not only are there different feet among hominoids, there are different hominoids! The Bigfeet/Sasquatch are giants 7 to 9 feet tall. Abominable Snowmen/Yetis are primitive types in the man-sized (6 foot) range. A different man-sized (6 foot) type is not so primitive. And a pygmy type stands in the 4 to 5 foot range.

A quartet always surprises those who know nothing about hominoid research, so the immediate urge is to hear more about them. You will. Later, all four will be described in detail, especially the two we in the West know next-to-nothing about. In general, we can say that from smallest to largest they have arms, hands, legs, feet, heads, and torsos that look—and are held together—quite differently from humans. All four are much heavier, thicker-boned, and far stronger (sound familiar?) than humans of comparable size.

The three large types (Bigfoot/Sasquatch, Snowman /Yeti, and man-sized) are quite different from the pygmy type, so we will set that group aside for now. However, the pygmy types have a unique musculature and lifestyle, which sets them well apart from their cousins and leaves their feet closest to humans in size and shape. They clearly are not human because they have such a high arch and narrow heel; but their forefeet and toe structures are surprisingly similar to ours.

***

Before we focus on the three large hominoids, let's consider how human feet would have to change if we suddenly became a much larger, much heavier-boned, much heavier-muscled species. First, their length and width would have to expand to enlarge the support base for our new bodies. Then our arch would have to go, flattening out to spread the increased load over the entire sole. (Understand that in humans flat feet are an aberration, not a variation, which causes numerous problems for those afflicted with them.) An expanded, flattened sole would require drastic modification in the ankle to stabilize the foot at its base. The ankle would have to widen, thicken, and move closer to the middle of the support area, which would mean reconfiguring the front and rear of the support area to reestablish a balance point. In short, the heel would have to enlarge rearward and the forefoot would have to be shortened and restructured.

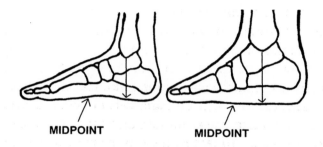

MIDPOINT   MIDPOINT

Fig. 36.

Not surprisingly, the three larger hominoids leave prints that show all those modifications. They have expanded soles with smaller length-to-width ratios than humans (2.5:1 vs. 3:1). They lack an arch. They have enlarged and elongated heels. The forefeet are shortened and widened. And their ankles are indeed wider, thicker, and set farther forward on their feet (which we know from the same kind of photogrammetric analysis used on the Laetoli tracks). We do not yet have the bones of a certified hominoid foot to study, but we have the next best thing: the bones of Neanderthal feet. As already shown in Fig. 28, these clearly exhibit each of the modifications necessary to support a hominid-type body that has much more size and bulk than typical humans.

Despite lacking the bones of a certified hominoid foot, we can still draw comparisons between their feet and ours by comparing tracks. For example, at any given stature Bigfoot feet are 23% longer than human feet and 33% wider. Given their size differential, this becomes an actual 65% wider, which means Bigfoot feet have roughly twice the surface area of human feet.

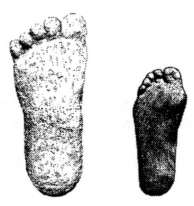

Fig. 37.

Photogrammetric analysis of hominoid tracks also shows they do not walk with anything near the human heel-strike, toe-off pattern. Their walks are much closer to whatever made the Laetoli tracks. Recall that those smallish (in the five-foot range) track makers walked with a flat-footed, bent-kneed, gliding kind of gait that was far more efficient than any human's lock-kneed, hip-rotating, discombobulated stride. What I knew then but didn't mention was that their ankles were also located forward of ours. Notice in Fig. 38 where the internal pressure points are for their ankles compared to ours. Hominoid ankles analyze quite similarly to theirs.

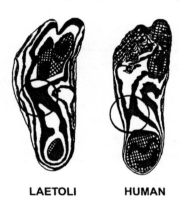

Fig. 38.   **LAETOLI**   **HUMAN**

It would have caused unnecessary confusion when we first encountered the Laetoli tracks, but now take note: the Laetoli Australopithecines of 3.5 million years ago and today's hominoids have remarkably similar feet carrying their owners in a similarly efficient way.

***

Another proof of the hominoids' ankle-forward position is supplied by encounter reports. Like footprints, encounter reports number in the thousands, and a consistent thread among eyewitnesses is that larger ones do indeed have ankles set noticeably forward on their feet. A third proof is seen in the famous film of a female Bigfoot taken by a man named Roger Patterson in 1967. As with hominoid bodies, the Patterson film will be discussed in detail in a later chapter, so please bear with only this passing mention of it now. It reveals that the creature he filmed had a markedly elongated heel and an ankle set well forward of ours.

All in all, hominoid feet reveal what is anatomically required of them, not what tends to be expected by hoaxers, the media, and the public.

BIGFOOT/SASQUATCH FEET

Some of the most convincing support for hominoid reality comes from tracks made by one nicknamed "the Bossburg cripple." Bossburg is a small town in eastern Washington State, near the Canadian border. Around it in the winter of 1969-1970, a lone Bigfoot's tracks were seen on several occasions. Once it scrounged around the town's garbage dump. Another time it left over 1,000 prints in fresh snow as it lumbered up hill and down dale, stepping over four-foot-high fences as if they were not there. Those tracks were large even for a Bigfoot—18 inches long by 7 inches wide (an 18 inch human foot would be less than 6 inches wide), and their depths in mediums revealed weight in the 700 to 900 pound range. Also, the best prints revealed exceptionally clear dermal ridges.

Here is a side-by-side comparison:

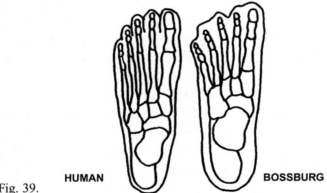

HUMAN   BOSSBURG

Fig. 39.

Apart from their number and clarity, what made those prints especially unique was their expression of the unusual—but anatomically correct—malformation that provided the nickname. The forepart of the Bossburg cripple's right foot was badly twisted inward by a severe dislocation of two metatarsals on the foot's outside edge. Also, the third toe was squeezed up and out from its usual position. That malformation meant he/she had received a crushing injury—possibly in youth—which healed without being repaired.

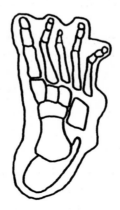

Fig. 40.

This is so convincing because of its anatomical accuracy. The metatarsal dislocations are not where they would be on an elongated human foot; they are where they would be on a foot redesigned to carry a much heavier load. Only an expert in foot anatomy would know how to create such a malformation in exactly the right places, in exactly the right manner. Combined with their dermal ridges, their unusual anatomy gives the Bossburg cripple's prints unassailable credibility.

***

Apart from enlarged heels and front-shifted ankles, Bigfeet have forefoot areas that are remarkably different from humans and—amazingly—different from each other! These differences occur in three main places: in the size and shape of the forefeet (the "ball" area); in the size and shape of the toes; and in the positions of the toes relative to each other and to the forefeet.

Actually, it is not accurate to say the three largest hominoid feet have a ball, in the sense of a human foot's ball. Their forefeet comprise platforms that act as unified thrust mechanisms to move them forward. In other words, their whole forefoot acts like the human ball. This is to be expected of a forefoot shortened and broadened in relation to humans, and which in Bigfeet must balance, carry, and transfer quadrupled weight over soles whose surface has only been doubled (though their thickness is increased by 2 to 3 times,

91

which is determined by analyzing how they push out print rims). With the smaller hominoids these factors remain, but to a lesser degree.

No Bigfoot forefeet correlate exactly to human forefeet, though one of the three types can be considered remotely human because it shows no crease in the ball region. Another type shows a partial crease in the lower portion of the ball, while a third type shows a full crease across the ball. However, be clear on the fact that none of these feet have a "ball" in the human sense.

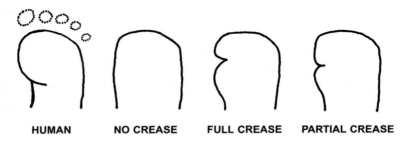

HUMAN   NO CREASE   FULL CREASE   PARTIAL CREASE

Fig. 41. Forefeet

Connected to these unique forefeet are three unique sets of toes. One has members that are about the same size all the way across. Another has a big toe that is noticeably but not significantly larger than its mates. The third has a big toe that is significantly larger than its mates. But in all cases their toes are much closer to each other in size than are the toes on human feet.

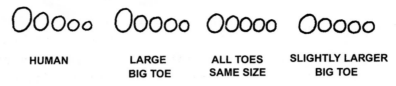

HUMAN   LARGE   ALL TOES   SLIGHTLY LARGER
            BIG TOE   SAME SIZE   BIG TOE

Fig. 42. Toes

Bigfoot toes line up three different ways: in a balanced arc across the entire top of the forefoot; in a gentle curve only vaguely reminiscent of the human's sharper curve; and a straight line set at an oblique angle across the forefoot (the so-called "peas-in-a-pod").

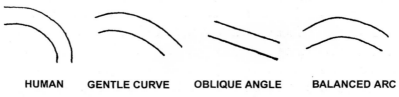

| HUMAN | GENTLE CURVE | OBLIQUE ANGLE | BALANCED ARC |

Fig. 43. Toe arcs

The peas-in-a-pod toes form the oblique angle in front of the fully-creased, double-balled forefoot. The somewhat larger big toe forms the arc, and it is attached to the partially creased, small-balled foot. The largest big toe forms the gentle curve and, not surprisingly, is attached to the vaguely human, uni-balled foot. All three kinds of toes are longer and land farther from the forefoot than human toes because their major role is to act as a series of forward stabilizers.

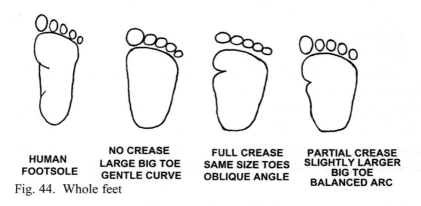

| HUMAN FOOTSOLE | NO CREASE LARGE BIG TOE GENTLE CURVE | FULL CREASE SAME SIZE TOES OBLIQUE ANGLE | PARTIAL CREASE SLIGHTLY LARGER BIG TOE BALANCED ARC |

Fig. 44. Whole feet

Whatever their degrees of divergence and congruence, all three represent distinct types of Bigfeet. In fact, a major focus of future hominoid research will be determining all the relationships and correlations between them. Maybe the differences are biomechanical, dictated by the relationship of their bodies to their feet. Maybe it has to do with the feet adapting to unique walking styles. Or maybe Bigfoot/Sasquatch populations have the equivalent of our races, but they don't or won't or can't interbreed. The truth is, they are such a radical departure from normal primate morphology—

indeed, from animal morphology in general—the reason(s) for them will not be known until we have detailed studies of how all three function (which will require captures), and how their internal structures differ (which will require CAT scans and/or dissections).

TOES, WALKS, AND GROVER KRANTZ

The next thing to say about Bigfoot/Sasquatch feet might be the most shocking of all: not only do they have radically different fore-feet, some have different numbers of toes!—three or four toes! For as incredible as that seems (even after years of knowing about it, I still have trouble accepting it), photos and casts attest to their apparent reality. If we are willing to accept the five-toed ones, we have to at least discuss the aberrations, so what might multiple toes mean?

Darwinists would say inbreeding in a small initial population could have produced micromutations that over time became fixed. However, we have no indications that hominoid populations are small. In fact, they must exist in fairly large numbers to inhabit as many places as they do. Nor is it easy to see how three or even four toes would be adaptively favored in a confined microevolutionary niche (a la finch beaks). So for now the best we can say about multiple toe types is the same thing we must say about multiple balls in feet: at present we have no idea what causes them, but we can be certain we will learn everything about them when Bigfeet are secured in enough numbers to provide samples of each type.

***

When humans walk, the foot's function is to absorb momentum in the heel, transfer it to the ball, regenerate in the ball any energy lost in the transfer, then keep the momentum moving forward while maintaining stability. Remove or alter any of those functions and our walking would change dramatically. The same holds true for Bigfoot/Sasquatch feet. By removing—or at least greatly reducing—the ball's function, they had to forego humanity's heel-strike, toe-off stride for the bent-kneed, gliding, "Groucho Marx" stride they have. Again, the proofs for that unique stride are the same three proofs for their forward-shifted ankles: photogrammetric analyses of their footprints; hundreds if not thousands of eyewitness descriptions; and Roger Patterson's brief film of a female Bigfoot striding away from his camera.

As of now, the best evidence indicates that Bigfeet—and, indeed, all hominoids—carry their greatly increased body weight (relative to humans) by gliding the whole surface of their feet to a relatively soft landing rather than coming down hard with our stiffened legs and heavy heel strikes. By having no concentrated point of impact, they absorb their weight over the whole of their thickened, widened, flattened soles, then transfer it along the midline of those soles into a markedly shortened and broadened forefoot.

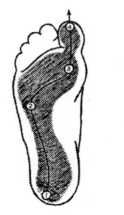 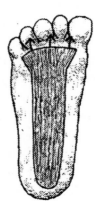

Fig. 45.

The forefoot works as a platform for transferring carried momentum forward into the next step, but it has to first pass through the toes. Because all five Bigfoot toes have to act with equal facility as both stabilizers and thrust generators during a step-off, it greatly improves balance and efficiency to have them close to (if not exactly) equal in size and muscular capacity. The laws of physiology and biomechanics demand such an array of modifications—and there they are.

***

There is, of course, much more to how and why Bigfoot/Sasquatch feet are built and function as they do. This is only an outline. A vastly

95

more detailed analysis can be found in Dr. Grover Krantz' book, *Big Footprints*, Johnson Books, 1992. *Big Footprints* is the best recent hominoid book available, and thus far Dr. Krantz—a respected physical anthropologist—is the only member of the scientific establishment to openly support hominoid reality. However, his membership in the establishment creates hardship for him at both ends of the spectrum.

During the thirty years Dr. Krantz has been supporting hominoids, his scientific peers have made his academic career a professional hell, denying him promotions and tenure even though his anthropological work apart from hominoids was beyond reproach. He has been made into a stark example for all other scientists who might consider joining him on the hominoid side of the fence. Because of that censure, he must be extremely conservative in everything he says and does regarding hominoids. In *Big Footprints* he stays focused on the Bigfoot/Sasquatch type, which dominates his home area of Washington State. As for the other three types, he goes out of his way to downplay them, explaining why on page 218:

"It is difficult enough to get most of my skeptical colleagues to listen to anything about the Sasquatch evidence, and almost impossible to make them take more than a cursory glance at a footprint cast. Still, some of them are curious enough to want to know a little more about the subject, and I am the person they often come to. If I were now to assert that there are multiple species of hairy bipeds out there that have not been demonstrated, then I would lose what little credibility I have now."

Another factor coloring Dr. Krantz's work is that his area of academic expertise is human evolution in the strict Darwinian sense. Ironically, that prevents him (of all people!) from accepting (at least publicly) the possibility that all bones in the so-called "prehuman" fossil record represent hominoid progenitors, and that human progenitors are entirely missing from the record. What Grover Krantz does best is overwhelm Bigfoot/Sasquatch doubters with technical data supporting what he knows to be true about their tracks, feet, and lifestyle. Taken in that context, and disregarding his personal constraints, what he has to say about them is about as convincing as it gets.

THE COUSINS

A primitive cousin of Bigfoot/Sasquatch is the Yeti/Abominable Snowman of the Himalayas, whose feet show the usual broad range of primate variation in length, width, etc. However, there are not nearly as many examples of them as of Bigfoot. (For that matter, there are not as many examples of any other type.) Nonetheless, on a snow-covered peak in the high Himalayas, British mountaineer Eric Shipton found and photographed a long string of Snowman/Yeti tracks that has become the standard model. By all accounts the photographs are authentic and show a startling divergence from what is normally considered bipedal feet.

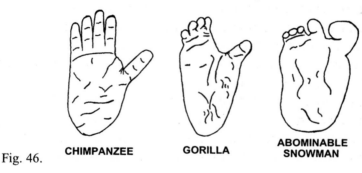

Fig. 46.   **CHIMPANZEE**   **GORILLA**   **ABOMINABLE SNOWMAN**

The comparison is to pongid (ape) feet because the Snowman seems closer to them than Bigfeet or humans. When the first one is brought in—dead or alive—it will baffle the scientists who study it because it is so difficult to make biomechanical sense of such a foot. It apparently is a product of pongid modification, yet it supports and propels a heavy, upright, bipedal body.

Part of the explanation is the Snowman's primitiveness compared to its hominoid cousins. Observers often describe its walk as shambling or lumbering rather than the smooth glide of the others. Observers also say when Snowmen want to move fast, their normally upright stride becomes a down-on-all-fours scramble. Others claim they take to trees when the occasion warrants.

These reports indicate the Snowman is considerably different from the other three hominoids. Maybe it is a "missing link" of sorts, but instead of being the long-sought, never-found link between humans and a primate ancestor, the Snowman is connected to the great apes (gorillas), and so maintains a more pongid-like, arboreal existence around trees. (Forget the popular image of Snowmen/Yetis living on snowfields atop Himalayan mountains. Large mammals cannot live in such harsh environments. The mistaken image comes from them being observed most often crossing high mountain passes to get from one life-sustaining upper valley to another.)

Whatever the Snowman's links to other primates—gorilla or hominoid—it has very odd feet for a biped. Rather than the usual heel-to-forefoot mode, they use thick bands of longitudinal muscles for both stabilization and locomotion. While those irregularities might explain its shambling, lumbering stride, such broad feet should be ideal for trekking snowfields in the high valleys of the world's highest mountains. Also, their heavy musculature should provide superior support and balance on steep, constantly rising and falling terrain. And the two big toes seem to have enough muscle power in them to provide a solid purchase on the narrowest rock ledges.

The Snowman's unusual feet might also explain—at least in part—why they seem confined to the Himalayan ranges (which, counting foothills, are approximately 2,000 miles long and 500 miles wide). The other hominoids have spread all over the globe, to six continents, but the Snowman's high degree of foot specialization works against overland treks to expand their range.

Whatever the reason(s) for those unusual feet, we can be certain that biomechanically they will prove to be just what the Snowmen/Yetis need.

***

The next hominoid cousin is the man-sized type (5 to 6 feet tall, 200 to 400 pounds). It is virtually unknown in the United States and Canada because it has no popular name like Bigfoot or Sasquatch, and because sightings of it are always lumped with their sightings. In other words, if a hair-covered, upright biped is spotted over here, no matter its size, it is considered to be and reported to be a Bigfoot/Sasquatch. In Russia, however, hominoid reports have a long history and are taken quite seriously (the old Soviet Union sponsored several official research teams), so they are well aware of distinctions and have separate names for all types. In Ivan Sanderson's *Abominable Snowmen*, he paid homage to the Soviet pursuit by using their term for this type—Almas. Hominoid researchers honor Sanderson by using it too.

Many researchers believe Almas will turn out to be living Neanderthals. As we learned from the supposedly extinct Coelacanth, just because scientists have not found (or admitted to finding; recall Part I's back-pocket spearpoints) Neanderthal remains for 30,000 years, that does not mean, necessarily, that no such remains exist, or that Neanderthals actually did become extinct. Evidence certainly supports a link with the Almas. Compare Figs. 12 and 13 with Figs. 28 and 29 to see how similar Neanderthal tracks are to those at Laetoli. Then check Figs. 38 and 39 to see how radically Neanderthal feet diverge from humans while comparing closely with a Bigfoot track. Now compare a Neanderthal track with an Alma's track.

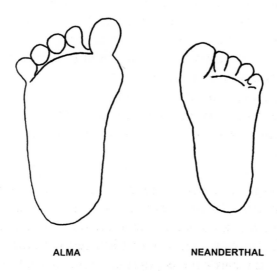

ALMA   NEANDERTHAL

Fig. 47.

Though their sizes are different (the Alma is a bit larger), the shape comparison is telling. However, as with the Bigfeet/Sasquatch, there is another type of Alma to consider; and, as with the Almas, we use a Russian name for them—Kaptars. While Almas are described as squat, thick, and muscular, Kaptars are said to be taller and slimmer in every dimension, looking more like robust, hair-covered humans than svelte, upright gorillas. And their footprints are clearly different.

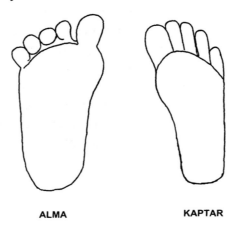

ALMA   KAPTAR

Fig. 48.

Kaptar feet are the closest to human feet of any large hominoid, and their wide divergence from the Almas indicates that in each group of hominoids (including Abominable Snowmen) there are some extreme variants from "normal" (assuming there are norms). Such divergence can be explained by several possibilities. For one, birth rate levels affect species variability. Prey animals that suffer high losses of young to predators will develop a high birth rate and a correspondingly narrow range of physical variability because microevolutionary pressures will act to keep the gene pool small, tightly packed, and functioning smoothly.

Conversely, if a species is a predator (lion) or suffers few losses to predation (elephants), the survival rates of offspring will be high and birth rates correspondingly low. As a result, physical variability can increase because microevolutionary pressures slacken enough to permit playing around in the gene pool. Thus, there can be as many physical differences among one gorilla troupe as there are in a whole species of monkeys. This probably accounts for much of the wide variations in all hominoid footprints, not to mention other variations among and between them.

***

Unlike the larger hominoids, there is only one basic pygmy type. Turning again to Ivan Sanderson, he reports that among the places this type lives, its longest and best-documented history is in central Africa, where they are called Agogwes. Agogwes are diminutive, in the 3.5 to 4.5 foot range; but, like all hominoids, they are heavily muscled and so weigh between 100 and 200 pounds. Observers say their most pronounced physical feature is the extraordinary development of their calf muscles. Agogwes have thick, powerful calves that help mold exceptionally high arches and equally thin heels, which gives them a distinctive footprint.

AGOGWE

Fig. 49.

Compared to true pygmy feet, the feet of Agogwes show a fair degree of humanity; but their extra-high arches and extra-narrow heels clearly set them apart, as do their powerful calf muscles, which seem to lift the arches to their unusual height while reducing

101

the heels. So the question becomes, what is it about their walking technique—which is fundamentally the bent-kneed posture of the others—that produces such robust calves?

One possible answer is that maybe they have a bit of a skulk in their stride, a front-heavy kind of tiptoe. Why would the Agogwes walk on tiptoes? If their lifestyle required frequent—if not nearly constant—stealth, for sneaking up on animal prey or—perhaps equally important given their small physical stature—to avoid becoming something else's prey. Also, when utilizing a front-heavy, skulking kind of stride there is less need for a heel to disperse weight and to aid with balance, while there is a corresponding need for a thicker, heavier forefoot to absorb increased stresses, which the Agogwes clearly show.

As was noted with the Abominable Snowman's unusual feet, for as odd as the Agogwes feet appear to us, they no doubt make perfect biomechanical sense to them.

SIZE AND HAIR

As with footprints, thousands of hominoid encounters are reported from all parts of the world, spanning from centuries past to the present. No matter what era reports come from, they exhibit remarkable consistency, whether those making them are cosmopolites trekking in a wilderness, or uneducated natives who cannot read but who know what they see. That consistency permits the creation of a composite profile of all hominoids, the kind police artists draw from eyewitness accounts. A person sees a perpetrator one way, while others see him/her differently; but in the end, with enough input from divergent viewpoints, an accurate rendering can be created.

***

The first aspect to consider about hominoids is the most obvious—size. Humans who encounter one—from giant Bigfeet to tiny Agogwes—are awestruck by their physical dimensions. All four are invariably described as being built much bigger, heavier, and more muscular than humans of comparable size. Related to that is the sexual dimorphism they all show, which is typical of the higher primates (including humans). Bigfeet males are in the 8-10 foot range; females, 6-8 feet; juveniles, 4-5 feet. Abominable Snowmen, Almas and Kaptars are roughly equal: males in the 5-7 foot range; females, 5-6 feet; juveniles, 3-4 feet. Agogwes show less dimorphism than the others. The 4-5 foot males are seen as taller than females by a half-foot or so, if that.

Regardless of height, every hominoid is immense in its body parts relative to humans (except for penises and ears, which are not outsized). They have big, thick limbs and enormous torsos, and their strength is incredible. Bigfeet have lifted and hurled half-ton boulders, while Agogwes can pull up fair-sized saplings by the roots. Bigfeet are known to kill/maim large animals like cows and horses by ripping out their tongues! (Most humans cannot yank out the tongue of a freshly dead rabbit or squirrel.)

Hominoid strength is difficult for humans to imagine because few of us understand the difference between our own strength and that of primates. Pound for pound any primate is vastly stronger than any human. If Mike Tyson and an adult male chimpanzee—a chimp, mind you, not a gorilla—were locked in a room for an unarmed battle to the death, a few minutes later the chimp would walk out. It might be missing an ear....but it would definitely be the one to walk out.

Please note this as the first in a series of human-primate comparisons (#1): All of Earth's indigenous primates have tremendous natural strength. All, that is, except humans.

***

The next most obvious thing about hominoids is the hair that covers their bodies from head to toe. Every primate (including humans) is hirsute to one degree or another, but hominoids seem to be more like monkeys or apes in texture, and those pelts span the typically wide range of primate colors: black, brown, light brown, yellowish brown, reddish brown, russet, gray, pale gray, steel gray, silver-tipped, to snow white.

Some primates are dominant in certain colors—chimps and gorillas, for example, tend toward basic black, while orangutans tend toward browns and russets—but all species have substantial variations. And the all-white ones are no different from other primate albinos (for example, Snowflake, the famous albino gorilla kept in Barcelona's zoo). Many reports describe certain hominoids as having gray-streaked or silver-tipped pelts, which is also a trait shared by every aged primate—chimps, gorillas, monkeys, orangs, and humans. We all get gray and whiten as we grow older, some faster and more thoroughly than others. In fact, it would be strange indeed if hominoids were consistently reported to appear in only one or two colors.

Whatever their colors, though, hominoids are covered with hair, not fur. Be clear on that. Fur is generally packed tightly against the hide it covers, with hundreds of follicles per square inch of surface area. Hair is more spread out on the skin and tends to compensate for that loss of insulating capacity by growing longer than fur. For example, contrast the hair of a horse's mane or tail with the fur on the rest of its body.

Hominoid body hair is reported at varying lengths, some of which may be seasonal (short in summer, long in winter). Within those variations are patterns for every group. Bigfoot/Sasquatch hair is most often described as short-to-medium (2 to 4 inches) and "thick" over most parts of the body. ("Thick" in this context means no thin or patchy areas where skin can be seen.) Almas/Kaptars and Agogwes are said to have long hair—4 to 6 inches—but often with thinner growths on their chests, abdomens, and parts of limbs.

Most observers say hominoid head-hair is generally longer than their body hairs, but there is great variation here, too. In Bigfeet the difference is slight, while in Agogwes it can be quite pronounced. Agogwes are said to grow thick manes of head hair that sometimes cascade down their backs to their buttocks; remember, however, that in small statures that is not very far.

The palms of hominoid hands and the soles of their feet are hairless. Equally hairless are the cheeks below the eyes and the bridge of the nose. Those areas of hairless skin are described as light when they are young and dark when they age. Some call their exposed skin black, while others call it dark brown (except in the case of albinos). The palms and soles of the feet are reported to be the same shades as the facial skin.

Hairs are sparse around hominoid mouths and ears, though their ears are sometimes draped with head hair. As for the ears themselves, they are typically reported as human-shaped and rather small, in no way exaggerated to match their other physical features. Their heads are reported as conical or bullet-shaped, with big, protruding browridges that support a forehead which slopes back and away at a sharp angle. (Note #2: The forehead sloping sharply backward from pronounced browridges is found in every upper skull of every fossil hominid from Lucy through Neanderthals, then it disappears quite abruptly with Cro-Magnons.)

BODY PARTS

The eyes under all hominoids' thick, heavy browridges are consistently described as small and beady and set close together in large, round sockets. Not surprisingly, that is how all primate eyes (other than humans) are designed and described by most observers. Also, hominoid eyes are often said to "shine" with intensity in daylight, and to have a "reddish glow" in the dark.

Like most primates, hominoids can be nocturnal, which means they can see at night. Any animal able to take in usable amounts of night's dim light has many additional rods in the retinas of their eyes. Those extra rods require extra blood and enlargement of the retinas, which enlarges eyeball size and socket size. Enlarged retinas, in turn, more efficiently reflect light coming into them, giving an illusion of shining in daylight and glowing at night. They also require an "awning" of bone as protection from sunlight during daytime (a built-in cap brim), which all primates except humans possess. (Note #3: Like thick bones and sloping foreheads, similar browridges and eyesockets are found in every fossil hominid up to Cro-Magnon.)

When we look at the eyes of primates like gorillas, chimps, orangs, and gibbons, we are seeing the same kinds of eyes hominoids must have. To describe them as otherwise would be suspicious. Unfortunately, the ridicule heaped on occasional mentions of "glowing" red eyes taints all aspects of every encounter.

Hominoid faces are invariably described as "flat" across the front plane of the profile. Noses are typically primate—pugged and spread wide across their faces with no noticeable "jut." (Note #4: Such noses indicate hominoids have the same enlarged nasal passages as all prehuman skulls up to Cro-Magnon.) Mouths project outward, giving their lower faces a muzzled appearance. Lips are thin and usually fit together in a line. [Note #5: Hominoid lips are much more like primate lips than the everted (turned-outward) lips of humans.] Behind those thin lips are large, wide incisors (front teeth), and some observers mention large canines (fang teeth). But others fail to mention canines, so some types probably have them while some do not.

No hominoid has much of a chin. (Note #6: Again, this is the same situation with all prehuman fossils up to Cro-Magnons.) What little chin they do have tapers down into virtually no neck at all. Their heads seem to rest flush on their shoulders, with a small separation between chin and collarbones. Of course, there is a neck in there, but in all apes the shoulders are set so high in relation to the head, the neck is obscured.

Fig. 50.

In part because of how their heads are set on their shoulders, all primates have rib cages with the shape of an upside down funnel. (Note #7: This is also true with every hominid prior to Cro-

Magnon.) That being the case, it seems safe to assume—if not conclude—that all hominoids will turn out to have funnel-shaped rib
cages rather than the more oblong rib cages of humans.

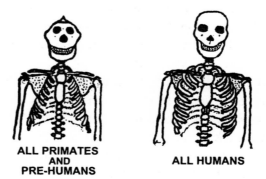

**ALL PRIMATES
AND
PRE-HUMANS**

ALL HUMANS

Fig. 51.

As for hominoid arms, witnesses mention those as often as they
mention great size and hair covering. Hominoid arms are invariably
described as longer than human arms—"hanging down around the
knees" is a frequent comparison. (Note #8: Again, this is true with
all primates and hominids up to Cro-Magnon.) In conjunction with
their long arms, hominoid shoulders are usually described as wider
and thicker than in humans. (Note #9: The few fossil hominids that
show shoulder width—principally the Neanderthals and the Homo
Ergaster boy from Lake Turkana—indicate the same extra width
that hominoids have.) Such shoulders are almost certainly an
adaptation for dealing with longer, bulkier arms.

Assuming that is the case, we can further assume hominoid
chests would need much added development to handle the extra
stresses caused by longer, heavier arms. In fact, that is just what
the encounter reports indicate: hominoid chests are consistently
reported as big and barrel-shaped. Males and females are both
said to have thick, heavily muscled upper torsos, which are
necessary biomechanical adaptations for dealing with long, bulky
arms. (Note #10: This might also explain some of the rib cage's
funnel shape; more muscle has to be packed in around the shoulder girdles, so there is less room for ribs.)

Because encounter reports consistently mention long arms, wide shoulders, and barrel chests; and because such biomechanical aspects are interrelated to a point of being interlocked, we can take those descriptions as strong evidence the encounter reports are true. Otherwise, how can we explain so many people from every point on the compass knowing long, heavy arms require wide shoulders and a big, barrel chest?

Another consistency in encounter reports is thick torsos, which also makes good sense when considering that all hominoids live in the open and most of them in climates that are normally cool and often cold. Thick torsos are useful—if not required—for insulation, but it is also difficult for any primate, including humans (as many of us know), to keep a trim waistline.

As for their hands, they have thick fingers and powerful grips (recall the ripped-out tongues of cattle and horses). The few available handprint casts support witness testimony that their thumbs are smaller than human thumbs (relative to their other fingers) and they rest close to the palm rather than slightly opposed to it. Those hand casts also indicate they either lack, or have a relatively small, thenar pad, the oval clump of muscle at the base of our thumbs which pulls them across our palms during activities that require gripping.

LEGS, NAILS, AND BREASTS

As might be expected for limbs required to support several hundred pounds of torso, head, and arms, hominoid legs are stout and heavily muscled. They are also often reported as shorter than human legs, probably an illusion caused by longer arms and/or a stooped posture.

As noted earlier, photogrammetric studies of their tracks indicate their feet do not function like human feet, which we can assume correlates to the function of their legs. Supporting that assumption are the biomechanical studies of the female Bigfoot in the Roger Patterson film, which reveal she had the same leg motion and function the footprints indicate. She had the same bent-kneed, extra-efficient, gliding kind of walk the available evidence indicates all hominoids utilize. (Note #11: In terms of the prehuman walking style, only the Laetoli tracks and Neanderthal prints left in caves are useful. Inasmuch as both employed a version of the hominoid stride, it seems fair to surmise the others probably walked that way, too.)

The unusual walk hominoids have may be yet another physical adaptation to their long arms (the Patterson female showed a wide, sweeping arm motion as she moved away). Or it could be a function of their great weight and superior muscle power. Whatever its cause, they walk with splendid efficiency, far more than humans, which, ironically, is how all animals except humans carry themselves on this planet. Watch any animal go about the business of its life and you will see a creature completely integrated into its environment. It will not waste motion or energy in anything it does. Contrast that with the distinct lack of grace and physical economy humans exhibit. Yes, we have the capacity to gain those attributes, but they do not come naturally to us. We have to train ourselves (dancers, acrobats, etc.) to achieve what all animals are born with.

This oddity sets humans apart from other species as much as our enlarged brains. We do not seem to belong here with everything else; we are, in effect, cuckoos in the nest of our world. (Cuckoos lay their eggs in the nests of smaller birds that cannot discriminate between egg sizes. The small birds brood the cuckoo egg with their own, then imprint on their hatchlings. The intruder is always larger than its "siblings" and relentlessly shoves them all out of the nest. Soon the adult "parents" are running themselves ragged feeding the insatiable monster they think they created. This is a chillingly apt analogy for the behavior of humans on Earth.)

***

We have examined hominoid hands and feet in detail, but a neglected point is what witnesses often say are their "copper" nails. As we noted, their fingers and toes are much larger than humans, so their nails show up clearly and sometimes appear to be copper colored. But because a few observers have speculated that they are *made* of copper, the whole notion of hominoids can be ridiculed.

Actually, primate nails are often copper-colored because they are made of a material called keratin (this includes human nails), which is stained quite easily by the juice of fruits and berries. There is nothing unusual—or laughable—about it.

Another laughable aspect of hominoid encounters used to dispute their reality is the size of female breasts. They are huge, elongated, pendulous blobs of flesh that dwarf the average human breast and obliterate primate breasts, which are basically enlarged nipples that supply milk. In addition, they are fully covered by hair, which no other female primate has—not apes, monkeys, or humans. They are so big and so droopy, in fact, females flip them up over their shoulders when they walk. (The Bigfoot in the Patterson film shows large breasts, but not superpendulous ones. This could mean she was a young adult yet to have her first offspring. It could also mean that when not lactating, hominoid breasts shrink to a more manageable size.)

Like the shining red eyes and copper nails, huge breasts make an easy target for critics. However, if a human female had a couple of feet of breast weight dangling off her chest as she walked—and more so if she ran—it would make excellent biomechanical sense to lift them up onto her shoulders to minimize their unbalancing effect. In addition to the logic of biomechanics, critics can be shown some of the most ancient sculpture yet discovered, which clearly (and many might say amazingly) depicts such a distinctive physical feature (along with outsized buttocks). Consider these examples of Cro-Magnon work dated between 20,000 and 50,000 years ago:

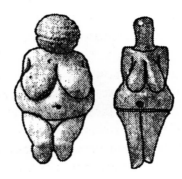

Fig. 52.

***

Like much else about encounter reports, the real reasons hominoid breasts are so pendulous and covered with hair would make them seem unreal if they were not described as they are. First, the hair. As recently stated, most hominoids live in cool-to-cold climates where winter temperatures can be fatal. Exposed breasts—especially large ones—in such an environment could easily cause hypothermia and death. Obviously, the breasts of hominoids from those climates have to be covered with hair as a matter of survival. Those that live in warmer climes (like the Agogwes) would not need thermal insulation, but would surely need protection from the Sun.

As for why they are so pendulous, that has to be caused by the physical limitations of their young. No primate needs extruded breasts because they nurse, and frequently carry, their young in a frontal position. (Humans do this, too, but may have developed extruded breasts for other reasons, such as sexually signaling males. They may also have "acquired" them as remnants of a process of genetic manipulation to be discussed in Part IV) This is not to say young monkeys or apes never go riding around on their mother's back, but at feeding time they easily swing around and cling to her chest to nurse, which usually occurs when she is sitting or at rest on all fours.

Even when mom is moving, nursing infants can hold on because they have that exceptional primate strength right out of the womb, combined with fully functional gripping ability in their hands and feet. In fact, lower primates probably stayed low because their infants could not get along without grasping feet. In comparison, hominoids have developed bipedalism, which required some radical microevolution in typical primate anatomy. Most radical, perhaps, was exchanging the foot-gripping ability of offspring for bipedality. With that change came the need for a new method of carrying young, because mothers still had to forage for their family's food.

If you are primarily a food-gatherer, you cannot afford a nursing infant tying up one of your major gathering tools. However, if you are an upright primate with an infant that can no longer cling to your chest, you either give up an arm to carry it or find a new way for it to cling to you as you work. The obvious answer is your back, where the tyke's powerful hands can cling to your trapezius muscles while gaining a weak purchase with his or her feet against your lower back. That divides the strain on the infant between its hands and feet, while you only have to lean forward a bit and keep your knees slightly bent to keep the ride fairly smooth. (Remember how all the prehumans and hominoids seem to walk?)

Because no other carrying position makes physiological sense for hominoid offspring, mothers had no choice but to microevolve breasts long enough to lift up and over their shoulders when a meal or a snack was called for. Again, from a biomechanical standpoint nothing else would work as well. And sure enough, encounter reports of mothers carrying infants do put them on their backs, so it all correlates as it should. In contrast, human infants walk before they have enough arm strength to cling to their mothers' backs, which means that for many months mom has to use at least one of her arms to carry and protect her little bundle of joy. That is an unacceptable loss of work efficiency for a food-gatherer and pre-parer, particularly when other offspring have to be managed and/or a demanding mate's needs have to be met.

Fortunately, even the most primitive humans are capable of con-structing devices to maintain infants in the on-back position, which is absolutely necessary to facilitate near-constant, two-handed daily work. Those devices are inevitably slings of one type or another, which secure infants for the periods between feedings. In short, humans have developed an artificial way to cope with one of the primary drawbacks of upright posture, while hominoids have chosen a natural physical adaptation to solve the same problem.

***

As for the outsized buttocks mentioned earlier, they have an equally logical explanation. Though not as outlandish as depicted in the ancient sculptures, the Bigfoot in Roger Patterson's film does display large buttocks, which—like all else there is evidence for—makes perfect sense from a biomechanical standpoint. The more you lean forward as you walk, the more your trunk must be supported by the buttock muscles at the base of your spine; and the more you stress your buttock muscles, the larger they will grow. Thus, large buttocks in hominoids are not as unlikely as they first seem, and coincidentally provide a convenient "base" for infants to rest their feet on.

ODOR, LIFESTYLE, AND COMMUNICATION

When humans encounter hominoids at close range, they use words like "garbage" and "sewage" to describe how they smell. Everyone in a position to know says that hominoid body odor is thoroughly repugnant. Considering how closely hominoids follow the general primate pattern (apart from bipedality and enlarged breasts), it is no surprise to learn that every primate has a strong, distinctive, individual scent. This includes humans, which we only tend to notice when we are clean and those around us are not.

Creatures living wide-ranging, open-air lifestyles (which hominoids do) can use pungent body odors in two useful ways: to mark a territory for others of their kind, especially potential rivals; and to advertise sexual availability and/or interest over a wide area. Both, either, or neither might apply to hominoids. There are no reports of territorial battles among any hominoid types, nor are males known to fight to mate with females, which indicates there is enough land and sex to go around. However, those behaviors do not represent the typical primate pattern, so it could later turn out that they do have such disputes.

***

Hominoids are omnivores (they eat most anything) who—as mentioned above—range far and wide to maintain what appears to be an essentially solitary, food-gathering lifestyle. Like primates and primitive humans, they subsist on the natural bounty of their ecological niches—in their four cases different kinds of forests— from which they can extract seasonal banquets of tree nuts, ground nuts, berries, fruits, vegetables, tubers and roots, supplemented by insects, fish, and small animals (often movement-restricted burrowers like gophers) they can catch by hand.

They are predominantly vegetarian, but concentrated animal protein has to be a significant part of their diets because of their great size and high levels of activity. If they confined themselves to vegetation alone they would be pot-bellied and relatively inactive, much like gorillas (who are strictly vegetarians). Their lifestyle seems to range from isolated individuals on extended walkabouts (which provides most encounters with humans), to nuclear families of parents with an offspring or two, to small groups (10 to 20) gathered on apparently rare occasions. The nuclear family—or some aspect of it—is probably the most common.

Like primates, hominoids do seem to have certain areas they range through. Those that live in tropical climates (the Agogwes and some Almas/Kaptars) seem to stay in one area year round. Those in higher latitudes (Bigfoot, the Snowman, and other Almas/Kaptars) seem to travel north and south with the seasons. Hibernation is unlikely for three reasons: no other primates hibernate; hominoids are not inherently fat; and their main rival in most niches—bears—do hibernate, leaving all winter food for them. When staying in one place, they inhabit hidden areas of protection such as caves, rock overhangs, or other natural formations that offer sufficient shelter. When on the move, everything they own is on their backs and everything they eat is usually within easy reach. When ready to rest, they make a bed of dry vegetation wherever they happen to be.

In summer they sleep as we do, sprawled any way they like. In winter they drop to their shins, lay their bellies and chests (and those breasts) along their thighs, put their foreheads on the ground, lock their fingers behind their heads, and tuck their arms against their sides. For as odd as it sounds, that position keeps the front torso protected by the upper thighs, exposes the back and outer arms to the brunt of the cold, keeps the palms flat against the rear of the head, and covers the ears with forearm earmuffs. (Note #12: The forehead-on-ground sleeping position could possibly account for at least some of the skull flattening found in hominoids and prehumans.)

Fig. 53.

Though most sighting reports come from daylight encounters, hominoids are considered mostly nocturnal. In fact, they seem to work a split-shift schedule with bears, who awaken in late morning and feed until just after sundown. Hominoids appear to rise in early evening and feed until just past dawn. This lets both creatures share the same ecological niches without conflict.

Their nocturnal lifestyle means they easily observe us whenever we venture into their world, but we are not naturally equipped to see them when they are most active. And when they do happen to be out in daytime, they have excellent vision to go with highly developed senses of smell and hearing, all of which can warn them of approaching humans—or anything else—well in advance.

Most human encounters with hominoids occur by accidental approaches from downwind. When they realize they are in a human's presence, they tend to hustle themselves out of sight. No signs of panic, though, like prey animals exhibit when taken by surprise. Just the make-yourself-scarce reaction of a creature used to being alone or exclusively in the company of its own kind.

***

Hominoids communicate by using a wide range of distinctive vocalizations that humans who hear them describe as screams or yelping cries or whistles that are loud enough and eerie enough to curl the hairs on the backs of their necks. The whistles are high-pitched and piercing, and mingle with blood-curdling screams and forlorn howls that can echo across miles of open country. Their meanings could range from, "Hey! Nobody get excited, I'm just passing through," to "Yo! Anybody looking for a date?" Actually, females may do the date calling, if we accept reports of them exhibiting periodic swelling of their genitalia. That is how sexually receptive primates announce their availability, so hominoid females may do it that way and verbally as well.

Apart from vocalizations, they do not seem to have speech as we know it, but there are two angles to consider. First, all primates other than humans (indeed all other mammals) have a larynx located high in their necks, which permits simultaneous breathing and swallowing but makes human-type speech impossible. Because of so many similarities between hominoids and primates (i.e. their "short" necks), it seems safe to assume they will turn out to have some (if not an identical) degree of voice-box limitation.

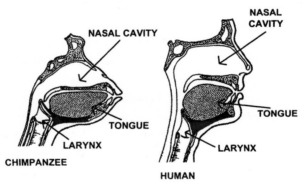

Fig. 54.

On the other hand, they clearly seem to communicate with each other, as do all primates (and most animals) in one way or another. In groups they direct a wide range of verbal sounds at each other—grunts, growls, and various glottal noises—to express what they want to "say." And others seem to understand them, so it can be argued that such communication is equivalent to ours, though that cannot be determined until some are under study. It may turn out they communicate as well as whales or porpoises—or even primitive humans. But however well they communicate, their capacity to master language will, more than anything else, determine if they are classified as animals or extremely primitive humans. And that debate will become volatile.

Right now science and religion stand united against hominoids, with scientists carrying the brunt of responsibility for keeping them ridiculed out of existence. However, as soon as one is brought in, those same scientists will be forced to publicly take their lumps and accommodate the new reality. But what is a routine—even inevitable—turnabout for science will be a crushing blow to religion. Ecclesiastics will be left standing alone, with no choice but to try to keep hominoids as far as possible from linkage to "God's image."

Ultimately, the debate will turn ugly. On the side wanting hominoids to be animals will be fundamentalists of every stripe, from calm theoreticians to strident, in-your-face radicals. Opposing them will be the usual liberal, humanitarian, and legalistic pressure groups equally determined to get hominoid "rights" established and protected by law.

Once again, the more things change, the more they stay the same.

LIVING AND DYING

With a fair idea of how hominoids look, it is time to talk about where and how they live and die. If, as previously stated, they live on every arable continent, thousands must be needed to maintain breeding populations. However, that flies in the face of scientific dogma that insists no creatures as large and distinctive as hominoids could possibly be living on the Earth today without their existence being "common knowledge." Furthermore, successful breeding populations mean hominoids need access to extensive habitats in which to live and mate and die. Here the dogma is that there is no room for hominoids anyway because humans occupy every available ecological niche on the planet. We have all been assured of that since our first day of school.

As usual, the truth is a far cry from the dogma. In the next chapter we will review the actual facts about our world's geography, which you will be largely—if not totally—unaware of (again, most of what you know about it is wrong). For now take my word: hominoids are able to live in virtual isolation in heavily forested areas, undisturbed unless they journey out to the edges—or beyond, as they occasionally do—and humans happen to be near or beyond those edges.

Another concern people have is this: If thousands of hominoids do live alongside us, why aren't their remains ever found when they die? Where are their corpses? Those seem like logical questions because most people—including scientists—have little understanding of how animals die in the wild. If you ask anyone with long experience in forest environments, "Have you ever come upon a non-prey animal who laid down and died in the open where it was easy for you to see it or its bones?" the answer will be, "No." This holds true for the largest to the smallest.

With the possible exception of Agogwes, who might be prey for big jungle cats, hominoids would only leave easily visible remains if they were shot (there are several of those on record), struck by vehicles (a few of those, also), or otherwise the victims of an untimely death (say, a fall off a precipice). In nearly all other cases they will reach old age, sicken, and die; and—like other non-prey animals—they will know when their time has come. When it has, they will seek out a secure, well-hidden spot to spend their last days and hours.

Living in heavily wooded areas on both mountainous and flat terrain doubtless makes it easy to find some pocket of rocks or fallen trees to serve as a makeshift "coffin" while they wait out their end. When it comes—soon or after an agonizing wait—Nature swiftly moves in to clean up the remains. Scavengers will get to fleshy parts and strip the body to its bones. Insects and worms will clean out what remains of marrow, etc. The bone itself will be attacked by molds and fungus that utilize certain parts of it; and what remains will be lying on the acidic soils of all forests. In time those soil acids will dissolve every scrap down to nothing, leaving a clean plate, so to speak, which gives no hint anything ever died there.

Remember, the forested areas that support hominoids are the same environments that have produced *no* fossilized remains of any chimpanzees, and most of those alleged to be from gorillas, monkeys, baboons, and orangutans are subject to dispute. The very same processes that scoured the fossil record clean of those animals are what act to prevent easy access to hominoid remains. So just because we don't find hominoid corpses lying around in the woods, it does not necessarily mean they don't live—and die—there in large numbers.

THE REAL WORLD

As noted earlier—and in keeping with this book's title—most of what you think you know about the world around you is wrong. It is simply not laid out the way people think it is.

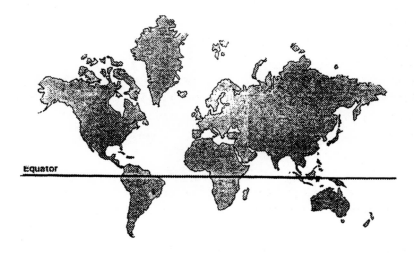

Fig. 55. Mercator world map (© Friendship Press)

This is the world map we all know from school—the Mercator projection map—a flat representation of the round Earth. Naturally, flattening a globe has to cause distortion, the least at the equator and the most at the poles. The problem with the Mercator—the

119

standard throughout the world—is that it is skewed to present a distorted picture favoring European cultures over those in Africa and Latin America. Notice the two hemispheres above and below the equator. In each half the physical distortion of land should be equal and the same relative sizes should be maintained. Are they? Check the north. See how much larger it appears compared to the south.

The reason such a farce exists is simple: this map was designed by Gerhardus Mercator, a Flemish cartographer, way back in 1569, when the European explorers who hired map-makers wanted Europe to be the center of the world. Mercator understood that and gave them what they wanted. He put Europe near dead center even though it is actually in the globe's northernmost quarter. This produces oddities like Europe's 3.8 million square miles looking much larger than South America's 6.9 million sq. mi.

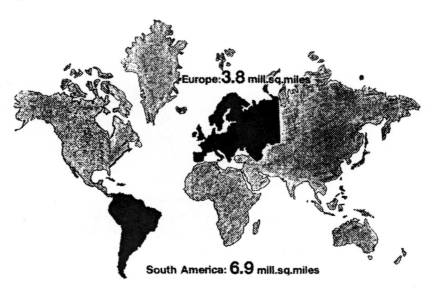

Fig. 56. (© Friendship Press)

America, too, contributes. Check the relationship between Alaska and Mexico. Alaska looks twice as big, but in reality is only 0.6 million sq. mi. compared to Mexico's 0.7.

Fig. 57. (© Friendship Press)

Greenland, which dwarfs China, is actually less than 1/4 of its size, 0.8 to 3.7 mil. sq. mi.

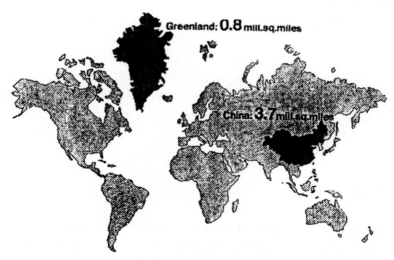

Fig. 58. (© Friendship Press)

I could go on and on with similar examples, but I hope these few have made my point. Now, here is a world map that is much closer to how things actually look.

Fig. 59. (© Friendship Press)

Like countless other pieces of basic information all of us should know the truth about and understand, we must ask ourselves why we are so incredibly misinformed about this? The answer is simple—and familiar: we have been brainwashed by a power elite serving their own purposes.

After Columbus discovered the Americas, geographers were under pressure to delineate a new, non-flat globe. Once every continent's coastlines were well-enough determined for everyone to agree on what they were, it was obvious that distortion would be needed to place the centers of economic, political, and intellectual power anywhere near the physical center. That hoax was easy to engineer because all it required was constant exposure (especially in schools) to beautiful maps that made Mercator's distortions seem real. Also, by brightly coloring every area depicted, those maps implied that every inch of land had been explored and inventoried, which reinforced the impression that nothing was left to know about it.

Mercator maps are a graphic example of the societal maxim that says what we *think* we know and what we actually *know* are often wildly divergent concepts manipulated by people serving agendas we never even suspect, much less understand.

***

Given all of the above, how much land on Earth—as a percentage—do you believe remains unsurveyed? Not unmapped, mind you, physically unsurveyed. Before you respond, understand that while satellites and reconnaissance flights take high-resolution photographs that can be developed into reasonably accurate topographic maps, only people surveying a piece of land on foot, verifying every dip and rise in the terrain, can truly map it. So, what do you think? How much of Earth's land surface remains unsurveyed?

Most people feel that inasmuch as we have been able to survey land for centuries—and especially since we began searching for oil reserves—the job should be complete or very nearly complete by now. Naturally, no one in authority does anything to disabuse us of that perception, but, as usual, we are wrong. A conservative estimate is that not more than 30% to 40% of Earth's surface—which includes the polar ice caps and all deserts—has ever been foot-surveyed. Much of that 30% to 40% was a quick once-over by early explorers traveling through for the first—and very often the last—time. Since the advent of flight, nearly all of it has been done from the air because dense forests make it too difficult to do on foot.

Not only is 30% to 40% all that has been surveyed on foot, only about 20% of that area can be called well-surveyed. And the unsurveyed 60% to 70% is more or less uncharted territory!

***

Earth's total land surface is 55 million square miles. Of that, one-third (18.5 mil/sq/mi) is icy wastelands and deserts essentially unfit for human habitation. Included in it are the huge ice domes covering Antarctica (5.5 mil/sq/mi) and Greenland (.85 mil/sq/mi); and the swath of frozen tundra that supports the coniferous forests (taiga) across the top of Russia and Siberia; and the similar swath of boreal forests that stretch across northern Canada. That global crown of forests extends from 55° N. latitude to 65° N., 90% of which

123

are unexplored and extremely difficult to penetrate. Few humans ever go there—much less live there—because it is so cold and inhospitable for nine months of the year. (Its three-month summers are wildly luxuriant with both plant and animal foods, so hominoids can and do migrate there in summer.)

Also in that 33% of uninhabitable land is open desert and scrubland. Despite the romantic image of nomads trekking across all parts of the world's great deserts, the truth is that desert dwellers stay close to watering holes (oases) and travel on direct lines between them. The vast, waterless areas in between remain uninhabited and unexplored. (Note: deserts can be surveyed from above because no trees block overhead views.) Apart from ice caps, tundras, and deserts, another 30% of Earth's land (16.5 mil/sq/mi) is covered by temperate forests. That includes thick montane growths of hard and soft woods, dense jungle canopies, and swampy bottomlands. And while huge tracts of forest (the Amazon basin for one) can be as numerically populated as a desert like the Sahara, in relative terms such areas are all but uninhabited.

The Sahara averages 5 people per square mile, the Amazon basin, 9; but such numbers are misleading because they include city dwellers. Remove those and chart boonie dwellers alone and the person-per-square-mile figure drops to near nothing. And as already mentioned, desert dwellers stay near oases, while jungle dwellers cluster near rivers and lakes. (Note: forest canopies give no access to surveying from above.) Apart from ice caps, tundras, deserts, and dense forests, what remains—36% (20 mil/sq/mi)—is the arable land on which humans can live comfortably. Let me repeat that: Only 36%—a bit more than one-third—of Earth's total land surface is easily and readily available for human habitation. Surprising, isn't it?

What it means is that we humans are quite far from being the masters of all we survey. We do not even survey all we claim to be masters of! Our vaunted "mastery" extends to only a bit more than one-third of Earth's landmass. Another third is too frozen or too parched to be of much use to anybody. And the last third clearly and without question belongs to the hominoids.

The humbling truth is that human ecological niches are fundamentally restricted, just like the niches of all the other creatures that live and die with us.

POPULATION AND VEGETATION

No one can deny humans reside in every ecological niche. However, their distributions in those difficult areas consistently put them in the safest, most accessible spots, which in nearly every case is on the environment's edges. To say a few hardy individuals can eke out a marginal living along the transition zones of a rugged wilderness area is not the same as saying they actually inhabit those areas. A little known, poorly understood, critical law of life for humans is that we can comfortably occupy only a few narrow vegetation zones we are biologically adapted for.

China, for example, is the world's most populous country, always depicted on maps as a red mass of people spread as smoothly over its land mass as batter on a griddle. This is a gross distortion of reality. China's surface area is roughly equal to the U.S., yet its population density is 4.5 times ours (120 people/per/sq/mi versus our 27). Yet that immense population is heavily concentrated in only 1/3 of their available land—only one-third! Vast tracts of high mountains, upland plateaus, and deserts are largely uninhabited because humans are not built for such rugged environments. Approximately 80% stick to where they inherently belong—on the two great river plains (Yangtze and Yellow) that spread out from the highlands. Despite massive overcrowding on a mind-boggling scale, which creates an endless array of problems and inconveniences for daily living, Chinese people stubbornly predominate where they are biologically designed for.

The same holds true in the U.S. For example, in the deep forests of Maine, New Hampshire, and Vermont, hunting parties can still get hopelessly lost. The same is true in parts of Appalachia and the southern Smokies. Few people venture into the swamps of Florida and Louisiana, and even fewer actually live there. In our western states men on foot have surveyed only a small part of the huge montane block that covers much of northern California, Oregon, Washington State, and Canada's western provinces. Camels lost in the Civil War are rumored to be running wild in Nevada's Panamint Mountains. This list is long.

More specifically, 383 million acres of western federal land have *never* been surveyed. That is 17% of the entire U.S.! Another 50 million acres—2.2% of the U.S.—were last surveyed, inadequately, over a century ago. The 1990 Census counted 143 counties in 15 western states with 2 or less people living on every square mile. That is 572,000 people in an area of 950,000 square miles, another 25% of the country! What all this tells us is that we know practically nothing about 20% of the western states of our country. Another 25% is so sparsely populated it is virtually uninhabited. That is almost one-quarter of the entire U.S.! So whenever you hear someone say America is running out of room, tell them you know better.

***

More than any other factor, distribution of plant life determines where and how Earth's creatures—humans, hominoids, everything—make their homes and earn their livings. Each creature is designed, or has microevolved, to fit in one or more ecological niches dominated by plant life in local food chains. To analyze plant distribution patterns we begin with the fact that Earth revolves around the Sun in a fixed, flat plane but spins on an axis tilted 23° from vertical. That tilting produces seasonal fluctuations in the northern and southern hemispheres, with different amounts of sunlight bathing different latitudinal bands that circle the globe from top to bottom. Those latitudinal bands are the key.

Imagine Earth without oceans or seas, its land scraped smooth as a beach ball. Then imagine the beach ball spinning vertically on its axis rather than at 23°. Then imagine everything else the way it is today: animals, weather, soil, and most importantly, vegetation. What we would have is all plant life growing in a pattern of 28 major bands that from space would make the new Earth look like a striped beach ball. Half of those 28 bands would be in the northern hemisphere, mirroring 14 in the southern hemisphere. That means at the equator there would be a double band of similar vegetation (those two would be a big, double-sized stripe colored jungle green), and at the top and bottom would be the white circles of ice caps.

Starting at the equator of beach-ball Earth and moving north or south, the bands we would find are:

1. Tall Equatorial Forest
2. High Deciduous Tropical Forest
3. Orchard-Bush
4. Savanna
5. Subtropical Scrublands
6. Hot Desert
7. Temperate Scrublands
8. Prairies
9. Parklands
10. Temperate Deciduous Woodlands
11. Boreal Coniferous Forest
12. Tundra
13. Barren Lands
14. Polar Icefields

Fig. 60.

If we stood at the equator of our imaginary beach-ball Earth and started traveling north or south, we would pass through each vegetation zone in the precise order of the list. Not only that, each zone would be the same width across, exactly one-fourteenth (1/14) of the hemisphere, or approximately 900 miles. If we went to the equator and found a mountain there, and if we began climbing it, we would pass through the exact same series of vegetation zones we would pass through heading north or south. However, instead of being 900 miles long, each zone would take up 1200 feet of altitude until a perpetual snowfield was reached at approximately 17,000 feet.

If we moved the mountain north or south before starting our climb, we would only pass through vegetation zones that lie latitudinally above the mountain's new position. For example, if we moved it to the fourth zone—savanna—we would start our climb there and move up through only the ten remaining zones. We would also find each zone lower on the mountain than it was at the equator, and the perpetual ice and snow would begin four zones lower, at about 12,200 feet.

***

Fortunately, Earth is not built like a beach ball. Besides its axial tilt, it has oceans, seas, mountains and valleys that disrupt its vegetation patterns. In addition, the dominant ocean currents influence global weather, which directly determines plant distribution. But despite all that, the vegetation zones listed above *do* cover the land's surface in the exact order listed, through every valley, across every plain, and up every mountain. They are not all the same width and do not run in tidy ribbons like colored stripes on a beach ball, but they always maintain a certain basic consistency by bending and folding into waves that move up and down and grow hugely fat or disappear altogether as they sweep around the globe. This map should make the process clear:

Fig. 61. (Opposite page)

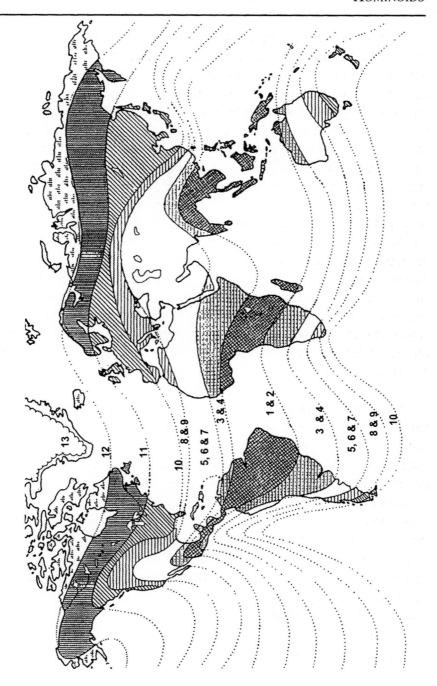

As for how all this relates to hominoids, look at Fig. 60 again. Each vegetation zone is a layering of ecological niches that supports only those animals designed by Nature (or whatever force drives the engine of life on Earth) to make a living off its plants or off the animals that live off its plants. In other words, a troupe of crocodiles deciding to try their luck outside wetlands will quickly come to regret their decision. Remember: nothing lives where it is not supposed to live—not humans, not hominoids, nothing. Everything alive is trapped in its ecological niche.

Of course, humans do live at the margins of every environment on the planet—but not in a natural state. Strip everyone naked and force us to live off the land and watch how quickly the tropical and subtropical zones will start to bulge. Our supreme adaptability is only the result of mechanical means we have devised to defeat the natural order of life on Earth. Deny us those means and it will readily become apparent that our niches adjoin but do not overlap the niches hominoids are best suited for. Here is the zone list modified to show those different niches:

Hominoid	1. Tall Equatorial Forest
Hominoid	2. High Deciduous Tropical Forest
Human	3. Orchard Bush
Human	4. Savanna
	5. Subtropical Scrublands
	6. Hot Desert
	7. Temperate Scrublands
Human	8. Prairies
Human	9. Parklands
Hominoid	10. Temperate Deciduous Woodlands
Hominoid	11. Boreal Coniferous Forests
	12. Tundra
	13. Barren Lands
	14. Polar Icefields

As you see, hominoids "own" the equatorial forests and temperate woodlands, leaving the prime open-country niches to humans and other animals that share them with us. And—wouldn't you know?—where our niches adjoin theirs is where the majority of hominoid encounters occur.

NICHES

Hominoids are easily capable of sustained trespass in human niches as they move from one of theirs to another, which could account for how they have become so widely dispersed. Humans have trouble simply penetrating hominoid niches (much less living in them), but hominoids have no trouble making their way in ours. So it seems hominoids are the true masters of planet Earth. They can live in all but the coldest or most barren environments, which far surpasses humanity's limited ability to survive in a natural state.

This leads to an obvious question: if Nature equipped hominoids to live in human niches, shouldn't they stay there rather than in their own difficult habitats? Yes, and they probably used to do just that. Let's compare hominoids and pongids (apes and monkeys). Pongids are tightly locked into their forest environments by their physical specializations (i.e. grasping feet) and their diets. They are designed by Nature to live just where they do—in the closed-canopy equatorial forests that provide an almost limitless supply of their principle food sources.

On the other hand, hominoids are as dietarily omnivorous as humans; and except for the Abominable Snowman/Yeti, they are as physically unspecialized. Consequently, they are not restricted to their current ecological homes. Unlike the crocodiles mentioned earlier, if hominoids decided to move into human niches they could easily survive the transition. In fact, living in the milder human habitats would undoubtedly be much easier on them.

***

With that thought in mind, let's backtrack to the previously discussed period between 20 and 5 million years ago, when several Miocene apes were seeking safe, comfortable environmental niches to inhabit. Some chose well and flourished, while others chose badly and died out. (Keep in mind, those that flourished did so by microevolution; they all remained within the same genus of Miocene apes, a la Darwin's finches.) Some chose the safety of life in trees and became monkeys. Others combined the safety of trees with the abundant food on the forest floors and became the large foragers we call apes. Still others chose ground-dwelling on the open parklands and savannas. They developed upright posture along with enough size, strength and cunning to cope with such a food-filled but dangerous habitat. These became hominoids.

Life went on like that for several million years, with no species stepping on anyone else's ecological toes. Then, for whatever reason and by whatever means, humans came along to upset the balance. Not only were the newcomers omnivores like the hominoids, they could live only in the hominoids' preferred niches. That gave humans a compelling motivation to prevail in any contest for control of those niches. Also, humans had superb analytical and tactical intelligence, a savage territorial imperative built into their gene code, superb tool- and weapon-making ability to complement their internal drives, and—most important—a tightknit social order that allowed them to multiply their meager physical strengths by combining into cohesive groups.

Though any hominoid could physically destroy any human, the humans would win every niche dispute because of their deadly weapons and group tactics. That would leave the hominoids facing two grim choices: stand and fight and get wiped out; or gracefully retire to less hospitable niches where they could at least survive, and where the murderous gangs chasing them would not or could not follow. Even for a hominoid, that was not a hard decision to make.

***

If we accept that Lucy and the other supposedly prehuman fossils were instead the ancestors of hominoids, then it is probable that something along those lines did occur. The presence of such fossils in what were once prime human niches tells us hominoids were homesteading "our" territory from 3.5 million years ago until the Cro-Magnons appeared, as late as 120,000 years ago. Assuming that is true, it means hominoids were well-adapted to a wide-ranging, food-gathering lifestyle in open, temperate country. When the human menace finally appeared, some hominoids were physically robust enough to take their life skills into the harsh but safer forests, jungles, and swamps. Also, it happened over a long enough period (no less than 120,000 years) for the survivor populations to stabilize and move ahead as if a major relocation had never occurred.

***

Regardless of how they got there, hominoids live in various of the world's heavily forested areas, which—excluding the ice caps, tundra, and deserts—comprise nearly half of the remaining land. [That is 46% forest, 54% savanna and parkland. By disheartening contrast, it is estimated that 500 years ago (when Columbus landed) the world was 60% forest, which tells us that since Columbus we have destroyed nearly one-third of the planet's trees.] So it is not as if hominoids have no room to live in or stay hidden in.

Fig. 62. World forests   (Next page)

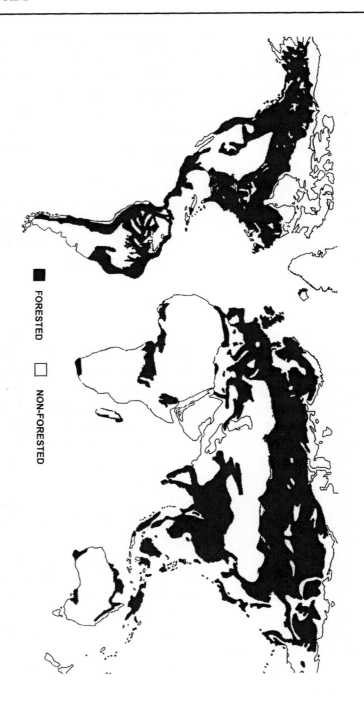

FORESTED

NON-FORESTED

Unfortunately, no map can accurately portray the vast range of habitats available to the hominoids. They can survive in any substantial tract of forested land, even in forests crisscrossed by human roads and sprinkled with human dwellings. However, despite numerous sightings in or near woodlands close to centers of human population, that is not considered prime real estate for them. It seems more likely they use such places as migration routes rather than as home areas.

No matter where a forest is located, its different niches are created by the effects of latitude (how far from equator or poles) and altitude (how high above sea level). Those are the two main factors determining the kinds of trees and supporting flora and fauna found in any habitat.

HABITATS

The highest, harshest habitat exploited by any hominoid is the home of the Abominable Snowman/Yeti—the Himalayas. The Himalayas are five sprawling mountain ranges that link together and drape across central Asia like a mutant five-legged spider. They are extremely rugged and, combined, are nearly the size of the U.S., which gives the Snowmen who inhabit them plenty of room to live and roam. Specifically, they exploit its upper montane forests, which contain tracts of two to four tiers of hardwoods and mixed deciduous trees that can blanket the sides of mountains anywhere from their snowlines to near their bases. (The kinds of trees and their relative densities are functions of the latitude and altitude influences mentioned in the previous chapter.)

Because of the extreme height of their habitat, Abominable Snowmen must cope with far more environmental stresses than their cousins, which has left them more physiologically specialized. They are said to be more brutish (many reports mention canine teeth); their bodies are covered by longer, denser hair (for obvious reasons); their strange feet and shambling walk probably result from steadily moving on steep, rugged terrain; and all that difficulty has, not surprisingly, given them belligerent dispositions. Unlike their cousins, Snowmen will stand their ground when confronted by a human, and with typical pongid bluster may bluff a charge at an intruder.

Apart from physical differences, their habitat also forces them to eat more meat than their relatives. In the first place, the frigid environment puts limits on the amount of vegetation they can find and exploit. Secondly, they need more high-energy animal protein to fuel their bodies (though their man-sized height is an obvious constraint on their need for fuel, and their extra-long body hair—in the 6 to 10 inch range—conserves heat). When not eating the limited choice of small animals (burrowers and scurriers) in upper montane forests, Snowmen will feed on sheep, goats, yaks, or cattle left unattended in the valleys they sometimes share with humans.

Sherpas of Nepal and Tibet will attest to losing livestock that way, finding carcasses torn limb from limb in a savage but efficient way. The killing wound is usually a crushing blow to the back, which severs the spine. (When I mentioned Bigfoot/Sasquatch tearing out the tongues of large animals, I did not mean to imply that is a preferred way to dispatch victims. The tongue is probably a delicacy consumed first, like a cherry on a soda.)

All in all, Abominable Snowmen are exactly what Nature seems to have intended them to be: rugged individualists living in and exploiting a difficult but life-sustaining environment.

***

Bigfeet primarily dwell within the lower montane belts that girdle mountain flanks and valleys all over the world. Unlike Abominable Snowmen, they are not trapped in one ecological niche. They can easily adapt to life in upper montane forests, and jungles and swamps will do in a pinch; so of the four hominoid types, Bigfeet probably have the widest habitat diversity.

Compared to upper montane forests, whose blankets of trees can be considered thinly woven, the lower montanes are more like a heavy carpet. They seldom have less than three or four tiers of trees, which leaves little floor area free of trunks and roots. Also, every tree in the canopy drops its dead limbs to the floor, many of which are as twisted as coiled tubing and as hard as forged steel. Those limbs combine to form a daunting thicket of undergrowth that laces over, under, around, and through the standard briar bushes and other brambles.

Apart from frigid weather, upper montane forests are more suitable to humans than lower montane growths. A hardy man with a sharp machete needs a tough morning of hacking to travel 200 yards through a typical stand of lower montane timber. It is not now and never was worth that much trouble for humans, so we have steered clear of lower montane growths, which is probably why Bigfeet/Sasquatch make them their home.

Despite widespread damage from overlogging by rapacious timber interests, lower montane forests still cover a huge swath of Earth. They supply Bigfeet with the cornucopia of plant and animal foods mentioned earlier, which provides a banquet each day as they migrate north and south with the seasons. (Any creatures—including humans—that know how to live off the land seldom have a reason to be hungry.) Wherever they go, Bigfeet remain dwellers in some of the most physically demanding environments on the planet, which may explain why they are built on such a heroic scale. Only time and genetic testing will tell.

***

Almas/Kaptars are the man-sized types that could be Neanderthals living in our own era. Like Bigfeet/Sasquatch, they range into multiple forest environments, but their primary habitat seems to be the temperate deciduous (non-evergreen) belts adjacent to lower montanes. Montane and deciduous forests have many of the same trees, but, as always, latitude and altitude differences determine their density. In general, deciduous belts are less wooded than lower montane.

Almas/Kaptars can also be found in mixed woodlands, and occasionally in the tropical rain forests known as jungle. Bigfeet can and do overlap into niches where Almas/Kaptars dominate, and Almas/Kaptars can return the favor. However, when that happens they do not seem to crowd—or to threaten—the other's living arrangements. This is ironic because Almas/Kaptars consume the same kind of diet Bigfeet utilize: fruits, vegetables, nuts, berries, roots, tubers, and small animals. (Actually, the diet patterns of all hominoids seem to be the same: eat whatever you want whenever and wherever you find it because there is plenty to go around.)

***

The Pygmy-sized Agogwes live in temperate and tropical rain forests, and occasionally in the swamps and bottomlands created by large river systems. Another term for rain forest is jungle, which most people think of in Hollywood terms: as a danger-laden, vegetation-choked, sweltering, insect-and-snake-infested hellhole. Real jungles are forests growing on elevated lowlands in tropical—and sometimes temperate—climates. (An example of temperate jungle is the rain forest in Washington State.) The majority of rain forests are tropical, as are most swampy bottomlands. (Florida's Everglades and the Mississippi's delta are exceptions.)

Like montane forests, rain-forest jungles are comprised of three and four tiers of trees with undergrowth bushes on the forest floor. However, its trees tend to be of much softer woods whose dead limbs quickly decompose. As a result, jungle floor is relatively open and much easier to travel through on foot. Also, the climate on a jungle floor is nearly perfect. The highest canopy of treetops casts welcome shade to the floor, reflects the heat of tropical climes, and keeps the air at ground level remarkably steady and comfortable—neither too hot nor too cold.

Despite Hollywood's stereotype, jungles are mostly free of noxious insects, equally free of disease and pestilence, and well-supplied with easy-to-obtain food and plenty of pure drinking water. However, the "snake-filled" stereotype is accurate. Overall, though, jungles are excellent places to live, especially for hominoids because so few humans choose to dwell in or near them.

Swamps, on the other hand, present a challenge. Swamp-*land* is the dry-ground areas within them, which can support trees, shrubs, Agogwes, and even a few humans (Louisiana's hard-core Cajuns, for example). Here noxious insects are a problem, and trees are generally dispersed so thinly that sunlight sends ground temperatures soaring. However, swampland is well-watered and teems with easily accessible foods. Swamp-*bottom*, or marsh, on the other hand, is the treeless, mushy verdure that is extremely inhospitable to humans and hominoids alike.

No Agogwes actually live in bottomlands. Like snowfields in the Himalayas, if they use them at all it is as a transit route between the dry areas of swamplands.

AGOGWES

Agogwes are able to live in jungles and on swampland because they are as specialized for it as Abominable Snowmen are for the high, cold, rugged terrain of the Himalayas' upper montane forests. In fact, Agogwes are as different from the other three types as the Snowmen are, but in different ways. Rather than their cousins' dominant shades of dark body hair, Agogwe hair is described in the light-brown to russet range, with most observers calling it reddish, no doubt because light colors reflect heat better than dark. (Orangutans in the steamy jungles of southeast Asia usually have reddish hair.) Agogwe hair is shorter and less dense than other hominoids, except on their heads, where the opposite holds true: many have thick manes of long, straight head hair that can spill down their backs to their buttocks (acting, perhaps, as a natural sunscreen).

Their faces are essentially free of hair, and their skin is, paradoxically, of lighter shades than other hominoid skin. (Dark skin seems more appropriate in tropical climates, as does light skin in higher latitudes. However, that is placing human parameters around distinctly *non*human creatures.) Their foreheads are somewhat higher than other hominoids; not nearly like humans, but not straight-back-from-the-eyebrows, either. (This could result from not needing to sleep in the warmth-conserving, torso-on-thighs, forehead-on-ground position; or from not needing enlarged sinus cavities to breathe cold air. Also, the above-mentioned orangutans have higher foreheads than any other primate.) Agogwes have typical hominoid facial features—round, deep-set, "glowing" eyes;

broad, flat noses; human-like ears; slightly protruding mouths; no chins; "no" necks; large teeth—but their lips do show evidence of human eversion (turning out).

Agogwes communicate by jabbering among themselves, which they do more than other hominoids. They are seen more often in groups, usually in pairs or family units. When upset or aroused, they call like the other types, with loud screeches and howls, to get quick responses from their own kind. This indicates they are more sociable than the others, possibly living in loosely confederated troupes that inhabit specific regions, which fits the classic primate pattern better than the isolated family units and basically nomadic existence the other hominoids employ. Because Agogwes live in niches that do not suffer seasonal fluctuations, it probably makes better sense for them to select a defined "home" territory and share it with others of their kind.

Another unusual aspect of Agogwes is that they seem to utilize the trees in their habitats more often and more easily than their cousins. However, they don't swing from limb-to-limb with their arms, in the typical primate fashion. Instead, they *jump* from limb-to-limb, virtually running through the overhead canopy. Recall the uniqueness of Agogwe feet: narrow heels, exceptionally high arches, expanded ball and forefoot area. Our first analysis of those feet—and the greatly expanded calves attached to them—was that they might have resulted from frequent walking on tiptoes, which would be required by equally frequent stealth. Now we see it could also be that those feet and calves are merely physical adaptations caused by leaping and jumping from limb-to-limb through trees.

Of the four basic hominoid types, Agogwes are the ones most observers describe as "human" looking. However, nobody claims they *are* humans. They still have their all-over covering of body hair, the same repugnant odor, the same loud vocalizations to communicate with each other at distance, the same pair-bonding to raise offspring, the same pendulous breasts, and the same fantastic strength. So, too, are they known to be swift runners and powerful swimmers. But they do not hunt with weapons, make clothing, use fire, or do anything else that can legitimately be described as human. They are simply hominoids, like the others, but a distinct group among that unique, as-yet-unrecognized subset of primate species.

ALMAS/KAPTARS

The old Soviet Union had its own version of Ivan Sanderson and Grover Krantz, a highly-credentialed academic who in the late 1960's completed a landmark study of his country's numerous reports of encounters with Almas and/or Kaptars. He was Dr. Boris Porshnev, a scientist and historian who carried out hominoid research in the same atmosphere of official repression that exists today. However, his research methods were of such unimpeachable quality, his peers could not deny him the right to publish his results in Russia's most respected technical journals.

Though he was predictably ignored, being allowed to officially make his case speaks volumes for his credibility. In one long paper published in *Soviet Ethnography* in 1969, he gave extensive details about the results of his research. The following are excerpts from that paper, which can be read in its entirety in some of the hominoid books in the bibliography of this one.

***

"We turn now to information gathered from local inhabitants in different ethnographic regions. Considered one by one, each story may be questioned. What cannot be questioned is that such reports exist as independent of one another. They do not contain many contradictions; rather, they support each other. And they confront researchers with three difficult questions:

"First, why is it that in each interview—though the topic under discussion, the situation, the whole circumstance may be different—references to the anatomical features of such creatures are consistent and biologically sound? Second, why are there no biological contradictions in information that has been gathered from widely-separated peoples with varying historical, linguistic, and religious backgrounds? Third, why is it that the enormous amount of 'folklore' (about these creatures) is in basic agreement with the observations of strangers (to an area) who have never heard of the local traditions?

"To my knowledge, none of the doubters has ever been able to provide a satisfactory answer to any of those three questions. (But) common sense provides an obvious answer: that the subject of the stories exists in each of the regions (in question).

***

"As a result of analysis of abundant information it is possible to give a preliminary description of the creatures. Their average height is from 5 to 6 feet, but with great size variation. This is also true with humans.

"The entire body is covered with hair from 3/4 to 3 inches in length, but uneven. For instance, the cheekbones are covered very slightly. There is no underlayer of hair, so that sometimes the skin can be seen. The hair grows longer in cold weather. Infants are born without hair. There is not much hair on the hands and feet, and none on the palms or soles. Witnesses often report they have a very distasteful smell.

"Color varies with age and locale, but can be black, brown, reddish, pale yellow, or gray. A few are white. Color is not always the same on all parts of the body, and hair does not turn gray evenly over the body. There is no hair on the face, usually no beard or moustache, but eyebrows are unusually thick. Sometimes there is sparse hair around the mouth and on the cheeks. The skin of the face is dark or gray or reddish-brown. Hair on the head is usually of a different color from that on the body, and noticeably longer. It is sometimes matted and sometimes falls onto the shoulders, or even down to the shoulder blades.

"The head leans forward more than a man's and is supported by strong muscles which make the neck appear short and wide with the head right atop the trunk. The back of the head rises to a cone-shaped peak. The forehead is low and receding, with protruding eyebrows, and eyes deeply buried in the skull. The bridge of the nose is flat, with the nostrils turned outward. Cheekbones are wide and protruding. The jaws are heavy, strong, and greatly protruding.

The mouth is wide, with the canines more widely separated. The ears differ little from a man's ears.

"The females have large, long breasts which they flop over their shoulders when they run or walk. Probably this enables them to feed their offspring while walking because they normally carry them on their backs. Their legs are slightly bent at the knees, as are the arms at the elbows. Difference in size of the hands and feet is less than in men (their hands are large), and the thumb is less opposed than man's, so they often grasp objects between fingers and palm, without using the thumb. The toes and fingers have primate nails, not claws. The feet have no arch.

"For their size they are significantly stronger than men. They can run as fast as horses, climb cliffs and trees, and swim in swift currents. However, they cannot climb something smooth, like a pole, where gripping with an opposed thumb is necessary. They move easily in varying terrain, and in snow, though snow is not typical of their habitat. They sit by squatting on their buttocks. In winter they sleep face downward, with knees and elbows drawn in under stomachs and their hands behind their heads. [See Fig. 53.]

"They do not have permanent homes, but often use caves or dig holes for shelter. Breeding pairs remain together, but the males are inclined to range over a wider territory, whereas females tend to remain in one area while their offspring are young. They give birth to offspring which resemble human babies. The young eventually leave their mothers to find territories of their own. Large old individuals, past the age of breeding, live alone in the most mountainous and heavily-forested regions.

"They are capable of many different sounds and call to each other over long distances, particularly at twilight and at dawn. Mooing, mumbling, whining, and whistling are reported, but nothing resembling speech. They do not make tools but can throw stones, and even carry them and use them to build windbreaks. They may break small stones one against another. They do not make fire, but are glad to warm themselves at the embers of a fire that has been abandoned. They may use sticks as clubs.

"They eat both meat and vegetable foods. They may dig up roots, they eat different sprouts and leaves, and all kinds of berries, fruits and nuts. Given the opportunity they will take cultivated vegetables and fruit, such as corn, sunflower seeds, hemp. They catch frogs, crabs, turtles, and snails, and will eat frogs' eggs, insects, worms, nestlings, and eggs. They may catch small animals such as gophers, moles, rabbits, and other rodents, and scavenge from the carcasses of larger animals, but they do not habitually hunt large animals. On the few occasions when they do kill larger animals, it is by breaking the back.

"They are active mainly in twilight and at night. Their senses of sight, hearing, and touch are acute, and they can move without making a sound. They are expert at concealing themselves and otherwise taking advantage of their surroundings. They are expert mimics, and have been seen to imitate men after an encounter. They imitate (calls of) animals and birds with great skill.

"Toward men they are usually not aggressive, though in ancient times Persians and others are supposed to have used them as fighting animals which showed great ferocity on the battlefield [Goliath vs. David]. Those domesticated in recent years have been quiet and complacent but hostile to domestic animals, particularly dogs. Horses and cows fear them. In the wild their relations with other animals appear peaceful."

[Their domestication will be examined in more detail later.]

***

Remember, Dr. Porshnev's academic credentials were above reproach. Because his evidence was too comprehensive and authoritative to be dismissed out of hand or ridiculed into triviality, critics have never mounted a serious attack against him, his methodology, or his results. They can only ignore all three and hope they stay where they are—lost on the "lunatic fringe."

HIDING IN PLAIN SIGHT

Because all experts hate to admit any lack of knowledge about their bailiwicks, many animals have at one time or another been forced to dwell with hominoids in cryptozoology's "limbo of the unacceptable." There they remained until evidence for their reality drowned out the bleating chorus of official nay-sayers. Among them are the absurd platypus, the long-rumored mountain gorilla, the legendary giant squid, and the Giant Panda. (The coelacanth we met earlier was never rumored to be alive before the first one was trawled from the Indian Ocean in 1938.)

The Panda's story is a perfect comparison with hominoids because they live in the same kind of habitat (montane forest) and terrain (mountainous) as Bigfoot/Sasquatch and the Almas/Kaptars (predominately Bigfoot). Also, as with early written references to hominoids, Pandas are mentioned in many old Chinese manuscripts. In those texts they were called Bei-Shung, which meant "white-bear," and they were typically described exactly as they turned out to be: black-and-white bears that lived high in rugged mountain ranges and ate bamboo shoots for a living.

Since every Western authority "knew" all bears were meat-eating carnivores; and since black-and-white coloring was so obviously a fanciful creation of benighted natives; and—most importantly—since no Western authority had ever braved the rigors of going to China to actually study the matter, they felt fully qualified to pronounce the Panda an amusing legend invented by the Chinese as a harmless woodland sprite. But then, after 2,000 years of unaccepted reports, in 1869 a French missionary and naturalist named Father Armand David made his way to Sichuan Province. Like most naturalists of his time, Father David had heard of the legendary Bei-Shung and believed the official assurances that mottled, bamboo-eating bears were a highly embellished Chinese crock. Then he saw the full skin of one hanging on a wall in a village elder's home!

At first stunned, then delighted at discovering such incontrovertible evidence that the legend was real, Father David hurried to the Bei-Shung's reported habitat, a bamboo forest high in a forbidding mountain range. Upon arrival, he promptly tried to hire a group of local hunters to bring him a living specimen. The locals were hesitant, saying the Bei-Shung lived in very rugged terrain and were extremely difficult to see, much less capture. Father David took their reluctance as a ploy to extract more money from him, which he offered. The locals shrugged, agreed to take a crack at it, and after just twelve days returned with a living Bei-Shung they professed to have found only by amazing good fortune.

Knowing the captive would make history, a delighted Father David did not concern himself with the circumstances of its capture or the high price he paid for it. However, in transporting his prize back to France, his luck soured. The wild Bei-Shung became so agitated it was beating itself to death in its cage, so for humanitarian reasons it had to be euthanized. Having to kill his prize was a terrible blow to Father David, who found solace knowing he could still achieve his main goal, which was to prove beyond doubt that Bei-Shung did exist. And he knew if he could do that much by himself, well-equipped field teams would follow with sufficient methods of extracting the living Bei-Shungs they would no doubt capture. So he forwarded the preserved remains of his dead legend to the Paris Museum, which created a predictable worldwide sensation.

In a preview of what will probably happen after the first hominoid is officially presented for inspection, the world's top dozen scientific institutions entered into a race to determine who would put the first living Bei-Shung on display. They sent legions of top-notch experts—hunters, trappers, scientists—swarming through the mountainous regions of Sichuan, an area about the size of Arizona or Italy. All waited anxiously to see who would be first to bring one in. And they waited . . . and waited . . . and waited. By 1900—31 years after Father David's find—all of the museums that financed expeditions had long since given up the chase. By 1910 the Bei-Shung had been renamed "Giant Panda" by the Western media and shoved by scientists back into the mists of legend. Though Father David's stuffed specimen remained real, 41 years without even so much as a follow-up sighting convinced most experts the Panda was, indeed, extinct.

Cavorting around Sichuan's mountains looking for phantom Pandas became a lark undertaken by plucky young sports with time and money to burn. Then, in 1915, one claimed to see a Panda that slipped into brush before he could shoot it. His sensational report was met with thunderous denouncement from official science, which had declared the Panda definitely extinct. One lone voice had no chance against such a credentialed chorus, so he was dismissed as a shameless publicity-seeker. If, during the next 14 years, any more sightings occurred, no one had the nerve to step into the hail of ridicule that had greeted the previous eyewitness. Then, in 1929, exactly *60 years* after Father David captured the first one, Teddy Roosevelt's two sons, Kermit and Theodore, Jr., were in Sichuan earning their spurs as Panda hunters. They spotted one in a hollow tree and shot it, sending their bullets through the poor Panda to puncture countless scientific egos.

Even with the passing of 60 years, not much changed after this second discovery of Pandas. Museums and zoos all over the world mounted full field expeditions to try to be the first to capture a living specimen. By then, of course, many Americans and Europeans had learned how to cope with the rugged montane forests of Sichuan. The earlier era's mistakes were eliminated or minimized, and successes began to occur. In 1931 a Panda was killed for the Philadelphia Academy of Natural Science. In 1934 another was killed for the American Museum of Natural History. In 1935 another was shot, then another early in 1936. That was five Pandas (counting the Roosevelts') in seven years—a tremendous record considering what the previous 60 years of effort had produced. Then the second living one (counting Father David's) was captured in 1936 by a man named Floyd Smith. He got it to Singapore before it died of natural causes.

Finally, in 1937, a remarkable woman named Ruth Harkness achieved what had begun to seem impossible. With literally no hunting or trapping experience, she led an expedition that captured a live Panda and returned it to Chicago's Brookfield Zoo. Naturally, the men who had been hunting Pandas for years claimed Ms. Harkness' success was an undeserved fluke, which prodded her into trying again the following year. Incredibly, she deuced the challenge, bringing back another living specimen and touching off the Panda craze that remains with us to this day.

***

I have gone into such detail about the hunt for the Panda because, as I said earlier, it perfectly illustrates the fundamental reasons why hominoids have managed to stay "undiscovered" in Western eyes. Imagine, 60 years of effort by the world's top wilderness experts to secure one specimen of a relatively numerous (at that time), distinctly marked, reasonably large, slow-moving, dimwitted animal inhabiting a rugged but confined area, living a daytime existence, while eating a highly restricted diet. Consider how infinitely more difficult it would be to locate and secure specimens of shrewdly intelligent, largely nocturnal, highly mobile omnivores that are absolute masters of enormous areas comprising some of Earth's most difficult environments.

Even with the highest of today's high-technology hunting and tracking devices, it would be a tough, demanding task. But it can be, and someday will be, done—on a regular basis.

WITNESSES

Earth is liberally plastered with extensive tracts of wild, essentially unexplored territory. Around the edges of those live humans who for one reason or other choose to dwell in the roughest parts of their own ecological niches—those which adjoin genuinely wild areas. In any country in the world, such people are far removed—physically and emotionally—from their neighbors dwelling in villages and towns and cities in the best parts of their niches. If, for example, someone living on an isolated farm encounters a hominoid and, for whatever reason, files an official report about it, a city dweller could easily dismiss the report as a befuddled invention of a well-meaning hick's overactive imagination. Which, not surprisingly, is exactly how such reports are evaluated by every status quo worthy of the name. The problem with dismissing such reports out-of-hand is that farm dwellers are usually near the scene of encounters day-in and day-out.

Anywhere in the world, people who live in the boondocks know and can recognize flora and fauna in their home region, and their imaginations are unlikely to be activated because their lives depend on constantly maintaining an undistorted perception of their surroundings. So upon seeing a hominoid in his front yard, so to speak, a farmer would probably do as he would with any other unusual phenomenon: study it and absorb its details. He would not realize what he was seeing was "impossible," so he could observe and evaluate it in the context he found it.

***

I have exaggerated this situation to make my point. The truth is that nearly everyone living near the edge of a hominoid niche will have heard of them, and most will assume—if not know for a fact—that they exist. Such people accept hominoids as simply another element of the local fauna and are not likely to know or care what the world's scientific and religious establishments, or the media's mavens, say about it. They also know hominoids have unaggressive, live-and-let-live natures (except the Abominable Snowmen, who will kick up a fuss), so they are not likely to panic at the sight of one. In fact, natives living alongside hominoid habitats are the least likely candidates to get flustered by, or become creative about, anything they experience in their environments, particularly hominoids they know for certain live among them.

Another interesting fact is that their stories corroborate from habitat-to-habitat, country-to-country, continent-to-continent. A trapper from backwoods Canada can easily describe the same type of Bigfoot as a shepherd in South America. Both would recognize a similar creature described by a Mongolian yak herder, or a Russian logger. This is true despite the fact that all four would typically be isolated and uneducated in the Western sense, which would severely limit the chance of them ever having heard or read descriptions of hominoids given by others. All they know how to express is what their eyes and ears and noses tell them, which they do with a consistency and conformity that is downright amazing.

***

Despite all that consistency and conformity, whenever natives report seeing hair-covered "humans"—giant or otherwise—in their neighborhoods, scientists dismiss their assertions as "colorful fabrications" that can be explained away as remnants of a "collective fantasy" dating back to the early prehistory of all primitive peoples. Regarding hominoids, that collective fantasy is known as the "primordial bogeyman" theory, which—whether plausible or laughable—does nothing to explain the fact that modern hominoid encounter stories correlate remarkably well with each other no matter where in the world they come from, and they correlate with similar stories from centuries past. In fact, the overlaps between such stories are so blindingly obvious (large, human-like, hair-covered, smelly, etc.), the only collective fantasy still in effect is the one among scientists who believe "collective fantasy" is remotely acceptable as an explanation.

FACE TO FACE

Tabloid newspapers and tabloid TV readily exploit the world's yearly crop of several dozen human-hominoid encounters. However, such encounters have occurred with similar regularity throughout the backward sprawl of history, and records of one kind or another exist for several centuries. No more than a few can be discussed in a general book like this, but a hundred or so are covered in Ivan Sanderson's *Abominable Snowmen* and John Green's *Sasquatch*. For this book I choose to focus on the most substantiated, which should make them the most interesting to novices (which I assume most current readers are).

Like the best tracks, the best encounter reports demolish the scientific position that hominoids cannot be real because no valid proof exists to support them. The truth is, the best encounter reports provide plenty of valid, convincing proof. However, as with tracks, such proofs are officially disregarded because of the syllogistic logic that says hominoids don't exist because they can't exist because they don't fit into the current status quo's world view.

150

Remember, in any court in the world other than the court of scientific opinion, hominoid tracks alone conclusively prove they exist. To further support that assertion, we will examine some of the best American and Canadian encounter stories, followed by reports from Russia, China, and the rest of the world. We will also probe a trio of classic encounters in detail. Then decide for yourself if you think hominoids can or cannot exist.

***

Jacko—Countless Bigfoot encounters have occurred in the huge sprawl of montane forest extending along North America's Pacific Northwest corridor, from northern California to southern Alaska. A prime area within that sprawl is in southern British Columbia, Canada, near Vancouver Island, just north of the U.S. border with Washington state. There, in 1884, a juvenile Bigfoot fell from a 30-foot rock ledge near a railroad track and was knocked unconscious. His injury allowed him to be spotted and captured by several men riding a train that passed the spot where he fell. The following account of the capture and its repercussions is taken from a report published in a Victoria newspaper called *The Daily British Colonist*:

"Yale, B.C., July 3, 1884—In the immediate vicinity of No. 4 (railroad) tunnel, situated some 20 miles above this village, was captured a creature who may truly be called (a) half-man, half-beast. Jacko, as the creature has been called, is something of the gorilla type, standing about 4 feet 7 inches in height and weighing 127 pounds. He has long, black, strong head hair and resembles a human being with one exception: his entire body, excepting his hands and feet are covered with glossy hair about one inch long. His forearm is much longer than a man's forearm, and he possesses extraordinary strength, as he will take hold of a stick and break it by wrenching or twisting it, which no man living could break in the same way.

"Since his capture he is very reticent, only occasionally uttering a noise which is half-bark and half growl. He is, however, becoming daily more attached to his keeper, Mr. George Tilbury, of this place, who proposes shortly starting for London, England, to exhibit him. His (Jacko's) favorite food so far is berries, and he drinks fresh milk with evident relish."

The article goes on in considerable detail about the means of capture, naming many names (along with Mr. Tilbury's) of local men who were involved. It also offers natural speculations about what the strange creature might be. But the main purpose the article served was to document an authentic hominoid encounter witnessed by many people in an established town, rather than one or two easily dismissed natives from the boonies.

Though it happened over a century ago, Jacko's story can be taken at face value. The area near Yale was far from primitive. It had telephone service (a call is mentioned in the article), and was settled by pragmatic, down-to-earth, westerners with no toleration for sensationalism. As for the story itself, it was published in a respectable journal with a wide readership and a tradition of even-handed, accurate reportage. It was quite thorough in its fact base, giving names and details which must have been carefully checked by an eyewitness to the events after the capture. Overall, it was a model of careful, non-speculative journalism.

As for what happened to Jacko, as the article stated, his keeper, George Tilbury, did in fact load him onto a train to accompany him to London—but neither was ever heard from again. We can speculate endlessly about what might have happened on that journey because betrayal, escape, kidnaping, and murder are all possibilities. However, regardless of Jacko's eventual fate, the point is that he did exist in Yale, B.C., for the few weeks it took Mr. Tilbury to arrange the trip to London. His disappearance is unfortunate in a historical sense, but immaterial to the fact that a young hominoid (probably a Bigfoot) was secured and held by a group of responsible people exactly like us but from another place and time.

It is a clearly documented, undeniable capture.

***

Ape Canyon—This encounter occurred in the summer of 1924, in Washington state, in the shadow of now-famous Mount St. Helens, the volcano that blew its top in 1982. In 1924 Ape Canyon was an unnamed, glacier-worn, steep-walled valley that drained runoff from the eastern slopes of the mountain. Its importance is that it shows a group of hominoids acting in concert to pursue a common end. Even more significantly, it shows them using "weapons" while exhibiting aggressive behavior toward humans—a genuine rarity, but in this case fully justified. What follows is from an account in the Portland *Oregonian* newspaper:

"Kelso, Wash., July 12—The strangest story to come from the Cascade Mountains was brought to Kelso today by Marion Smith, his son Roy Smith, Fred Beck, Gabe Lefever, and John Peterson, who encountered the fabled mountain devils or mountain gorillas of Mount St. Helens this week, shooting one of them (in late afternoon) and then being attacked through the night by rock bombardments from the beasts.

"The men had been prospecting a claim on the Muddy, a branch of the Lewis River about 8 miles from Spirit Lake, 46 miles from Castle Rock. They declared that they saw four of the huge animals, which were about 400 pounds and walked erect. Smith fired at one with a revolver. Thursday Fred Beck shot one, the body falling over a precipice. That night the animals bombarded the cabin where the men were stopping with showers of rocks, many of them large ones, knocking chunks out of the log cabin.

"The animals were said to have the appearance of huge gorillas. They are covered with long, black hair. Their ears are about four inches long and stick straight up. They have four toes, short and stubby. The tracks are 13 to 14 inches long and have been seen by forest rangers and prospectors for years."

***

This article is not nearly the factual equal of the one describing Jacko because the *Oregonian* reporter was relating a second-hand tale. Nevertheless, it was enough to make the world take notice because the situation in 1924 was much different than when Jacko was captured 40 years earlier. In 1884 the Victoria *Colonist* was a regional newspaper, so information about Jacko never spread much beyond the area of his capture. By 1924 the Portland *Oregonian* was linked to the rest of the country's news network, so the reigning scientific establishment was forced to get involved. Naturally, they came out hard and fast against the miners, depicting them as ignorant backwoods yokels who probably shared a jug one night and suffered a common delusion. In typical fashion, no scientist bothered to actually investigate the incident. They simply obliterated all relevant or subsequent facts by the overwhelming force of their ridicule.

Shortly after the incident, however, two search parties were formed to return to the cabin to have a look. One group included two detectives from Portland, plus one of the miners. The other was led by the Sheriff of Cowlitz County. Both groups found the cabin wrecked, its log walls and roof torn to pieces despite it being a sturdily-built place designed to withstand the crushing weight of winter snow at that elevation. They also found broken rocks scattered everywhere, several of them bloody. And around the cabin's perimeter they found hundreds of those improbable four-toed tracks discussed earlier, the longest of which was 19 inches (large even for a Bigfoot). So regardless of all the scientific ridicule, no one who went on either search party had any doubts that events had indeed occurred substantially as the miners related them.

***

Now we move to the famous Roger Patterson film, whose star is the lady depicted here:

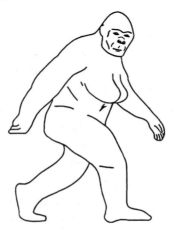

Fig. 63. "Patti"

154

THE PATTERSON FILM

Shot in 1967, Roger Patterson's 24 feet of 16mm home movie film remains one of the most convincing pieces of evidence for the existence of hominoids—namely Bigfeet. Everything about it points to absolute authenticity, yet from the day it was filmed scientific authorities have used the "track" treatment on it: "Like tracks, all films and photographs can be faked, so we syllogistically conclude that any film or photograph or track of something we feel does not exist is, ipso facto, a fake." And the reply remains the same: "Just because something *can* be faked, that does not mean it can be faked *convincingly*."

***

Roger Patterson was a vigorous little man who loved horses and the outdoors around his ranch in Washington state. There, in 1964, he saw some Bigfoot tracks near a place called Bluff Creek, and that experience turned him into a dedicated Bigfoot hunter. He believed Bigfeet were primitive humans that should not be killed, so he always searched with a camera rather than a rifle; and he always went mounted, sometimes with armed companions who agreed not to shoot any Bigfoot they saw unless an emergency dictated otherwise. That was the case October 20, 1967, when a good friend named Bob Gimlin joined him.

It was early afternoon on a bright, sunny day. As Patterson and Gimlin rode around a bend in Bluff Creek, the gurgling of the creek's running water muffled the sound of their horses' hooves to a point where a Bigfoot squatting at the side of the creek did not hear them. As they rode near enough for the horses to catch its powerful scent, Patterson's horse reared and fell on its side. He had to scramble around to get his camera out of the saddlebag while Bob Gimlin—who had managed to stay on his horse—pulled out a rifle to cover his companion. By then the Bigfoot—a female—had seen them and was up and on her way back into the woods fronting the creek, walking across the bend's sandbar at a fairly rapid clip.

Patterson grabbed his camera from the saddlebag and hurried after the retreating Bigfoot, filming as he ran. That produced blurry, shaky shots, so when he got 80 feet from her he stopped. She had ignored him up to that point, but as soon as he paused she turned her upper body back toward him for a single good look at him. Then she turned back toward the woods and maintained her measured pace into the trees, giving Patterson clear shots of only nine strides before she disappeared. In all nine her arms (shoulders and elbows) clearly articulated; but in several, her feet and parts of her legs were obscured by driftwood on the sandbar. However, in a few strides her feet and legs showed well enough to give analysts clear views of how she walked; how her legs, knees, and ankles worked; and how her feet were built.

After Patterson and Gimlin were sure the Bigfoot was gone, they filmed their own tracks beside hers for comparison. Their feet did not sink to any appreciable degree in the hard-packed sand, while hers were about an inch deep, indicating tremendous weight. Her tracks were 14 inches long, 5.5 inches at the ball and 4 inches at the heel. They were flat, with five toes in the partially creased, small-ball arrangement. Patterson and Gimlin later made beautiful casts of some of the best impressions of the left and right feet. Then, knowing his film would be condemned as a fake by officials of every kind, Patterson rushed from the scene back out to civilization to send it to his brother-in-law for careful processing. Then he phoned the British Columbia Museum to ask their scientists to come to the scene and bring tracking dogs with them.

***

One of the strongest elements supporting this film's authenticity is Roger Patterson's actions after taking it. Nothing he did is consistent with fakery. First, he told where he shot it, which fakers cannot afford to do because knowing a location allows comparison measurements of a subject's height to be made against bushes and such, along with verification of what cannot be faked convincingly —tracks. In addition, he specifically requested the presence of scientists and tracking dogs to try to follow what he filmed to its lair.

Even if a faker could somehow defeat the location problem, he would never call for tracking dogs because their sensitive noses could easily tell the difference between a human in a hominoid costume and a genuine hominoid's powerful scent, which all dogs— even hunting dogs—instinctively fear. So despite how easy the film would have been to debunk if it had been a fake, no scientist bothered to examine the evidence. It was much easier—and safer from a career standpoint—to toe the party line that such a thing could not possibly be legitimate, and leave it at that.

The only track expert to visit the encounter site was a taxidermist named Bob Titmus, who arrived the day before the whole scene was erased by a heavy rainfall. Titmus examined the tracks carefully and found most in good condition. Several that Patterson and Gimlin had covered with slabs of bark were in excellent condition, showing the usual differences in size and morphology. Some revealed a great deal of foot movement, some only a little, and some virtually none.

Titmus took plaster casts of ten consecutive imprints, each showing clear differences in toe placements, toe grip forces, pressure ridges and breaks, weight shifts, weight distributions, depths, etc.— the kinds of subtle changes that simply cannot be faked. Besides casting a compelling set of tracks, Titmus had his 200 pound brother-in-law walk near the tracks to make a depth comparison. The best his brother-in-law could do was sink 1/4 inch at his heel strike and 1/8 inch everywhere else. The Bigfoot sank a full inch, indicating a body weight of 600 to 700 pounds.

***

Later, the film was taken to Hollywood to see if top movie technicians could determine how it might have been faked. They could not, because the clearest frames reveal the Bigfoot's shoulder and leg muscles rippling as she walks, which is not possible to reveal in any kind of body suit, much less one with such outlandish body proportions. Also, when she turns to face Patterson for that brief moment, there is a perfectly natural sway to her breasts, which would be extremely difficult to fake. They concluded that if Roger Patterson had somehow managed to fake that incredible piece of film, he was wasting his time as a hard-scrabble horse rancher. By exploiting his skills in Hollywood, he could have died a multimillionaire special effects wizard.

Another fact strongly supporting the film's authenticity is what eventually happened to Bob Gimlin, the friend with Roger Patterson when the film was shot. Rightly or wrongly, Patterson considered the film his own personal property and made sure Gimlin was cut out of any monetary rights to it. Both men became bitterly estranged over the money issue, so Bob Gimlin could easily have squared things with Patterson and made a tidy bundle of his own if he would have explained how the film was faked—but he never did. The story of what happened at Bluff Creek that fall day in 1967 remains the same in all details as when it was first told.

***

Because the Patterson film is so compelling, over the years several credentialed scientists have examined it in depth. One was Dr. Grover Krantz of Washington State University, and his results are offered in considerable detail in his book, *Big Footprints*. Also studying it closely was England's Dr. Donald Grieve, an anatomist who specialized in the human gait. And a third high-level analyst was Russia's Dr. Dimitri Donskoy, a biomechanical engineer. All three experts studied the Patterson film extensively and ended up strongly supporting its authenticity.

In general, they say the creature's exaggerated arm movements indicate her arms are far more massive than humans, the muscles in them are much stronger, and the elbows articulate in a distinctly non-human way. The leg movements are typical of massive limbs with smooth, springy muscles. The amount of her knee flexion (bend) is significant in that it far exceeds a typical human walk. Her bent-kneed walk, in fact, resembles humans cross-country skiing, which is reputed to be the most efficient way we can travel. In contrast to our normal up-and-down bob over locked knees, her bent knees and thick thighs carry her great weight through each step in a graceful, gliding stride that gives her a far more efficient transfer of energy. It also shows no indication of being forced or unnatural.

In short, the movement of the Bigfoot in the Roger Patterson film indicates she is much heavier than humans, her muscles are much stronger, and—despite the wide diversity in human walks—she walks in a way that is absolutely, unarguably different from ours. Not surprisingly, her walk most closely resembles that of the creatures at Laetoli, 3.5 million years ago.

ALBERT OSTMAN

Without question the best classic hominoid encounter happened to Albert Ostman. He was a young Swede who immigrated to Canada in 1920 to find work as a lumberjack, the profits of which he used to finance prospecting trips into the back country of southern British Columbia, east of Vancouver Island. Lost gold mines were rumored to be in that rugged country, and intrepid young men like Albert Ostman occasionally went out to try to rediscover them.

Coincidental to the Ape Canyon incident, Ostman's encounter also occurred in 1924. Typically, after it happened he told no one for fear of being ridiculed (a well-founded concern among encounter participants). He kept mum for 33 years, which strongly supports his contention that he never intended to capitalize on it. Then, in 1957, he finally came forward after reading a published affidavit by Canadian William Roe, who encountered a female Bigfoot in October, 1955. After seeing Roe's affidavit, Ostman knew someone else had had an experience like his own, so he wrote Roe that he had a similar story to tell. Roe suggested that Ostman put his story on paper, which he did, filling two spiral binders with a carefully pencilled account.

Albert Ostman's apparent and stated motive for finally speaking up was his desire to help solve the Bigfoot/Sasquatch mystery just beginning to emerge full-blown in America's Pacific Northwest and in Canada's western provinces. His story created an immediate sensation for two reasons: first, he knew vastly more details about Bigfeet than anyone who had ever encountered them; and he himself was so genuine. He was a plain-spoken, straightforward man who was well-read, had traveled extensively before settling down, and understood the ridicule his story would generate and the negative effect it would have on his hard-earned reputation. By the time he came forth he was retired, owned his own property, had many good friends, and always shunned the publicity that later came his way. There is little doubt his motives were purely altruistic.

As for the degree of truth in what he said, any police procedural will attest that liars tend to confuse details when they tell fabrications over and over, particularly in long, complex tales. Even at his advanced age (65) and three decades after the event, Albert Ostman never faltered or got confused when relating the minutiae of his story. He had a marvelous eye for detail and a clear memory to support it. This held true even when he was questioned by a physical anthropologist and a veterinarian—both specialists in primates. They asked him numerous questions about primate physiology that would have only one correct answer, while several other answers would seem equally feasible but would be wrong. Ostman answered all their queries perfectly.

Later, he was interrogated by a magistrate who specialized in making people crack under the pressure of persistent antagonistic questioning, what some people call "the third degree." Under that pressure the old man never gave an improbable reply, never offered an uncalled-for elaboration, never gave an unrequested fact that did not have a logical place in the picture. Most importantly, he produced information that was not then known in any hominoid literature, but which has since been corroborated by other witnesses.

In short, Albert Ostman told the truth.

***

In Ostman's penciled account he first explains why he took his prospecting trip, then he goes into detail about the supplies and equipment he took. (A key element was three tins of snuff, a finely powdered form of tobacco.) On the rock-strewn shore of a sheltered inlet he chose a good site, set up camp, and laid out his sleeping bag. During the first three nights he noticed there were disturbances around his camp while he slept, but he was a heavy sleeper and had not seen the culprit, which he assumed was a porcupine or a raccoon.

The fourth night he was asleep in his bag when he suddenly found himself being lifted off the ground. By the time he fully regained his senses he was wedged tight at the bottom of the bag and being hauled away like a sack of toys on Santa's back. Jostling against him was his camp sack with his stores, so whatever was stealing him was taking his supplies, too. And because he had heard Indians talk about what they called Sasquatches, giant hair-covered people who lived deep in the forests, he assumed one of those was what had him.

He could hear his captor breathing hard and occasionally coughing as it lugged him up a steep mountainside (he could feel himself rise with every step). Luckily, its hands were not big enough to completely encircle the top of the bag, so he barely had enough fresh air to keep from suffocating. He calculated he was in the bag for about an hour, and by then he was suffering terrible cramps in his legs and feet from their awkward positions at the bottom of the bag. Finally, though, he and his camp sack were put on the ground and he slowly, painfully crawled out.

It was still dark so he couldn't see what had him, but he could smell them and hear them moving in the darkness, continually chattering, and what he heard was four distinct "voices." He finally asked them what they wanted with him, which brought more chattering but nothing he could understand. Finally it became light enough for him to see them: an "old man," an "old lady," a "girl," and a "boy," all covered with hair and wearing no clothes. The old man seemed to be trying to explain what he had done, while the old lady seemed to be chewing him out for it.

Ostman could also see he was in a roughly ten-acre basin surrounded by high mountains. It had only one opening, a V-shaped notch about eight feet wide, opposite from where he and his supplies had been deposited. As soon as he could see that, he started planning how to get away, but he could also see he was much too far from it to make a break and run. Even worse, he found his captors' "home" was close to the opening. It was a shelf in the mountain with an overhang of rock that was like an undercut in a tree—10 feet deep and 30 feet wide. The proximity of that home area to the single opening dimmed his immediate prospects for escape.

Soon Ostman realized his captors were not out to do him harm, but were inviting him in a crude way to stay with them. He began to organize his new campsite, first taking an inventory of the supplies the old man had brought along. He found most things there, including enough food to last about a week. He also found the three tins of snuff. The boy and girl watched him from nearby as he worked, more out of curiosity than to keep him in place. He figured there must be water in the basin and went looking for it, finding a spring nearby. He got a canful and amazed all four captors by making a fire with the matches in his supplies. Then he made coffee and ate.

The next day Ostman packed and tried to leave, but the old man lifted his hands and gestured for him to go back. Among his supplies was a 30-30 rifle, but it had only six shells, and his captors were so big he was not sure he could kill them all with six shots. So he went back to his camp to rethink his plans. The next day the old lady left the enclosure and was gone all day, gathering "grass and twigs and all kinds of spruce and hemlock, and some kind of nuts that grow in the ground." The boy, who could scale the canyon's rock walls with as much agility as a mountain goat, offered him a stem of grass with a long sweet edible root. Ostman ate it and in return gave the boy a snuff tin with a teaspoon of snuff in it. The boy tasted that and then took the remainder to the old man, who promptly licked it clean.

While waiting for a chance to escape, Ostman studied his captors carefully. He described the old lady as "a meek old thing," the boy as "quite friendly," and the girl's chest as "flat as the boy's, no development like young ladies." The boy was "between 11 to 18 years old, about 7 feet tall, weighing 300 pounds. His chest would be 50 to 55 inches, his waist about 36 to 38 inches. He had wide jaws and a narrow forehead that slanted upward, round at the back and 4 to 5 inches higher than the forehead." (Keep in mind that when his encounter occurred, Albert Ostman was an experienced lumberman who made part of his living by visually calculating the girths of trees and weights of logs, so his estimates in this regard can be considered highly reliable.)

The hair on all of their heads was "about 6 inches long. The hair on the rest of their body was short and thick in places. The old lady's hair on the forehead had an upward turn like women have. They call it 'bangs' nowadays. The old lady could have been anything between 40 to 70 years old. She was over 7 feet tall and would be about 500 to 600 pounds. She had very wide hips and a goose-like walk. She was not built for beauty or speed, and she really needed a brassiere. Her chests [sic] were as big as kegs."

The old man he described as having "eyeteeth longer than the rest of his teeth, but not long enough to be called tusks. He must have been near 8 feet tall. Big barrel chest and big hump on the top of his back, with powerful shoulders. His biceps on his upper arms were enormous and tapered down to his elbows. His forearms were longer than ordinary people have, but well-proportioned. His hands were wide, the palms were long and broad, and hollow like a scoop. His fingers were short in proportion to the rest of his hand. His fingernails were like chisels. If he were to wear a collar it would have to be at least 30 inches.

"The only place without hair was inside their hands and the soles of their feet, and the upper part of the nose and eyelids. I never saw their ears, (because) hair hung over them. I have no idea what size shoe they would need. I (studied) the young fellow's foot one day when he was sitting down, and the big toe was longer than the rest and very strong. All he needed was footing for his big toe and he could climb anywhere.

"To sit they turned their knees out and came straight down. To rise they came up without help of hands or arms. They always seemed to do things for reasons, wasting no time on anything they didn't need to do. When they weren't looking for food, the old man and the old lady were resting, but the boy and girl were always climbing something or (having) some other exercise."

Ostman then describes how they ate, saying he never saw them eat meat or do any kind of cooking, but they did wash all vegetable foods before eating them. By then, however, another day had passed and the old man had been intrigued enough by the snuff to start moving closer to Ostman's camp area. He would watch as Ostman took pinches of his snuff, but he kept his distance.

On the sixth day Ostman's food was low and he realized he had to escape soon—or else. By then the old man and the boy would watch his morning routine from only ten feet away, so as he made his morning coffee he started working on his plan. After breakfast he took his usual dip of snuff, then offered the nearly full remaining tin to the old man, who eagerly took it. Then, as Ostman hoped, "instead of taking a pinch he swallowed it all in one big gulp."

"After a few minutes his eyes began to roll over in his head. He was looking straight up and I could see he was sick. Then he grabbed my coffee can that was cold by then and emptied it in his mouth, grounds and all. That did him no good, either. He stuck his head between his legs and rolled forward away from me. Then he began to squeal like a stuck pig. I grabbed my rifle and got ready for him to rush me, but he headed for the spring, wanting water. I started putting what I had left in my pack sack while the young fellow ran over to his mother. She began to squeal as I left for the opening in the wall. She came after me, so I fired a shot over her head."

That shot was enough to discourage the "meek"old lady. She turned back to care for her stricken mate, while Ostman ran downhill as fast as he could. When he finally came to a logging camp he told them he was a prospector who had gotten lost, not mentioning what had happened because he felt they would think he was crazy. Understandably, that was his last prospecting trip.

THE MINNESOTA ICEMAN

The next classic encounter story began several months before the Patterson film was taken, in the summer of 1967. A Minnesota man named Frank Hansen began exhibiting what he claimed was a primitive type of human he had acquired to make money as a sideshow attraction. It was exactly what he claimed, too, a hair-covered, primitive-looking "humanoid" that had been killed and laid out in a block of ice in a refrigerated coffin he carried around to shopping centers and county fairs in the back of a trailer truck.

Known as "The Minnesota Iceman," controversy swirled around it from Frank Hansen's first explanation that it was owned by a mysterious Californian who demanded anonymity. The Californian claimed he acquired it in Hong Kong, where it was sold by fishermen who found it frozen in an iceberg floating in the Bering Sea. When people pointed out how ridiculous that story was—mainly because of obvious bullet holes in the corpse, but also for technical reasons a dim bulb like Frank Hansen could never be expected to anticipate—he reversed course and confessed to killing it himself in the woods of northern Minnesota.

That was much more believable than the ice floe fable, but by getting caught in such an outlandish lie, Hansen had tainted the whole affair with a permanent stench of hoax. Also, he had given scientists precisely the kind of excuse they needed to avoid having to take the Iceman seriously. Had Frank Hansen been a different kind of man, the issue of hominoid reality might be far behind us today. But he wasn't and it isn't, so here we all are, still trying to come to grips with it.

***

Hansen's claim of personally killing the Iceman alerted the FBI that he might have murdered a primitive human being. When he heard he was being investigated, he went farther off the deep end and announced the whole affair had been a money-making scam from the start and the "monster" had been manufactured by Hollywood model makers. Predictably, he never provided believable details about how such an anatomical miracle could be created, so the net result was that he came off as a latter-day P.T. Barnum, engaging in a bit of honest showmanship to make a dishonest fortune at the expense of a guileless, gullible public.

Because of Frank Hansen's absurd shenanigans, official interest in the Iceman soon died out. However, two things did not change: people continued paying to see the ice-entombed creature; and early on, when Hansen was still trying to generate publicity, he allowed none other than Ivan Sanderson (the godfather of world hominoid research, and a widely-renowned zoologist/botanist/biologist) to make a highly detailed, highly technical analysis of it. That analysis—which we will closely examine in a moment—was and remains a sterling proof of hominoid reality.

***

Hansen claimed he acquired his trophy during a winter deer-hunting trip. After wounding a deer, he tracked it into a clearing where he found three hominoids feeding on its carcass. One of the three attacked him, forcing him to shoot it in the right eye in self-defense. Even though that shot blew away the back of its head, he played things safe and shot it again—in the chest. While there may be grains of truth in that, most of it is a lie. First, encounter reports indicate that hominoids are generally not aggressive unless provoked. Also, the chest wound was a gaping, fist-sized hole more typical of an exit than the small opening of an entrance. And last, a bullet had passed through the left forearm just above the wrist. None of that jibes with Hansen's story.

A far more likely scenario is that Hansen was deer hunting and spotted a young hominoid on its own, exploring its neighborhood the way kids do. The experienced hunter waited until his unsuspecting prey turned its back, then—unlike many others who have drawn a bead on a hominoid and failed to fire because they felt it would be killing something nearly human—Hansen suffered no such pangs of conscience and cold-bloodedly shot it.

The heavy-caliber deer bullet slammed home, severing the victim's spine and ripping through its chest to make the gaping exit wound described earlier. The bullet's impact spun it so it landed on its right side, in shock, mortally wounded, gasping for breath, unable to move more than its left arm. If it could see its attacker creeping forward to execute the coup de grace, even in its profound state of shock it might have sensed what was coming next. It might have turned its face to its left so its left forearm could cover its eyes for protection from the rifle barrel pointed inches from its head. Or it might have just wanted to turn the lights out a few seconds early.

166

In any case, Hansen fired again, sending a bullet ripping through the lower left forearm, into the left eyesocket, blowing out the back of the head while exploding or dislodging the right eye. The deed was done. Frank Hansen was at a point where he could become one of the greatest contributors to scientific knowledge in all of recorded history . . . or a grubby little sideshow con artist. Unfortunately, to a man like him the choice was obvious.

* * *

Based on what was visible later, Hansen dumped the body in the freezer soon after killing it and made no effort to arrange it properly or make it easier to view. Then he filled the "coffin" with tap or well water, which froze in some parts with crystal clarity while other parts were left clouded by a milky haze of minerals. That gave excellent views of some parts of the creature, and from poor to literally no views of other parts. However, most of it was clear.

I went to see it when I was a young man with perfect vision, and to my eyes its skin looked real and its hair looked real—as real as anything I had ever seen. There seemed to be a literal million hairs visible, each one growing from a pore at the exact same angle as the ones around it, the spacing between them consistent and uniform wherever I looked. Even today there is no means of fakery that could produce such a phenomenal level of symmetry while executing such a broad canvas in such minute detail—no way.

Apart from the clear reality of its body hair, what cinched it for me was that because Hansen dumped it in the freezer and covered it with water so soon after killing it, its wounds were still oozing blood and plasma, which floated up in long, string-like tendrils as the water went through its freezing process. Those vivid tendrils extended like filaments from *inside* the wounds (and from both outward pointing nostrils) to the top surface of the ice. I cannot imagine a brain clever enough to think such details should even be part of a hoax, much less solve the technical problems involved in making them look so authentic. Again, no way.

As for what became of the Iceman, both it and Frank Hansen dropped from sight sometime in the late 1970's. It is probable that because freezing a corpse only slows down the process of decomposition (rather than arresting it), by then the Iceman had decayed to an unpresentable degree. Who knows? Considering the fortune it made for him, Hansen might have sprung for a decent burial. Considering his blatant lack of morals and character, I doubt it.

SANDERSON'S ICEMAN ANALYSIS

Ivan Sanderson's scholarly paper about the Minnesota Iceman was published in 1968 under the imposing title: "A Preliminary Description of the External Morphology of What Appeared to be the Fresh Corpse of a Hitherto Unknown Form of Living Hominoid." Its 36 pages are reprinted in full in Peter Byrne's excellent book, *The Search For Big Foot,* Acropolis Books, 1975, and Pocket Books, 1976. To enhance Dr. Sanderson's analysis of what he examined, Fig. 64 is a slightly altered (for clarity's sake) copy of a drawing he made of it. Understand that a Bigfoot this size—about 6 feet and 250 pounds—would probably be in the 10- to 12-year-old range, which means Ice*child* would be a more appropriate name.

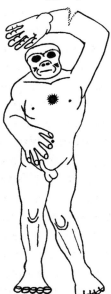

Fig. 64.

As you read Sanderson's report, notice his emphasis on the close physiological ties between this creature and monkeys and apes—not humans. Also note that many of its finer details had never been seen before, yet none were outlandish or impossible to accept in conjunction with each other. So who could fake such a highly detailed yet totally plausible hybrid of ape, monkey, and human characteristics? A hybrid utterly new and different, with no pattern to follow? And do it without making a single obvious—or even a subtle—blunder?

***

Sanderson begins by explaining that the Iceman was viewed from no closer than one foot, through four sheets of plate glass and varying amounts of clear, frosted, or totally opaque ice. He compared the process to viewing an insect stuck in amber, but with roughly half the exposed surface visible only as a shadow under fog. In general, the Iceman was preserved in ice in a rectangular block 6 feet 11 inches long by 2 feet 8 inches wide and 3 feet 6 inches deep. Though parts of the coffin contained clouds of ice crystals, very strong floodlights directed from low angles above the coffin's glass top revealed many otherwise unclear or even obscured details.

As with most people who see hominoids up close, Sanderson's dominant impression was of its great bulk. The hands in particular seemed out of all proportion to the body, and even to the large arms. (This was probably an adolescent Bigfoot, and all primates verging on adulthood have enlarged extremities—hands and feet—they "grow into" as the rest of their bodies catch up.) His second dominant impression was the uniform blanket of hair that covered virtually the whole of its body. Those hairs averaged 2 to 3 inches long, and in some places even more. (If it was actually killed in winter, in summer they may be shorter.) Most hair that was visible had been suspended upward in the water before it froze, permitting many exceptionally clear views down to the skin.

Sanderson estimated it carried 250 muscular pounds on a six-foot body, though weight was hard to pinpoint because the legs were bent up at the knees. Careful measurements proved the legs were of normal length, matching the torso from collarbones to scrotum. The torso was large in width compared to its length, though not excessively so for humans or apes. It flowed from the chest down to the abdomen and continued—as in apes—to the hips rather than stopping at a defined waist, as with the human torso. The length of the penis was not great for a man, but was large for the average ape. Though not well-seen, the scrotum seemed small and wrinkled, with smallish testicles (an additional sign of immaturity) obscured by shadows and hair.

The proportion of face to body was not excessive for humans, but was small for apes. The face itself was exceedingly wide, with prominent cheekbones and an equally wide jaw. Especially notable were a series of folds and wrinkles around thin lips that showed little outward eversion. The head was tilted back because its crown had been blown away by the bullet through the left eyesocket, so nothing could be seen behind the low forehead visible above slight browridges. (As much as anything, those undeveloped browridges indicate a juvenile. All adult primates have pronounced brows.) The eyesockets were unexpectedly round and large (a la the fossil hominids). The left eyeball was missing and the right had been dislodged from its socket by the shockwave caused by the bullet passing through the brain. Both sockets had blood streaming up in thin tendrils into the clear ice above the face, with more coming from the left (shot) eye than the right.

The face itself had a light yellowish to pinkish color (another sign of immaturity) and was naked of hair except for short bristles on the browridges and an odd track that ran up the septum between the nostrils. There was no moustache, but a few faint cat-like whiskers were on the upper lip's outside edges. (Again, this seems adolescent.) The nose was pugged upward like a Pekinese dog, with large round nostrils pointing forward. The nostrils were fleshy and rather heavy, and flowed into the upper lip with no crease. (They also streamed tendrils of blood and plasma.) The whole nasal structure was like a young gorilla, but there was more nose jutting up instead of being flattened. Though wide, the nose was in proportion to the exceptionally wide face.

As noted earlier, the torso was quite bulky, with broad shoulders that tapered only slightly down to the hips—not to a waist. There were no visible pectoral muscles, and the nipples were a bit far to the sides. There was the fist-sized bullet hole in the middle of the chest, from which the same kind of blood and plasma tendrils flowed upward into the ice. There was very little neck in front— only an inch or two covered over with dense hair—despite the head being thrown back. Opaque ice made it impossible to see how the head attached to the shoulders on either side.

The arms appeared massive, with the upper arm more slender than the forearm (a la Popeye), which had a heavy hair covering and an extremely wide wrist. Only the left arm was fully visible, with a compound fracture three inches from the wrist caused by another bullet wound. Like the chest and eye wounds, blood streamed up from it, and pieces of the arm's radius and ulna bones were visible on its outer side. As also noted, the hands were enormous. They were slightly more pink than the rest of the skin, and in no way gnarled or worn-looking (a further indication of youth). They looked like those of a huge man with a bad case of dishpan hands. That effect could not be due to postmortem bloat because the sub-digital pads on the inside of the fingers were not swollen, and the folds between them were clear and prominent.

The back of the right hand was heavily haired, but the individual follicles were well apart and curved gently over the sides and tips of the fingers above the nails. The nails were cropped as if manicured, yellow in color, flat, and almost square. The thumb seemed to be as opposed as a human's thumb, but it was exceptionally slender and reached to near the tip of the index finger. It also tapered rather than expanding like a typical human's. Knuckles were not prominent or well-defined. On the upturned palm's surface there was a most puzzling feature: an enormous and prominent pad on the heel at its outer side behind the fifth digit's base. That pad greatly exceeded the thumb pad in dimensions and protuberance, which meant the Iceman was either carrying it as an anatomical holdover from his ancient

171

past, or he had a use for it (sleeping?) not readily apparent.

As for the legs and their bent knees, the right knee was more elevated than the left, with both ankles hidden beneath opaque ice. The thighs and shanks were deeply buried in the cloudy ice, and their heavy covering of hair masked their outlines. The knees, however, were easily seen and bore only sparse, short hairs above a typically human kneecap, the kind a habitually upright walker had to have. The forward-projecting feet were pink in color, had bulbous terminal pads, and horny yellowish nails that were also cropped, in that they did not curl over the ends of the toes as ours do when left untrimmed. The hair atop both feet was profuse, long, and curved over the toes and the soles. The toes were roughly equal in size and proportion and formed an almost straight front, ideal for walking in snow or loose soils. Sanderson believed he could see a crease in the foot pads in the ball area, which would mean this creature was a "double-ball" Bigfoot.

The body hair's growth patterns were elaborate. Hair on the lower arm flowed up to the elbow, as it does with many primates (chimps in particular). Hair on the upper arm flowed down from the shoulder to the elbow, forming a "drip-tip" on the outside of the elbow. Such an unusual yet plausible arrangement would be most difficult to conceive and execute convincingly. The armpits were filled with the same type of hair as the surrounding areas, with no sign of the axillary hair humans have. There was also no pubic hair as we know it, though there was a thick, fine hair all over the pubic region. This absence of those types of hair is typically ape-like and even monkey-like. No ears were visible because the head was thrown back into the region of opaque ice. The head rested lower than the torso because its rear was blown away. Under the raised jaw was a dense, forward-pointing mass of short hairs filling in the 1- to 2-inch neck area between the collarbones and the wide jawline. This made the neck area look more ape-like than human.

The backside seemed to contain a longer-haired "cape" that extended from shoulders to buttocks. It emerged around the sides of the torso to form a continuous incurved eaves, as on a house.

Meanwhile, the chest was covered by widely scattered, long, lank, straight hairs. These were thickest above and below the wound in the sternum, slightly parted in the median and flowing down into a sparse covering of the belly. The difference between the eaves of the back cape and the sparsely-haired chest and front was quite striking, yet it was completely in accord with ape hair arrangement. It may also be explained by the hominoids' chest-on-thighs sleeping position. In direct contrast, humans manifest hair growth first on the chest and front of the belly, and only later on the back; and such hair is curly rather than straight.

Leg hairs were straight, averaged over 2 inches long, and were separated by follicles 1/8 inch apart. All flowed down to the tops of the feet, which were heavily haired to the ends of the toes. Body hairs were quite coarse and thick and straight except for those that curved around the hands and the feet. All of it was colored dark brown. One incredible aspect of the Iceman's hair was that it all seemed to be dully banded in what mammalogists call the "agouti" manner, which means each hair had successively lighter bands that started wide at the base and decreased in width toward the tip. That made the Iceman a phenomenally unique creature because, while that type of coloration is found among certain monkeys, no apes or humans have it.

***

Ivan Sanderson's concluding opinion was that the Iceman was a fresh corpse, not a composite manufactured from parts of human corpses and/or other animals. Nor was it a construction made of wax, latex, and animal hair because the technical requirements of such a feat were so daunting. The body was neither ape nor human, nor did it conform to any known artist's conception of fossilized men or apes. In other words, there was no model to copy. It would have had to be constructed from scratch, mixing some parts that belong solely to humans, some solely to apes, some solely to monkeys, some to all three, and—amazingly—some to none of them!

Like the Bossburg cripple's uniquely shaped tracks, which Grover Krantz feels would be impossible to fake without highly detailed knowledge of hominoid foot morphology, Ivan Sanderson believed the Iceman's odd mix of traits could not have been put together without intimate first-hand knowledge of what was to be constructed. To create something so incredibly different yet so remarkably plausible would be all but impossible, even with the acquired knowledge of a lifetime of study such as his own. Because he was convinced he never could have dreamed up such esoteric combinations, he felt no one else could have, either.

FOREIGN ENCOUNTERS

Russia and China have a much richer history of hominoid encounters, and acceptance of and research into those encounters, than the U.S. or Canada. Two of the best books dealing with Russian and Chinese sightings are: *In Pursuit Of The Abominable Snowman* (1970) by Odette Tchernine; and *Still Living? Yeti, Sasquatch, And The Neanderthal Enigma* (1983), by Myra Shackley. What follows is a brief glimpse of several stories I found intriguing.

***

In 1661 (this shows how far back such reports reach) in the forests of Lithuania, soldiers acting as hunter's beaters flushed out what was called a "bear-man." It was caught and sent to Warsaw as a present to King Jan Kasimir II, whose wife tried to educate the captive. It never learned to speak or do more than a few kitchen duties, but it was a well-known case at the time.

In the mid-1800's a widely-renowned lama lived at the monastery of Lamyn Hegen in Mongolia. He was called "Son of Almas" because his father had been captured and held prisoner by a group of Almas. During his captivity he fathered a child by a female Alma, then ultimately escaped with his son in tow. The boy later joined the monastery as a monk, where he became famous for his high intelligence and learning.

In 1914, in the forests of southern Manchuria, a famous Russian hunter named N.A. Baykov met a Chinese hunter named Fu Ts'ai, who had a domesticated Alma for an assistant. Baykov was a lifelong naturalist who wrote remarkably accurate natural history books. He said the wild assistant had been given the name Lan-Zhen, which meant "wolf-man." He described Lan-Zhen as hair-covered and lacking speech, but remarkably successful at catching birds and animals in snares and traps set by Fu Ts'ai.

Baykov said, "He would mumble animal sounds, and his wild, insane-looking eyes shone in the dark like a wolf. When reproved by his master, he replied with a snarl and went over to the wall of the hut to lay down and curl up like a dog. For a long time I observed this strange being, half-man and half-beast, and it seemed to me he had more the beast in him than the human."

In 1925 a man named Mikhail Topilskiy was a Commissar of the Red Army forces chasing White Army troops through the Pamir Mountains. At one point his soldiers started firing into a cave they thought was being used by White forces. To the great surprise of the soldiers around the cave, a crazed creature came running out and was promptly mowed down by machine-gun fire. At first they thought the corpse was an ape because it was covered with hair, but then they called Commissar Topilskiy to check it out and he told them no apes lived in the Pamirs. In addition, the body looked and had moved like a human. After burying it under a heap of rocks where it fell, the Red forces resumed their chase of the White forces, making no note of their victim's exact location so that later researchers could return and try to recover its bones.

In 1928 a very old Mongol woman reported that as an infant she was "kidnaped" by a female Alma and nursed by it until her parents found them both and drove the Alma away. The old woman claimed she had never been sick a day in her life, and the people of her village always attributed her robust good health to the fact that she had once nursed at the breast of an Alma.

(If it turns out hominoid milk actually provides humans with resistance to disease or illness, the gold-rush lust for it would dwarf the recent taxol-driven devastation of Yew trees. Hominoids would be found and captured at incredible rates, each selling for a king's ransom so that breeding programs could be established. Females would

175

be housed where they could not escape, impregnated when not lactating, and milked like cows when they were. This is not a welcome prospect, but the upside is that it should prevent hominoids from being killed like big game.

(Speaking of big game, in that regard I am not underestimating the powerful effects of money, or the equally powerful need of certain wealthy men with massive insecurities to prove their manhood by killing large distinctive animals. However, in a showdown with millions of people with serious health concerns, I like to think the hunters' needs would be served last—at least until a synthetic replacement for hominoid milk could be manufactured.)

In December, 1941 (for Europe, well into World War II), Dr. V.S. Karapetian, a Lieutenant Colonel in the Russian Army Medical Corps, was stationed with an infantry battalion thirty miles from Buisnaksk in Dagestan Province. One day two representatives of the local authorities asked Dr. Karapetian to come examine a man-sized but fully hair-covered suspected enemy "spy" caught in the surrounding mountains and brought to the district center. A medical opinion was needed to determine whether they were holding a cleverly disguised enemy or a freak of nature.

Dr. Karapetian was taken to an unheated shed to examine the prisoner. When he asked why he had to work in such a cold place, he was told the prisoner could not bear to be kept indoors. When that was tried he had sweated profusely and struggled to breathe. (Remember the mucous-membrane-covered flanges of bone in the nasal passages of Neanderthals?) So the doctor set aside his misgivings and went to work, later detailing observations that add little to what we already know. He concludes his report by saying, "I learned he had accepted no food or drink since he was caught. He had asked for nothing and said nothing. While I was there water and then food were brought to his mouth, but there was no reaction. I gave the verbal conclusion that this was no disguised person, but a wild man of some kind." (Karapetian later found out that despite his medical opinion, the prisoner had been executed anyway, as a spy, "just in case." But, unfortunately, subsequent research found no record of the execution or the disposition of its corpse.)

In the mid-1950's in Kabardinia, a female Alma had been owned and trained by a priest who died. The bereaved Alma was so miserably unhappy, she simply sat in a field waiting to die. A young man named Khabas Kardanov saw that and took pity on her, bringing her food. Like a stray dog given kind treatment, the Alma quickly attached herself to Kardanov by following him home. He was not thrilled about his new "pet," but taught her a few tasks to earn her keep around his home. He found her a good student and a willing worker, and very strong, loading hay on his cart with ease. In her inarticulate way she did all she could to please him, but at times her efforts were embarrassing, such as when she would steal vegetables for him from neighborhood gardens.

After three years the problems created by the faithful Alma outweighed the advantages of having her around, so Kardanov decided to get rid of her. He tried exchange offers and then outright sales, but no deal was ever consummated. He finally ended up taking a job in Siberia, and like a henpecked husband, Kardanov had to sneak off to get away from his loyal charge. After realizing he was not coming back, she drifted away and was never again seen in Kabardinia.

***

Here is a good place to address an obvious question: If so many people throughout the world have killed or captured hominoids, why hasn't at least one been turned over to proper authorities? There are several reasons: (1) fear of prosecution for wanton murder or some lesser degree of that crime; (2) superstitions about bad luck and/or bad karma; (3) the lucrative black market trade in hominoid body parts, which are extremely valuable in Eurasia for "medicinals" such as aphrodisiacs. Another reason is that on the rare occasions when hominoids are killed (much rarer now than in previous eras because humans venture less and less into hominoid territory), it is done by natives living at the edge of their habitat. To such natives it is roughly equivalent to killing a bear—certainly unusual, but "normal" within the world they know and understand.

Remember, though remarkably knowledgeable about their immediate environments, natives tend to be out of touch with the world beyond. They are unaware that outsiders would care about something that to them is just a part of the local fauna—a very rare part, but a natural part.

[Speaking of bears, Grover Krantz has calculated that bear tracks are found in the wild 100 times as often as Bigfoot tracks (100 bears = 1 Bigfoot), which extrapolates to a U.S. population of 10,000 to 20,000 Bigfeet, which seems an incredible amount for a creature so seldom glimpsed and almost never encountered. However, Dr. Krantz's conservatism is at work again. If his home state—Washington—alone held his upper projection—20,000—its 30,000 square miles of forests would contain one Bigfoot in every 1.5 square miles (1,000 acres), a reasonable figure. But if we consider the actual Bigfoot habitat, the forested areas of Washington, Oregon, northern California, and British Columbia, the number drops to one in every 20 square miles, not enough to maintain even one breeding population, much less three. So a more accurate Bigfoot total could well be 200,000—or more!]

ZANA

Zana was a female Alma that was caught and tamed and lived and died within the memory of many people still alive in Russia in 1970, when Odette Tchernine published *In Pursuit Of The Abominable Snowman*. The roots of Zana's story were first collected by a professor named A.A. Mashkovtsev, whose early work was brought to fruition in the mid-1960's by Dr. Boris Porshnev, Russia's equivalent of America's Ivan Sanderson—a highly qualified academic who also investigated hominoids. Dr. Porshnev talked to dozens of people who knew Zana when they were children, and they remembered her quite well. They lived in a region of Russia noted for the longevity of its inhabitants, so many of those he talked to were over 100 years old. He found ten people who had attended her funeral, though they could not agree on exactly when she died or her exact burial spot. They did agree it was sometime in the late 1880's or early

1890's, in the cemetery of the village of Tkhina, where Zana lived for most of her life.

No one knew how she was captured, but certain hunters of that era were skilled enough to catch and train Almas for sale—the males as work slaves (hard physical labor) and the females as sex slaves and/or wet nurses—or they were killed and their desiccated body parts sold for medicines (mostly aphrodisiacs). It was a rare but well-accepted event in the 1600, 1700, and 1800's. After Zana's capture she became the property of the ruling prince of the Zaadan region, a man named D.M. Achba. Essentially a wild animal, she had to be shackled by chains to a heavy log, and gagged by felt to muffle her loud cries. Prince Achba soon tired of his crazed possession and gave Zana to one of his noblemen, a man named Chelokua. Chelokua then gave her to Edgi Genaba, a nobleman from the village of Tkhina, on the Mokvi River, 78 miles from Sukhumi.

Edgi Genaba took her, bound and gagged, to Tkhina, where she was put in a strong enclosure. Because of her continuing wildness, food and water had to be shoved to her through cracks in the enclosure. Inside it she dug a hole in the ground in which she slept for the first three years of her captivity. Gradually, she became tamer. At the end of three years she was moved to a mud-fence enclosure under an awning near Genaba's house. She was tethered at first, but eventually was allowed to wander around freely. By then she had become totally dependent on those giving her food, so she never wandered far from Edgi Genaba's house.

Physically she was a tall, thick-set, hair-covered creature with the often reported gigantic bosoms, heavily muscled arms and legs, and fingers longer and thicker than human fingers. Her face was ugly at best and terrifying at worst: broad with high cheekbones; a broad, tipped-up (pug) nose; and dark eyes with a reddish tinge. Like the hunter's flunky described by N.A. Baykov, her expression was far more animal than human. Her skin was dark and covered with reddish-black hair. Her head hair was thick, tousled, and stood up on her head like a top hat. It was shiny and hung like a mane down her back. She could not speak, apart from uttering various murmurs, yelps, howls and growls, and she never learned the local language; but she did understand simple orders from her master and would carry them out. She also had acute hearing.

Zana did not like dogs and they did not like her (for some reason a consistent pattern with hominoids). She would toss sticks and stones at them (a very human activity) to keep them away. Like the Alma examined by Dr. Karapetian, she could not tolerate being in heated rooms (indicating a nasal structure like Neanderthals). Her teeth were large and strong enough to crack any nut. She was incredibly swift afoot, fast enough to keep pace with a running horse! She was also powerful enough to swim the Mokvi River when it raged during spring thaws.

She often played—sometimes obsessively—with rocks, grinding them together or flaking and smashing them into chips and cores. Apparently some deep-seated instinct drove her to create edges and/or points on stones, which not surprisingly resembled the Mousterian "tools" made by Neanderthals (some of whose skeletal remains were later found near Tkhina). However, she was never known to use them for more than the previously mentioned projectiles at dogs.

Surely the most astonishing part of Zana's history is that on several occasions she was made pregnant by various men of the village, and she always gave birth without difficulty or assistance. Then, following her own instincts, she would carry her half-breed newborn to the nearby river to clean it, and the shock of being dunked in the ice-cold water would kill it. Four times that happened. After the fifth birth the villagers stepped in and took the infant to rear themselves because the newborns looked remarkably human, and every pair of hands in a village was a valuable asset. Zana produced four children that lived—two daughters and two sons—to grow up and be far more human than whatever she was. They looked and acted like normal people, with full powers of human speech, intelligence, and reason. Of course, certain of their mother's traits were evident in them, too. All four were more robust than usual, much stronger, and had darker skin and broader, rougher outlines in their faces. However, on balance they were fundamentally human.

Zana and the half-breed lama, Son of Almas, prove that Almas and humans can successfully interbreed. Humans and their current nearest genetic relatives, chimps and gorillas, cannot, which means that if the Almas do prove to be living Neanderthals (an idea well-supported by evidence), then they must be "primitive" humans . . . or, conversely, humans are "advanced" Neanderthals. Information in Part IV will indicate it is far more the latter than the former.

***

Zana's eldest son was Dzhanda; her eldest daughter, Kodzhanar. No villager knew much about the later lives of either one. However, her second daughter, Gamasa, was known to have died in 1930, and her youngest son, Khvit, the best-known of all, died in 1954. All four left descendants scattered across various regions of the Abkhazian Republic, and in Tkhina it was rumored that Edgi Genaba was the father of Gamasa and Khvit. They were put in the Russian census under a different surname, but it is significant that they were raised by Genaba's wife, and Zana and Gamasa and Khvit were buried in proximity to the Genaba family's cemetery plot.

Local people remember Gamasa and Khvit as robust, powerfully built people, with dark skins and vaguely Negroid facial features, but without an overabundance of body hair. In fact, they inherited little of their mother's more pronounced hominoid features. Human characteristics dominated in every meaningful aspect, which skews well away from how hybridization normally works. [The blending of traits typically expresses a balance of parental dominance, which indicates there is something highly unusual about the genetic linkage between Almas (Neanderthals?) and humans. This, too, will be addressed in Part IV.]

Khvit, who died at around 70 (again, no old-timer Dr. Porshnev interviewed could be certain of his birth date), was described as overall quite human, with a few diversions. He had dark skin and thick lips; his head was small in proportion to his body; though not Negroid, his hair was stiffer and straighter than usual.

He was extremely strong, which combined with a contentious

181

personality to make him difficult to deal with. He lost his right hand in one of many fights with local villagers, but his left sufficed to mow and do farm work—he could even climb trees! He had a high-pitched voice that was melodious when he sang. When he died he was buried near Zana.

In 1964 Dr. Porshnev visited with two of Zana's grandchildren in the town of Tkvarcheli (where Khvit lived the last years of his life). They were a son and daughter of Khvit by his second marriage with a Russian woman, and both worked in a mine. Dr. Porshnev found they had dark skin and slightly Negroid facial features. Shalikula, the grandson, had unusually powerful jaw muscles and could pick up a chair with someone sitting in it using only his teeth! He could also dance well and was a deft impersonator of wild and domestic animals.

Later in 1964 Dr. Porshnev excavated part of the Tkhina cemetery trying to find Zana's grave. Since Moslem tradition permits no grave markers, he had to rely on the memories of the aged residents who had attended her funeral, and they could not recall exactly where it was. However, the graves of son Khvit and daughter Gamasa were found. In *Big Footprints* Grover Krantz discusses his personal examination of Khvit's skull, which he felt was "within human parameters," showing only "slightly stronger jaws and more flare to the zygomatic arches (cheek bones) than is usual." Before you accept that, however, recall that Dr. Krantz—despite his courageous support of Bigfoot/Sasquatch—is a rock-ribbed evolutionist committed by academic inclination and peer pressure to preserving the Darwinian model as much as possible whenever possible.

To someone capable of a more objective analysis, Khvit's entire skull reveals Neanderthal traits, from its heavy jaws to its wide zygomatic arches to its clearly enlarged browridges and its wide nasal passage. However, apart from what Grover Krantz or anyone else thinks about Khvit's skull, or about whatever Zana and her descendants were and are, far more research about all of them is—and has been since their discovery—demanded by Dr. Porshnev's evidence.

SUMMATION

In Part II we examined the allegedly prehuman fossil record and found not a single bone remotely resembling human bones until we reached the Cro-Magnons. That means humans are not found among the fossils of their own planet until only about 120,000 years ago, which further means humans definitely have not had enough time to evolve in classic Darwinian fashion. That fact forces all concerned scientists to seize every opportunity they find to pound the fossil record's square pegs into the round holes Swiss-cheesing the minds of the media, who then pass those distortions directly to us, the duped public. However, despite the countless absurd ways scientists pretzel logic, they cannot obscure the truth at the bottom of it all, which is that Charles Darwin's long-sought "missing link" remains missing and is certain to stay that way—forever.

In its place stands the hominoids, patiently awaiting their turn on the world stage. When the first hominoid(s) is/are brought in, it will prove beyond doubt that humans did not evolve on planet Earth. In fact, genetic testing of it/them will prove they are indigenous primates that *developed* (a still-mysterious process that can include extensive microevolution but not macroevolution) here alongside monkeys and apes. Having to accept hominoids as real will require having to acknowledge that the prehuman fossil record is comprised entirely of their bones, rather than ours. That admission will then force each of us—including, however reluctantly, all Darwinists and Creationists—to confront a truly awesome question:

Where *did* humans come from?

That question will crush scientists and religious leaders around the world because it can have only one possible, plausible answer: *Somewhere other than here.* Four simple words, yet fraught with terrible implications for science and religion and, peripherally, governments (who, by the way, are in charge of keeping an equally crushing truth stuck in tabloid limbo—UFO's).

UFO's and hominoids are inextricably linked because one guarantees the existence of the other. The day hominoids are established as real, scientists will have to forget about explaining how humans *evolved* here—all they can do then is explain how we *got* here. Once that line is crossed there can be no turning back because the path leads directly to "creation" in the manner our very first civilization—the Sumerian—says occurred: Humans were created to be slaves for multiple gods (with a small "g") who came to Earth from the heavens in flying ships to achieve a specific purpose, and while doing that they lived here for an extended, well-defined period.

For as "radical" and "far-out" as that might sound to you now, be assured that by the end of Part IV you will realize that the ancient Sumerians provide vastly more plausible explanations for our beginnings than the misguided wishful thinking of today's scientists and theologians.

PART IV

THE TRUTH?

INTRODUCTION

"Truth" is an extremely deceptive word, subject to endless shadings by all who profess to know some version of it, so let me begin this final section with a caution: it will contain the truth as I currently understand it. I realize today's fact can easily become tomorrow's fallacy; I accept that history is written by the victors; and as I said at this book's outset, in a universe as strange as ours it is difficult to know what is real, much less undeniably true. However, 2 + 2 does equal 4, and the sky is blue, so we know certain basic truths do exist.

I hope by now you can accept one such basic truth is that no creatures even remotely resembling humans appear on Earth until the Cro-Magnons at least 120,000 years ago (and almost certainly earlier than that, as we shall soon see). This can be considered a truth because for the prior 4,000,000 years the hominid fossil record contains only thick-boned, heavily-muscled creatures who are brutes compared to humans. That leaves an implausibly brief time (by *any* standard) for them to have "evolved" our much slighter frames and the supercharged brains guiding them.

That truth—if we accept it—means humans absolutely cannot be natives of Earth in any Darwinian sense, which in turn means we *got here* in some way, a process with only three options: (1) We arrived of our own volition and under our own steam (i.e., we migrated) from somewhere outside the planet. (2) We were brought from somewhere else by some entity who placed us here to live, with or without our cooperation. (3) We were developed/created by some entity who utilized genetic manipulation, crossbreeding, or a combination of both.

Coming on our own seems the least likely of the three because if humans lived on any planet that was seriously overcrowded, or in some way becoming uninhabitable (the staple of so much science fiction), and they had the brainpower to get here, it is hard to imagine even a small colony of settlers degenerating into Cro-Magnons before rebounding into humanity. It seems far more likely that settlers from another world would bring along whatever they would need to establish themselves and live as they were accustomed, and would simply keep developing from that point forward. If indeed that was how it happened, we should be much more technologically sophisticated and emotionally mature than we are. Also, unless the single-planet colonists were multiracial (which is possible but seems improbable), we should not be multiracial.

The second option, that we humans were brought here against our will to "go forth and multiply" (which we are badly overdoing), is more likely. It could account for the primitive state of the first arrivals (Cro-Magnons), and it can even account for the diversity of our races (whoever brought us chose a "sample pack" approach). In fact, if there were no other option, this one would be a hands-down winner. However, there is that third choice, and it is the one that works best for me. I believe humans were developed/created on Earth by human-like "aliens" using a combination of genetic engineering and crossbreeding with native hominids (hominoids).

Yes, I realize that of the three choices that one is by far the most

186

seditious, the one most certain to raise defensive hackles among scientific and religious establishments everywhere. So why would I choose that one? Because it is well-supported by a truly substantial, truly legitimate, truly plausible body of visible, tangible evidence. That evidence comes from the oldest civilization so far discovered on planet Earth, the high culture of Sumer, which was located in present-day Iraq (of Gulf War fame). It is overwhelming in its scope, its quantity, its quality, and—most importantly—in its availability. It is not a scarce record of highly debatable fossils, nor the more abundant, more accessible, but far more ignored evidence for the reality of hominoids. It is an extensive collection of well-documented historical artifacts left to us as writing and as pictures.

Using the Sumerians' own accounts of their history, we will examine the many remarkable things they had to say regarding the very questions we have been examining in this book, from the beginnings of the solar system itself, right through to the creation of the human beings on it. Once we understand what the Sumerian viewpoints are regarding these things, we will examine the evidence on hand that supports their claims. I guarantee you will find it enthralling.

***

Apart from hard evidence, in Part IV you will meet a brilliant thinker and scholar who has done more for my own enlightenment than anyone I have ever encountered—Zecharia Sitchin. Zecharia Sitchin's legacy is his ongoing seven-volume (so far) work in progress called *The Earth Chronicles*, which may sound like some of Ray Bradbury's fiction but is actually based on the historical accounts of the Sumerians. If you know that a chronicle is defined as "a listing of events in the order they occur," you have an idea of how precise Mr. Sitchin tends to be with his choices of words. His seven volumes are indeed a chronicle of events on planet Earth in the order they occurred. He starts at Earth's primordial beginnings and carries through to the present day, covering everything in between with scrupulous attention to detail. His is an awesome intellect, and I suspect as you get to know him during the course of this section—and especially if you take my advice to read at least some of his work—you will end up agreeing with my assessment.

All that keeps Zecharia Sitchin from being recognized as the innovative genius he is, is that his area of scholarship—humanity's ancient prehistory—is so painfully sensitive to science and religion. Otherwise, we would all sing his praises as I am doing in this introduction.

GENIUS AT WORK

Zecharia Sitchin was born in 1920 in Russia, but his parents soon emigrated to what was then Palestine (today's Israel), where he grew up. He was a brilliant student who focused on learning the ancient and modern languages of his area, along with its history and myths. His brilliance took him to London, then the center of world academic achievement, where he attended the School of Economics and Political Science. He graduated from the University of London with a degree in economic history, then returned to Palestine and became a writer/editor for economic and historical journals (which explains the depth and precision of his research and the high quality of his writing). At age 28, in 1948, he moved to New York and became an American citizen, where he continued his career as a journalist and editor while filling the volumes of notes about ancient history that would eventually form the basis of *The Earth Chronicles*.

Sitchin enjoys telling the story of how he got tracked onto his life's work. He was a boy in Palestine, ten or eleven years old, studying the Old Testament in the original Hebrew. As they studied Chapter 6 of Genesis, the teacher read the part about the days when "there were giants upon the Earth." Young Sitchin lifted his hand to ask a pertinent question. "Excuse me, teacher, but why do you call (the Hebrew word) Nefilim 'giants' when that word really means 'those who have come down from heaven to the Earth'?" His observation was disturbing because the literal meaning of Nefilim is: "Those who from heaven to Earth have come down."

Instead of giving the precocious young student the praise he felt he deserved, the teacher scolded him by saying, "Sitchin, shut up and sit down! You must never question the Bible!" Of course, no

188

ten-year-old in Palestine at that time would have dared to question the Bible, which is not what young Sitchin was doing. He was simply trying to make sense of an obvious mistranslation in what was (and remains) a crucial passage in Genesis. However, that unwarranted rebuke began Zecharia Sitchin's lifelong quest for the real truth about the Bible, which in turn has led him to make important discoveries about that revered document and many others.

As a young adult, Sitchin became fluent in the ancient Semitic languages which had produced works such as the Old Testament. By learning to read them in their original formats, he was able to determine for himself every nuance of every word, comparing and contrasting the translations of other linguists in order to be able to select the most accurate translation of any given passage. Like all who have followed that path, he came upon many puzzles and contradictions in the Bible's text, which drove him farther and farther afield in his quest for answers that made sense. That led to him becoming fluent in several more ancient languages, including Egyptian hieroglyphics and Akkadian (the language of historical Sumer), with its written text, cuneiform.

In the cuneiform of Sumer he finally found answers that made sense.

***

After thirty years of diligent study and admirably comprehensive research, Zecharia Sitchin had made numerous decisive breakthroughs in his understanding of Earth's ancient past. At that point he felt ready to share his discoveries with the world, so in the early 1970's he began working on Book I of *The Earth Chronicles—The Twelfth Planet*—published in hardback in 1976 by Stein and Day, then a year later in paperback by Avon Books (which has published paperback versions of the entire *Earth Chronicles* series). Like most genuine breakthroughs in our knowledge base (Continental Drift, pre-Ice Age spearpoints, etc.), *The Twelfth Planet* was not immediately understood for what it was, much less accepted by those it aimed to instruct.

Much of that rejection resulted from Sitchin drawing readers into a world so different from their daily reality, it was more like reading a science fiction novel than an historical analysis. *The Twelfth Planet* is based on the world's oldest writings, the cuneiform texts preserved on clay tablets found in the excavated Sumerian cities of the Tigris-Euphrates Valley (historically known as Mesopotamia, which is today's Iraq). Because of their great antiquity (3,500 to 5,500 years old) and the difficulty of learning to read them, some words and lines are subject to interpretation by the few dozen recognized scholars in the field. However, certain core facts are considered solid, and it is around those core facts that Sitchin has fashioned his *Earth Chronicles* series.

***

The Sumerian culture dates to 3800 B.C., exceeding by nearly 1,000 years the next oldest civilization—Egypt. Because it is so ancient, its traces in the historical record were scant until the mid-1800's, when discovery and excavation of its long-buried cities began. Despite the late start, they provided a vast wealth of information. Hundreds of thousands of clay tablets (most the size of a man's hand) were found scattered through every city (mostly in libraries). Researchers were amazed at the scope of the writings (in cuneiform) on those tablets, which contain remarkably complete records about politics, economy, law, medicine, mathematics, astronomy and history. Of the many thousands that have been transcribed, most are administrative, legal or economic documents. But about 5,000 are considered literary, and many of those are labeled "myths and fables."

The emphasis is on "myths." Researchers and translators found that nearly everything the Sumerians said about their cosmology (the way they viewed their beginnings) bore almost no resemblance to the world as it was understood in the late 19th and early 20th centuries. In fact, the things Sumerians talked about were *so* unusual they were downright bizarre, so all cosmological texts were dubbed "myths" and ignored. This is where Zecharia Sitchin's genius came into play. He took the Sumerians at their word regarding what they believed about themselves. He is modest about his achievement, pointing out that any scholar working with Sumerian material from 1850 to 1900 would have little inkling of how to interpret references to "winged chariots" and "gods that sailed the skies" and "life everlasting beyond the firmament," and any number of other concepts that require modern knowledge of aircraft and spacecraft to fit into a world view.

Like Alfred Wegener's "heretical" research into scientific disciplines beyond his own bailiwick of meteorology, Zecharia Sitchin approached Sumerian mythology as a scholastic outsider. By lacking formal training in the field, he did not go into it "knowing" the so-called myths had to be exactly that, fanciful creations of a brand new civilization (the world's first!) that, for whatever reasons, was incapable of distinguishing fact from fable. He did not approach his task assuming he would find what every scholar before him had found. He went into it looking for the simple, unvarnished truth, and ultimately that is what he discovered.

THE SUMERIANS

The high culture of the Sumerians was not only the world's first true civilization, it was arguably the best and certainly the most inexplicable. Why inexplicable? For two reasons. First, the Tigris-Euphrates Valley was not prime real estate. Yes, runoff from the surrounding mountains meant there was always water in the two main rivers and their tributaries; and yes, the land between them was fertile alluvial soil. However, there were no easily accessible trees or stones for building shelters, so it is difficult to imagine the primitive founders of Sumer gazing at such a denuded landscape and saying, "Right, this is the spot, this will be perfect!"

The other inexplicable puzzle about the Sumerians is that their culture, like so much else throughout history, appeared full-blown at around 3800 B.C., with their only precursor being a primitive agrarian society called the Ubaids. The Ubaids were village-based farmers who exhibited only a few of the hallmarks of the highly advanced Sumerians, who provided all subsequent civilizations with models of over 100 of the most important cultural "firsts" ascribed to every superior society. In addition, many of those firsts have not been equaled until modern times.

***

In Chapter 2 of *The Twelfth Planet*, Zecharia Sitchin spends 38 pages recounting in great detail the amazing "firsts" of what he terms "The Sudden Civilization." And so it was. Sitchin quotes from noted Sumerologist Samuel Kramer's seminal work, *From The Tablets Of Sumer*: "The table of contents (describes) twenty-five Sumerian 'firsts,' including the first schools, the first bicameral congress, the first historians, the first pharmacopoeia, the first 'farmer's almanac,' the first cosmogony and cosmology, the first proverbs and sayings, the first literary debates, the first library catalogue, the first law codes and social reforms, the first medicine, agriculture, and search for world peace and harmony." That is the quote. Then, as if it is all simply too much to comprehend, Sitchin adds for good measure, "This is no exaggeration."

Protestations aside, Sitchin goes on to point out: "The schools taught not only language and writing but also the sciences of the day—botany, zoology, geography, mathematics, and theology. Literary works were studied and copied, and new ones were composed." The language itself was a marvel, with its "precise grammar and rich vocabulary." The world's first writing, cuneiform, ultimately evolved into a surprisingly simple and efficient technique.

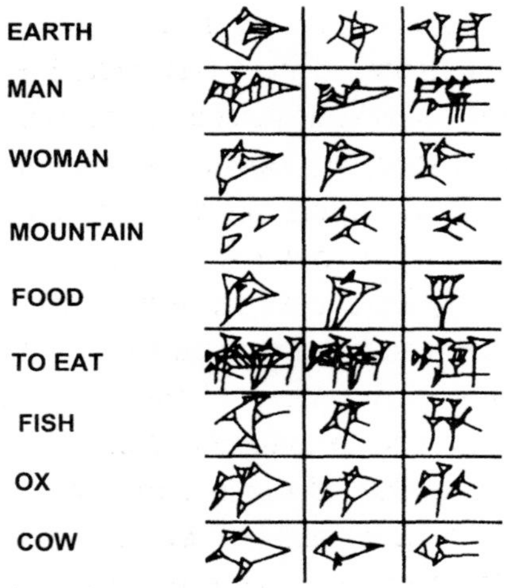

Fig. 65.

Using it, Sumerian scribes covered a remarkable range of topics, including "cosmological tales, epic poems, histories of kings, temple records, commercial contracts, marriage and divorce records, astronomical tables, astrological forecasts, mathematical formulas, geographic lists, grammar and vocabulary school texts." So it bears repeating: "This is no exaggeration."

***

Sumerians founded the first true cities, each having 10,000 to 50,000 inhabitants. When a city became too large to be easily manageable, part of the population left to create a new city that could grow without constraint. (Such wise urban planning is seldom practiced today.) Cities themselves were laid out in grids, with streets easing congestion between houses and buildings, and facilitating movement and commerce. (Post-Sumerian cultures tended to sprawl haphazardly around a village-sized center.) Sumerian city centers were dominated by magnificent high-rise palaces and temples (ziggurats), which were built to exact specifications outlined in detailed architectural plans. For defense they built walls around city perimeters. Water was supplied by brilliant canal and aqueduct systems, and they had equally clever drainage and sewage disposal.

Somehow they got the idea of reinforcing clay bricks with chopped reeds and straw, to which they added the kiln furnace to "fire" those reinforced bricks, making them strong enough and durable enough to construct their high-rises and temples (some over 100 feet tall!), as well as to pave streets. Sumerian kilns also forged the first durable pottery, such as cups, bowls, plates, urns, storage vessels, etc. However, the kiln's chief contribution was that it led directly to the first age of metals, the Bronze Age, because it allowed intense but controllable temperatures to be contained in furnaces without contamination from dust or ashes. Metallurgy in turn led to the first money (coins) and banking. However, Sumerian land contained no raw ores to make metals.

What Sumer did have was naphtha, which was asphalts and bitumens that seeped to the surface all over Mesopotamia. So Sumerians had to locate and retrieve mineral ores from wherever they existed to supply their well-fueled furnaces, which led them to develop the first extensive international trade routes by using naphtha as their principle medium of exchange. They also used naphtha for other purposes, such as road surfacing (as we do today), waterproofing, caulking, cementing, painting, and molding. In addition, their extensive use of petroleum products led to the development of advanced chemistry needed to create a wide range of paints and pigments, pottery glazes, even the artificial production of semiprecious stones like lapis lazuli!

Bitumens were also used in certain medicines, some of which enabled Sumerians to set high standards in surgery. In a policy we might profit from today, Sumerian doctors and surgeons were paid only if treatments were successful; if not, there was no charge, and if damage was done, doctors and surgeons had to pay their patients.

Sumer was first to develop advanced weaving techniques, producing highly refined textiles from both fur and fiber. Their basic garment was called a "tug," which Zecharia Sitchin feels was the forerunner of the Roman toga. Sumer developed the first widespread agriculture in a basically semi-arid plain, so an extensive system of irrigation canals was mandatory. (We will anaylze Sumerian agriculture later in this section.) They were also deep-water seafarers, partly from their need to obtain ores from far-flung countries, but also because they had no wood or stones nearby. This led them to develop the first means of open-water navigation, the first wharves, the first granaries, and the first marketplaces. Marketplaces and international trade meant the first standards of weights and measures. For overland transportation they invented and widely used the first wheeled carts, wagons, and chariots.

Perhaps the most interesting Sumerian "first" was the great care they took to insure fairness and good order within their society. They had written laws, courts, judges, lawyers, trials by juries, business contracts, marriages, divorces (with equitable settlements to both parties), police, jails, and punishments to fit crimes against persons, property, and the city-state (a crucial first). However, they strove for a higher purpose. Political evils were considered "unfair use by supervisors of their power to take the best for themselves; the abuse of official status; the extortion of high prices by monopolistic groups." Also covered were rights of the blind, the poor, the widowed, and the orphaned. They had a social safety net 5,000 years ago!

The Sumerians developed a wide array of musical instruments—lutes, harps, flutes, pipes—and a playing system much like the heptatonic-diatonic scale used today. Such complex, subtle music was long considered to have originated with classical Greeks, but now we know they received it from the Sumerians, who elevated all arts to remarkable heights of refinement and subtlety. Their statuary and pottery are still astonishing in their beauty and technical execution, as is their precious-metal jewelry (yet another offshoot from the development of metallurgy). They produced poetry, songs, and dances, through which, the Greek scholar Philo claimed, they sought to gain "worldwide harmony and unison."

Sumerians also created an efficient system of mathematics based on the number 60 (called sexagesimal). It enabled them to easily divide into tiny fractions and to multiply with equal ease into the millions, to calculate roots and raise numbers by any power. The 60-second minute and 60-minute hour are two vestiges remaining from the original system. So are the 360-degree circle, the 12-inch foot, and the dozen. Closely related to their mathematics was their geometry, which permitted their engineers to survey, level, and construct highly intricate and efficient irrigation systems for their widespread agriculture. That geometry also contributed to their astonishingly complete astronomy, which for our purposes is the most important of all the many firsts they achieved. Having an understanding of the cosmos at the level they did is not only incredible, by all accounts it should be flatly impossible . . . Yet there it is.

It must be said one more time: *This is no exaggeration!*

***

The full extent of Sumerian astronomical knowledge will probably never be known, but based on the hundreds of relevant tablets that have been transcribed thus far, their knowledge might have rivaled—or even surpassed—our own. They had accurate calendars

195

fashioned around the mind-boggling timeframe of 25,920 years, the "Great Year" based on a sophisticated celestial phenomenon known as precession (the time Earth's polar axis needs to circle the sky and point again at the same North Star). They had long lists of celestial bodies, some of which were invisible from Earth! They had tables of Sun risings and settings that were accurate enough to predict eclipses. Also necessary to predict eclipses was knowledge of the shapes, movements, and relationships between the Earth, Moon, and Sun. They did that using the heliacal system we use today, measuring the rising and setting of the stars and planets in our skies relative to the Sun. This means they were able to distinguish between fixed stars and planets, which wander around the skies at night. It also means they knew the Sun and the Moon were not ordinary celestial bodies.

The Sumerians kept accurate ephemerides, tables that predicted future positions of celestial bodies. Those ephemerides were not based on observations, which were impossible with the naked eye, but on mathematical formulas governed by rules handed down from some as yet undetermined source. (We know what they did but have no idea how it was possible.) The Sumerians also understood the complicated celestial phenomenon known as retrograde, which is the erratic motion of the other planets relative to Earth caused by Earth's faster or slower orbital speed around the Sun. What is interesting about this is that it requires an extremely long period—several centuries—to grasp the idea of retrograde and successfully track it.

The Sumerians did their astronomical tracking using a complex method of spherical geometry which postulated a round Earth with an equator and poles, and those concepts were extended to encompass the infinite heavens. They knew Earth and the other planets moved around the Sun in the flat plane of an ecliptic, which over the course of a year resulted in gradual north-south shifts of sunrises and sunsets along Earth's horizon, producing equinoxes and solstices. Remarkably, these sophisticated concepts are utilized by modern astronomers in the same manner.

The Sumerians fashioned the first zodiac, which divided the heavens into twelve distinct "houses." Our zodiac closely approximates theirs, as this list from *The Twelfth Planet* shows:

1. GU.AN.NA (heavenly bull)—Taurus
2. MASH.TAB.BA (twins)—Gemini
3. DUB (pincers, tongs)—Cancer (the crab)
4. UR.GULA (lion)—Leo
5. AB.SIN (her father was Sin [a god])—Virgo
6. ZI.BA.AN.NA (heavenly scales)—Libra
7. GIR.TAB (which claws and cuts)—Scorpio
8. PA.BIL (defender)—Sagittarius (the archer)
9. SUHUR.MASH (goat-fish)—Capricorn
10. GU (lord of the waters)—Aquarius (water bearer)
11. SIM.MAH (fishes)—Pisces
12. KU.MAL (field dweller)—Aries (the ram)

The Sumerian name for this heavenly configuration was, of course, not "zodiac." It was UL.HE, which meant "shiny herd," even though not all twelve represented animals. The important point about it, however, is that all twelve houses were sighted along Earth's central region, from 30° North latitude to 30° South latitude. Again, this shows full knowledge of a spherical planet moving in an ecliptic orbit around a relatively stationary Sun.

Sumerian text AO.6478 lists the 26 stars visible along the line we now call the Tropic of Cancer—achievement enough in itself. However, it then calculates the distances between those stars in three different ways! That tells us the Sumerians placed a high value on being able to accurately measure celestial distances. Yet who among a "primitive" people barely out of the Stone Age would conceivably need such knowledge, much less know how to calculate it?

***

If the Sumerians knew so much about astrophysics, to a degree unmatched until our own spacefaring era, what might they have known about our solar system? Could they possibly have known about "invisible" Uranus and Neptune, or minuscule, erratic Pluto? Indeed they did! Not only that, they had a significantly different understanding of the solar system than we have today. In a text

known as K.3538, they give this explanation of how they viewed it:
"The number of its celestial bodies is twelve.
The stations of its celestial bodies (is) twelve.
The complete months of the Moon is twelve."
This tells us the Sumerians knew there were the eleven bodies we know as our solar system—Sun, Mercury, Venus, Earth, Moon, Mars, Jupiter, Saturn, Uranus, Neptune, Pluto—but they also knew of a twelfth member. This, obviously, was the basis for the title of Zecharia Sitchin's first book: *The Twelfth Planet*. We will discuss that "missing" 12th planet in the next chapter, but first you should hear the following anecdote:

When *The Twelfth Planet* was published in 1976, Zecharia Sitchin related what the Sumerians claimed to know about the outer, invisible-to-the-eye planets of Uranus, Neptune, and Pluto. They described Uranus and Neptune as "watery twins" with a "blue-green" color, which Sitchin duly reported. Naturally, in 1976 every astronomer on Earth believed Sitchin's account was utter nonsense. They were convinced that the large neighbors of Jupiter and Saturn would prove to be equally gaseous, and certainly would not be dominated by *water.* So the few who bothered to review his book used that single "crackpot" idea to dismiss it entirely as worthless.

Now flash forward a decade, to 1986, when the Voyager satellite passed Uranus to photograph it for the first time. What did it find? Lo and behold! Uranus *was* watery (its surface was a kind of slushy ice) and it *was* colored blue-green, exactly as Sitchin had recounted the Sumerian claims! Needless to say, none of his earlier detractors bothered to offer any kind of apology. Then, three years later, in 1989, Voyager reached Neptune, which the Sumerians called a "twin" of Uranus. A few months earlier, Sitchin had written an article detailing precisely what Voyager would find, based on the Sumerian texts. He submitted it to magazines around the world, several of whom published it; however, none in the heavily co-opted U.S. dared to. Sure enough, Voyager found Neptune was just as the Sumerians had claimed: a blue-green ball of slushy ice!

No one bothered to apologize about that one, either.

***

What the above tells us is that—clearly and without question—the Sumerians knew exactly what they were talking about when they discussed the deepest reaches of our solar system. They put their money where their mouths were 5,000 years ago, then left it up to us, with our infinite ability to delude ourselves, to blithely disregard their stunning accuracy and call everything they had to say "myths." Well, there is nothing mythical in what Zecharia Sitchin wrote about in *The Twelfth Planet* (nor in any of his other books). As he says of himself: all he does is report what people wrote at a time when our species was just beginning to blossom on Earth. As you read further in this section, keep in mind that none of it is based on fantasy or speculation. It is based on facts as the Sumerians understood them, not facts turned into myths by scholars desperate to avoid confronting any reality their training has taught them is "not acceptable."

EPIC OF CREATION

The Sumerian "Epic of Creation" is a text with obvious parallels to the Old Testament's Book of Genesis. Called Enuma Elish after the fashion of naming some Sumerian texts by their opening words ("Enuma Elish" means "When in the heights . . . "), it is an allegory that relates a complex, thrilling tale of battles raging between fearsome "gods" in heaven. Much has been written about those parallels to Genesis, not least of which is that the six tablets that comprise its active storyline are considered by many to be the basis of a translation glitch in Genesis that caused "creation" to be reported as occurring in six literal days rather than in six varied periods lasting an indeterminate number of eons. (Many religious scholars now accept that more plausible interpretation.)

Enuma Elish was the most revered Sumerian epic, the one they saw as the quintessence of their most ancient knowledge; yet virtually every contemporary scholar interprets it as pure fantasy, with no conceivable grounding in reality. Instead, some consider it the earliest version of the classic struggle between good and evil, while others see it as an "imaginative" metaphor for life, death, and ultimate resurrection. Rather than follow the deep-rutted path of scholastic tradition, Zecharia Sitchin accepted Enuma Elish as what it purports to be—an allegorical account of our solar system's formation. Viewed in that context, Sumerian knowledge about that formation is even more amazing than their astronomical knowledge!

***

Zecharia Sitchin comprehensively discusses the Sumerian "Epic of Creation," Enuma Elish, in Chapter 7 of *The Twelfth Planet.* What follows next is my own generalized interpretation of his very detailed interpretation of how Enuma Elish recounts our solar system's creation. Much compression of events has been required, so any distortions and/or mistakes occurring in that process are, of course, unintentional on my part and should in no way reflect on Mr. Sitchin's work.

"In the beginning" the Sun, Mercury, and a large planet called "Tiamat" were formed.

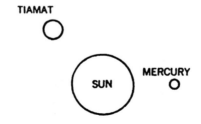

Fig. 66. (© Z. Sitchin, *The Twelfth Planet*)

Next formed were Venus and Mars, taking places between Mercury and Tiamat.

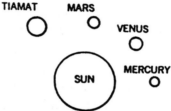

Fig. 67. (© Z. Sitchin, *The Twelfth Planet*)

Then came Jupiter and Saturn, with Pluto originally formed as a moon of Saturn.

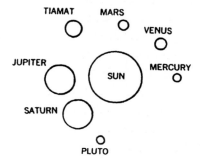

Fig. 68. (© Z. Sitchin, *The Twelfth Planet*)

Uranus and Neptune were the last to be formed.

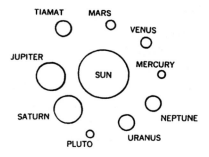

Fig. 69. (© Z. Sitchin, *The Twelfth Planet*)

Once the solar system was established but still primordial (in the phase when it was mostly hot, seething magma), another planet called "Nibiru" approached from deep space. Nibiru was unattached and isolated, possibly sent hurtling through the galaxy by surviving, rather than being destroyed by, its protosun exploding during formation. But no matter how it arrived in our still-coalescing solar system, Nibiru was as large as Tiamat (which was smaller than Saturn but larger than Uranus or Neptune), and it came in on

201

(or near) the ecliptic from a clockwise direction, as opposed to the other planets' counterclockwise motion.

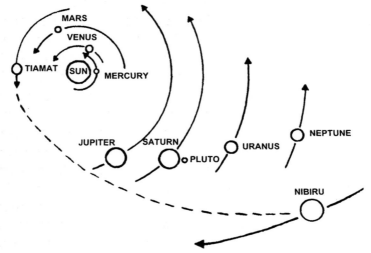

Fig. 70. Nibiru's arrival (© Z. Sitchin, *The Twelfth Planet*)

As Nibiru neared the solar system, it was drawn from its headlong path by the gravitational pulls of Neptune and Uranus. All three bodies were still somewhat plasmic (unsolidified), so their increasing nearness created electromagnetic disturbances that culminated in a bulge forming at one side of Nibiru. By the time it reached Uranus, enough material had been drawn from its body to create four moons orbiting it. When it reached the far more powerful gravitational fields of Jupiter and Saturn, it was drawn even more toward an orbit around the Sun. Also, three more moons were pulled from its body and began orbiting around it.

Small Venus and smaller Mars had little effect on it, but soon it faced an object its own size—Tiamat. That confrontation created more electromagnetic disturbances, which caused Tiamat to produce eleven new moons, the chief among them called "Kingu." Now Nibiru was fully in the grip of the Sun's powerful gravitational forces and its fate was sealed: it had been captured as a new member of this solar system; new, but unlike any of its other "natural" siblings. It would have an orbit and sidereal period completely unrelated to any of theirs, making it unique in all the heavens. However, it was not safe and secure in its new orbit.

While being captured by the Sun and sent on its first orbit around, Nibiru barely missed colliding with Tiamat. But several of its seven new moons (the text is imprecise about how many) did smash into Tiamat, at least one at its "head" and one or more at its "belly." Those monumental collisions shattered the still-cooling protoplanet to its core, but left it physically intact. However, all but the largest of its eleven moons—Kingu—were swept away in Nibiru's strong gravitational wake. On its next orbit through the solar system, Nibiru itself collided with previously cracked Tiamat, an event of such cataclysmic proportions it can barely be imagined. Chief among the results was a *mingling of the waters* of both planets (more about this later—keep it in mind). Even more dramatic was that unlucky Tiamat was broken completely apart—cleaved in half!

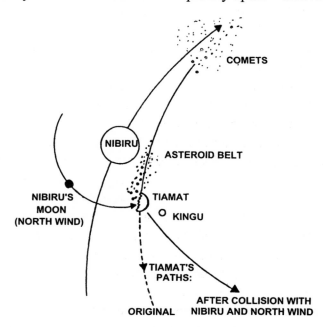

Fig. 71. Nibiru-Tiamat collision   (© Z. Sitchin, *The Twelfth Planet*)

After the cleaving, three major events occurred. First, the remaining half of Tiamat was struck by one of Nibiru's moons, which—combined with the ricochet effect of the collision with Nibiru—propelled it and its surviving moon, Kingu, into a new orbit between Mars and Venus. Then the plasmic body of the remaining half began slowly folding in on itself (as all fluid bodies do in space), becoming a new planet substantially smaller than the old Tiamat. (Whether Nibiru's moon ricocheted away or melded with the new planet to become part of it is not made clear in the text, though melding is most likely because the text does say that in the earlier collisions Tiamat "devoured" the moons that struck it.) The new planet was Earth, and Kingu became its Moon.

The second major event was that the half of Tiamat struck by Nibiru's "windshield," so to speak, splattered into millions of smaller plasmic globs (some many miles wide but most mountain- to boulder-sized) while streaming into a long arc behind the speeding survivor of the collision. As those millions of globs quick-froze into rocks in the sub-zero vacuum of space (all with irregular shapes because none had enough mass to resist hardening long enough to form into a sphere), they established an equilibrium suspended between the Sun's pull and the nearly equal (and much closer) pulls of Jupiter and Saturn. In other words, they became the Asteroid Belt.

The collision's third major effect was to ricochet Nibiru into a new orbit that carried it around the solar system in a giant "loop" (the precise word in Enuma Elish) that required 3,600 years to complete. It was also knocked off the ecliptic (above or below is not made clear, though several indirect references put it at 30° below), which left it entering and exiting the solar system at an oblique angle that all but eliminated the chance of a collision with another planet. Its path around the Sun and through the solar system was established between Mars and the Asteroid Belt.

**

Nibiru's last act before settling into its new life as a permanent member of this solar system was to pass near Saturn on its way out and capture a large moon ("Gaga" in the text, now known as Pluto).

It too was pulled off the ecliptic by an unspecified amount, but eventually found a home at 17° above the ecliptic. This, of course, argues against Nibiru pulling it away in its gravitational wake if Nibiru orbits 30° below the ecliptic. However, it could be that Nibiru first pulled Pluto below the ecliptic, then later some other celestial force moved it to its current location. Today we know Pluto has a tiny moon, Charon, unmentioned in Enuma Elish, which orbits so close to Pluto that some astronomers speculate it might be a piece of Pluto knocked off in a collision that occurred long after it solidified into a planet. On the other hand, Nibiru pulled Gaga away when it was still plasmic, so Charon could also have been pulled from its body at that time.

As of now we cannot come down on either side with any certainty. We will simply have to wait for more information about Pluto, or for a clearer explanation in one or more of the thousands of undeciphered Sumerian texts. But however it happened, Pluto has assumed a wildly erratic orbit that sees it careen between deep space and inside the orbit of Neptune. Astronomers accept that its small size and strange orbit strongly indicate it began life as a satellite of one of the large outer planets, but they do not know which one, nor how it could have been removed to its current location. So it boggles the mind that the Sumerian epic of creation, Enuma Elish, written down 5,000 years ago, accurately describes and plausibly explains Pluto's orbital eccentricities!

With Pluto's capture from Saturn and removal to the far edge of the solar system, Nibiru had done its work of reshaping the Sun's entire "family." All the members—now numbering 12 with the addition of Nibiru, Pluto, the new planet, Earth, and its Moon—settled into establishing the orbits needed to stabilize the entire celestial dynamic. And so they continue to this day.

* * *

Clearly the 5,000-year-old Enuma Elish is a tale to give one pause. However, couldn't the scientific establishment be right about it? Couldn't it actually *be* a brilliantly inventive fable? An improbable series of incredibly lucky guesses? Scientists would surely argue that anything—even something as unlikely as that—is possible. Logic, in turn, would ask how such supposedly primitive people could conceivably have imagined anything so astonishingly prescient? How could they "guess" about Uranus, Neptune, and Pluto, the outer planets we ourselves discovered only in the last 150 years? Reason tells us that *has* to be impossible, yet there it is—again.

PROOFS AND SPECULATIONS

At 4.0 billion years ago two monumental events occurred on Earth: (1) life appeared; and (2) plate tectonics began acting on the primordial crust. It is at least coincidental, if not downright suspicious, that two such critical milestones should be reached simultaneously. But whether coincidence or something more, we can analyze each event in light of Enuma Elish. First, life.

In Part I we found it was literally impossible for Earth's first life forms (the two fully developed prokaryotes) to have spontaneously generated themselves from a prebiotic soup. Darwinism forces scientists to insist they did, but anyone who studies the subject soon discovers the charade. That leaves only one other option: life was *introduced* here—accidentally or deliberately, but definitely introduced. Assuming it arrived from outside Earth, how might it have come? As was also mentioned in Part I, many scientists now accept that life could not possibly have developed here, so they are turning to comets and asteroids as the possible initiators of life. That is all well and good, but there is an even more plausible scenario: the one described in Enuma Elish.

According to Enuma Elish, Nibiru could not have been much more developed than the primordial solar system it encountered. Otherwise, the gravitational forces of the large outer planets could never have pulled seven moons from its body. Thus, we can assume Nibiru was still somewhat plasmic, but not nearly as plasmic as Tiamat (from which it drew eleven moons, in the same way it might have drawn out the unexpected, inexplicably high number of moons still found orbiting around Neptune, Uranus, Saturn, and Jupiter).

206

This leaves us assuming Nibiru was somewhat older than the solar system that captured it, but not so old it was no longer plasmic.

We know Earth's crust did not harden to its present density until around 2.0 billion years ago. That means it took 2.5 billion years to go from a seething plasmic blob to a still-seething core surrounded by a cracked but hardened shell. Given that, let's just wing it and assume a half-billion years (500 million) would be a reasonable guess (but only a guess) at the age difference between Nibiru and our solar system. (500 million is only 20% of how long Earth's crust needed to harden, so at that point it would still be fairly plasmic.) Also, 500 million years is about how long it took for Earth to acquire the unicellular life forms that dominate its history.

Remember, only prokaryotes and eukaryotes existed for seven-eighths (7/8) of life's timeline on Earth, with the Cambrian Explosion occurring only around 530 million years ago. So the entire history of complex, multicellular life on Earth is contained within roughly the timeframe we postulate for Nibiru being older than our solar system. It is thus reasonable to assume 500 million years is enough time for primitive life forms (the two kinds of prokaryotes and/or their precursors) to appear on Nibiru, take hold, and flourish. So assuming all of the above—that Nibiru's surface was teeming with prokaryotes it passed to Tiamat in the collision that "mingled their waters" (as Enuma Elish says)—we still face the difficult question of how prokaryotes got in position to be transferred during the collision? In other words, how did life get on Nibiru in the first place?

This again confronts us with the great cosmic riddle of life's ultimate source, only now we are one step removed from Earth. But no matter where we draw that contentious line, in the end it comes down to deciding if life is divinely created, or does it somehow, someway, spontaneously generate itself from inanimate molecules? Either method would allow it to be seeded onto Earth (and across the entire universe for that matter), which leaves the ultimate question unanswered.

It can be argued that inorganic molecules are inorganic molecules throughout the universe, so spontaneous generation is as unlikely on Nibiru (or anywhere else) as Fred Hoyle's tornado is to sweep through a junkyard and assemble a Boeing 747. It can likewise be argued that all biological processes we are currently aware of, from lowest to highest, obey fundamental laws based on organic chemistry rather than divine fiat. So decide for yourself what you prefer to believe.

***

As for plate tectonics beginning 4.0 billion years ago, Enuma Elish provides an explanation for that, too. 4.0 billion years ago is when Enuma Elish says the still-plasmic proto-Nibiru entered our coalescing solar system, whose large outer planets drew from it seven moons, some of which slammed into an even more plasmic Tiamat. Tiamat's newly formed primordial crust cracked like the eggshell it basically was, but its viscous interior was able to "devour" (Enuma Elish's exact word) and absorb the smaller moons that crashed into it.

On Nibiru's next pass it collided with Tiamat. Assuming it was 500 million years older, its crust was that much thicker and firmer, making it better able to withstand the collision. Meanwhile, previously "shattered" Tiamat was "split into two parts," one of which was swept away into space. What remained was like a gaping wound oozing magma, which could only fold in on itself like the edges of a deep gouge in flesh. And because of the cracks pounded into its surface by the collisions with Nibiru's moons, Tiamat's remaining crust was indeed able to stretch and cover its wound, forming a much smaller planet in its new position.

Naturally, this was not a rapid process. It could have required hundreds, thousands, or even millions of years to complete. However, given what and where Earth is now, and assuming Enuma Elish is correct in its basic essentials, something like it could easily have taken place. And there is more evidence to support it. An intriguing geological fact is that today's Earth is missing a huge portion of its crust. All other planets and moons so far studied have essentially uniform surfaces that contain approximately 10% outer crust (the part that wraps around their interior cores, whatever those interior cores happen to be). Earth has something like 1%. So the obvious question arises: Where is the huge missing portion (if only 1% remains, it means 9/10 is missing!) of Earth's crust?

A significant part, surely, is the deep gouge represented by Earth's oceans. Nothing else in the solar system is remotely comparable. Admittedly, the "uniform" surfaces of other planets and moons illustrate varying degrees of volcanic- or tectonic- or collision-caused blemishes. But Earth stands alone with such an enormous part of its surface missing and filled in with water. So could Earth's oceans be a physical remnant of the collision with Nibiru? Could they be a gaping scar left by the wound? To answer that we need to understand that today's oceans are not the oceans Earth has always had because plate tectonics keeps land and sea in constant flux.

Plate tectonics is the modern name for Alfred Wegener's "Continental Drift." It is caused by the roiling (like thick stew in a pot) of the viscous magma just below the surface of the crust. Huge plumes hundreds and sometimes thousands of miles across come up from the core, literally nudging and shifting the broken crustal plates above them. Very gradually they move the land (the length a fingernail grows each year), which over the scale of cosmic time adds up. At least twice in Earth's past (and possibly at other times not yet clear in the geologic record) all land has been driven together by plate tectonics to form one supercontinent (first "Gondwana," then "Pangea," named by Wegener when he postulated Continental Drift). In the same way, plate tectonics then tore them back apart and drifted them across the oceans to gather again at a new rendezvous.

No matter what course the lands above the oceans are forced to take by the action of the magma roiling beneath both, they provide clear evidence of the deep gouge inflicted on Earth, a wound that will remain unhealed, a visible reminder of the collision with Nibiru. (Nibiru also must carry similar evidence of the collision, which has to be how the Enuma Elish story was arrived at in the first place. But arrived at by whom? That will be discussed later.)

Now we must consider what happened to Tiamat's "removed" portion. And prior to that, what happened to the ten newly formed

209

moons Nibiru pulled from Tiamat and then swept away (leaving "giant" Kingu behind) on its first pass-by? Promising answers to those questions are offered by comets and the Asteroid Belt, two of the most unusual aspects of our solar system.

COMETS

Comets come in a wide range of sizes (mountains to moons) and an equally wide range of orbits, including many that defy the solar system's prevailing counterclockwise motion by moving clockwise (an inexplicable anomaly in an otherwise linear universe). No matter their size or orbit, all comets are comprised of rocks (boulders to pebbles) and ice, fused together in varying proportions by their own internal gravity and the cohesion of the ice's crystals. So how did they get that way? How did gigantic "dirty snowballs" (a typical description of them) come to be flying around in all parts of space? To answer that in terms of Enuma Elish we must assume Nibiru and Tiamat contained large quantities of water at or near their surfaces. Is that reasonable? Absolutely.

As any seething protoplanet coalesces, it releases vast amounts of water vapor as steam, which atmospheric cooling condenses into liquid water. This is evident in currently arid bodies like the Moon and Mars, whose surfaces show water once coursed over them and which now have patches of ice near their poles (the Moon's have been recently discovered). Thus, even as protoplanets, Nibiru and Tiamat would have contained substantial amounts of water at their surfaces. This means any collision between them and/or their moons would fling vast sheets of water into space with other debris from the impact(s). That water and debris would disperse in a wide range of amounts and sizes, with the water quick-freezing as it entered subzero space. Any rocks (boulders to pebbles) in the water would be trapped, forming aggregates that by size alone would attract other, smaller bits of ice and debris, creating the raw material of comets as we know them.

(Another recent discovery is proof of astronomer Louis Frank's radical theory that Earth is under a steady bombardment of cometary iceballs the size of houses. Dr. Frank first proposed his theory in 1986, basing it on hard-to-interpret images received by a NASA satellite in the late 1970's. His colleagues uniformly condemned it as preposterous, particularly because it called for much more water being loose in the solar system than they could readily account for. It was bad enough trying to explain all the water carried by ordinary comets; Dr. Frank was trying to add millions of additional tons by dubiously interpreting inconclusive data. However, as often happens in such cases, time and better data have settled the argument in favor of the "radical" with vision. Now astronomers speculate that Dr. Frank's iceballs are why Earth does not gradually dessicate like Mars or the Moon. And that, of course, begs the question of why Earth would be under such a continual bombardment, but not its "nearby" neighbors? Yet another vexing conundrum.)

As for cometary orbits, they are as varied as the stars they imitate when they come near enough to the Sun to be lit by its solar rays. As mentioned earlier, they can have the prevailing counterclockwise motion or the anomalous clockwise motion; they can originate from any direction, from all four quadrants of the heavens; and they can have either short periods (less than 200 years) or long periods (over 200 years). Halley's Comet is a well known short-period comet with a 75 to 76 year period. Others like Kohoutek are many thousands of years long. (Obviously, such extended periods have not been calculated from appearances in past eras; they are determined by measuring orbits when comets appear for the first time in the modern era.)

Prior to 1950, no one presumed to guess how many comets existed or where they stayed when not swooping around the Sun. In that year a Dutch astronomer named Jan Oort postulated a giant cloud composed of millions of comets hovering all around the solar system at about 1,000 times its radius (from the Sun to Pluto). Oort said that as stars from other solar systems passed close to the cloud (now known as the Oort Cloud), they agitated its comets and sent them hurtling across space toward our Sun, which would then capture them and assign them orbits.

For as far out (excuse the pun) as Oort's theory sounds (imagine the time needed to traverse 1,000 times the solar system's radius!), and for as much as it left out of the equation (no short-period comets could possibly originate so far away), the fact that it explained periodicity in all quadrants (another confusing paradox in our established linear universe), and was impossible to disprove (again, too far away), left most astronomers feeling comfortable slipping behind the Oort Cloud. After that, all they needed was a short-period explanation.

**

Because the Oort Cloud went over so well in 1950, the next year another Dutch astronomer, Gerald Kuiper, postulated a similar effect starting just beyond Neptune and extending only about 10 times the solar system's radius. But instead of hovering in all quadrants like the nebulous Oort Cloud (again, please excuse the pun), the Kuiper Belt (as it came to be known) laid and rotated in the flat plane of the ecliptic. In 1951 such a notion was a serious intellectual reach, but astronomers were obliged to close ranks behind it because it at least provided a potential home for short-period comets to come from and return to. What it did not do was believably account for the many short-periods that had orbits above or below the ecliptic, and motions that were more clockwise than counterclockwise (which, once again, was incompatible with a linear universe).

Kuiper's tentative explanation was that any short-periods traveling clockwise and/or off the ecliptic were "strays" that collisions had knocked away from where they belonged—the Kuiper Belt. This had a strong hint of shoehorning about it, so it was accepted with a large grain of salt. [Another apparent Kuiper shoehorn was Pluto, which he designated the largest stray from his Belt (17° above the ecliptic), but in a special category of rocky bodies rather than comets.]

Salt or not, when scientists grab at straws as thin as Kuiper's "stray" theory, you know they are in trouble. However, in astronomy the Kuiper Belt served a purpose similar to what Darwinism does for anthropologists: It was coherent enough to generally explain the broadest parameters of a multifaceted problem, while staying vague enough to permit the flexibility needed to shoehorn in aspects that did not readily fit. The only thing it could not accommodate was the ice.

***

Today, using modern techniques, astronomers have partially vindicated Kuiper by finding wide, thin bands of cosmic dust similar to his Belt. These bands surround several nearby stars (Beta Pictoris and Vega are two), which indicates our Sun is probably surrounded by a similar band—the Kuiper Belt. Such dust bands also indicate planet formation is common throughout the universe, and that whatever fails to aggregate into a planet or moon ends up in a thin platter of debris severely lacking in water (much less ice) beyond where the interior bodies form. This was recently supported by the Hubble Space Telescope taking supersensitive measurements that prove at least Jupiter-sized planets are orbiting several stars in our general galactic neighborhood.

Further evidence is supplied by dozens of supposedly "precomet" (a specious term at best) dirty iceballs that have been catalogued in a confined region of space beyond Neptune. Assuming Kuiper's debris is as evenly dispersed as that seen around the other stars, astronomers estimate there are 200 million or more "precomets" scattered throughout the entire Belt. However, for as compelling as the dust evidence is, dust is not rock, and the Kuiper Belt scenario asks us to accept that 200 million incipient comets—all composed of rocks (many of enormous size) bound together by ice crystals—were somehow created within a smear of cosmic grit so thin it did not have enough mass or gravitational attraction or adhesion to coalesce into a planet or a moon.

There is no question space dust like that in the Kuiper Belt can and does sweep itself into larger aggregates. In fact, that is how everything in the universe seems to have formed. However, ice is not a part of the equation. Ice is a by-product, something created once a planetary body has formed and come "alive" with internal reactions. By lacking the means to produce even one crystal of ice, the Kuiper Belt is reduced to no more than a stopgap explanation for the origin and periodicity of short-period comets, something for astronomers to officially promulgate until the truth becomes evident. And for all we—or they—know, it already has.

***

According to the Enuma Elish scenario, it is possible some comets were formed in the Nibiru-Tiamat collision, while others formed by the particulation of Tiamat's ten plasmic moons when Nibiru's gravity swept them away and likely pulled them to pieces during its first pass-by.

Let's imagine that first pass-by. Nibiru sweeps through along the ecliptic and sucks up the ten smaller-than-the-Moon moons that have recently been drawn out of Tiamat's plasmic body. Because all ten have come from near the surface, they will be composed of fresh, steam-drenched magma and thin pieces of hardening crust. Nibiru pulls them along in its gravitational wake, speeding at high velocity in the slingshot manner of any celestial body whipping around the Sun. Acceleration elongates the very plasmic protomoons, stretching each so that the entire mass resembles a gigantic head with ten long braids of hair. Out past Uranus and Neptune, Nibiru loses its angular momentum and begins slowing. As that happens, its hold on its "braids" also slackens, and their elongated forms (hundreds, if not thousands, of miles long) have enough mass and surface area to create enough drag against the Sun's solar wind to break free of their captor.

So far, so good. But now the protomoons' plasmic magma, which allowed them to elongate enough to break free, has now hardened too much in the deep-freeze of space for them to be able to pull themselves back into a round shape. And as the water in them freezes, it expands and cracks apart the rocks containing and surrounding it, which creates smaller and smaller pieces that spread out and gravitate to the only region celestial mechanics leaves available to them—along the planetary ecliptic where Nibiru dropped them off. (Remember, Nibiru does not get knocked off the ecliptic until the next trip around, when it collides with Tiamat.)

The ecliptic's relentless gravitational sweep would gradually alter those pieces' orbital paths, which would be following Nibiru's clockwise motion, to the counterclockwise flow of the rest of the solar system. Meanwhile, that slow, steady reversal of motion would tend to sweep the small pieces of ice and rock into larger and larger aggregates. Now we see that Enuma Elish provides a plausible explanation for why the Kuiper Belt might contain as many as 200 million "precomet" dirty iceballs, and why they float around in a thin smear of cosmic dust where they—and especially the ice that holds them together—theoretically do not belong.

As for the comets that do not originate along the ecliptic (most do not), Enuma Elish provides an equally plausible explanation. Imagine the explosive nature of the collision between Nibiru and Tiamat: like millions of H-bombs going off at once. As the proto-planets "mingled their waters" and then ricocheted to their new orbits, unknown amounts of Nibiru's water (imagine a round wet sponge thrown against a wall) along with countless pieces of Tiamat's early, water-soaked outer crust would go hurtling in all directions, out to every quadrant. Much of Nibiru's water and millions of Tiamant's exploded pieces could be expected to form into Dr. Frank's recently confirmed, more-or-less "pure" iceballs, while other millions would aggregate into the stone-filled "dirty" iceballs that find their way home as short- or long-period comets.

Despite its remarkable plausibility, Enuma Elish is not officially acceptable as an explanation for comets because science cannot permit such a deviation from its naturalistic dogma. It much prefers to stand behind something as flimsy as the Oort Cloud; something no human has ever seen or ever will see; something for which there is not a particle of tangible evidence, much less valid proof; a theory with only two real merits: it was created "in-house," and it predicts the unpredictability of cometary orbits that could not otherwise be explained.

(Compare that to how science treats hominoids: hundreds of sightings; thousands of tracks; scads of evidence easily acceptable as proof. If only they *could* be real, they would be.)

ASTEROIDS

Bode's Law is a mathematical formula based on the distance from Earth to the Sun (93 million miles, called an Astronomical Unit, or AU). The Bode's Law formula, which purists feel is merely a numerological quirk and not a true "law" of the universe, predicts the solar system's planets should follow the progression 0, 3, 6, 12, 24, 48, 96, 192, and 384, adding 4 to each and then dividing by 10. Quirk or not, the formula predicts planet locations with uncanny accuracy. Mercury is predicted at 0.4 AU, and it is actually at .387. Venus is predicted at 0.7 AU; it is actually at .723. Earth, of course, is the base, so it is 1.0 in both cases. Mars is predicted at 1.6 AU and is at 1.524. Jupiter is predicted at 5.2 AU and is actually at 5.2, right on the nose. And between them, at 2.8 AU, is supposed to be a planet, but no planet is there. Instead, at 2.794 AU, we find the Asteroid Belt, which is the wrong thing at exactly the right place.

The Asteroid Belt is composed of what astronomers assume to be millions of pieces of rocky debris (as opposed to the Kuiper Belt's dominance of dust) that range in size from hundreds of miles in diameter (Ceres, the largest, is 500 miles wide, and Pallas, the next-largest, is over 300 miles) down to pebble-sized. It is a band approximately 93,000,000 miles wide (coincidentally, one AU), although some asteroids drift in and out of it, coming as far toward the Sun as inside the orbit of Earth. This creates a real possibility—and, indeed, has been a past grim reality during many major and minor extinction events—of future Earth-asteroid collisions.

(For the record, there are two clusters of "leftover" asteroids that orbit along Jupiter's path, in front of and behind it at "Lagrange points," regions of gravitational stability where the centrifugal force of the asteroids' orbits counterbalances the gravitational pulls of Jupiter and the Sun. These two clusters, called the "Trojan" asteroids, are so small in number and size relative to the entire Asteroid Belt, they are seldom figured into calculations that define its parameters.)

Upward of 10,000 asteroids have been charted within the Belt, but those are only the most visible. Countless millions invisible from

Earth are assumed to make up the bulk of it, and that "bulk" is the major problem explaining it. Early astronomers assumed the Asteroid Belt was the remnant of a planet that for some reason had exploded, but skeptics eventually realized that if a celestial body were to explode it would send pieces flying in all directions, not lay them out uniformly in a 93 million-mile-wide band. Astronomers went back to the drawing board and then decided the Belt was the remnant of a planet that for some reason had failed to coalesce properly. Skeptics of that theory pointed out the extreme improbability of something failing to aggregate between four planets in front and four in back that coalesced perfectly.

Later, calculations became precise enough to show the amount of matter in the Asteroid Belt (including the Trojans) added up to no more than a Pluto-sized planet, which did not fit the Bode's Law pattern of Mercury, Venus, Earth, Mars, Jupiter, Saturn, Uranus, and Neptune. So what went wrong between Mars and Jupiter? The current official theory is that during the solar system's "formation" period, Jupiter somehow (precisely how or why is uncertain) sucked up the inexplicably missing mass. What little remained was then "trapped" in another Lagrange point created by the strong gravitational pull of Jupiter and Saturn, and the Sun and the inner planets. That suspension somehow (again, precisely how or why is uncertain) forced the remainder to fragment into small, discrete pieces rather than aggregating those pieces into a larger and larger entity.

As before, this ignores the fact that there is no such fragmentation at any other Lagrange points in the solar system. (Saturn's rings are similar, but localized around the planet itself.) Nor is there any reason to expect finding anything like it elsewhere. Thus, the Asteroid Belt remains an enduring mystery as yet unsolved. Or is it? As with comets, we find a plausible explanation for the Asteroid Belt in the story of Enuma Elish.

***

Assuming Nibiru seeded the Kuiper Belt with cometary material (Tiamat's ten elongated, fragmented protomoons) on its first journey through the solar system, its second orbit put it on a collision course with its same-sized counterpart, Tiamat. Traveling in opposite directions (clockwise vs. counterclockwise), Nibiru and Tiamat collided at planetary velocities. Today Earth travels at 68,000 m.p.h., so even if both protoplanets (which were much larger than Earth today) were significantly slower at 4.0 billion years ago, it still would have been a shattering collision.

Deep beneath Tiamat's water/steam-laced surface would be the seething, viscous magma of its mantle. That would be much denser and drier than the light, near-to-the-surface magma that would have been drawn out earlier to make up its ten moons captured on the previous pass-by. Though dense and dry, the mantle magma would not be solid enough to be propelled into space, like the crust, or light enough, like the surface magma. Rather, like clumps of thick mud striking a windshield, it would momentarily stick to, then slide to the edge(s) of, then splatter apart into various-sized pieces (in this case by the millions) that—because of their viscosity—would freeze into odd-shaped rocks before the rounding forces of space's vacuum could turn them into spheres.

Captives of Nibiru's momentum and gravity, those rocks would initially travel in its wake, gradually slowing as the greater mass of Jupiter counterattracted, then "stole" them, tugging them away from Nibiru's clockwise orbit onto its own counterclockwise path. That made them perfect candidates to occupy the Lagrange point between the Sun and Jupiter. In fact, spreading into a thin, wide band between the two giants was probably the only way they could gain internal and external equilibrium while simultaneously fulfilling the dictates of Bode's Law.

***

One more indication that Enuma Elish can be considered an accurate portrayal of how our solar system formed is found in Zecharia Sitchin's *Genesis Revisited*. In it he notes this:

"Bode's Law, which was arrived at empirically, uses Earth as its arithmetic starting point. But according to Sumerian cosmogony, at the beginning there was Tiamat between Mars and Jupiter, whereas Earth had not yet formed. (This was before the collision.) Dr. Amnon

Sitchin (Zecharia's brother) has pointed out that if Bode's Law is stripped of its arithmetical devices, and only the geometric progression is retained, the formula works just as well *if Earth is omitted* (emphasis Sitchin's)—thus confirming Sumerian cosmogony."

In other words, comparing distances between Enuma Elish's original lineup—Mercury, Venus, Mars, Tiamat (where the Asteroid Belt is now), Jupiter, Saturn, Uranus, and Neptune—reveals a more fundamental mathematical progression than Bode's Law! This indicates the solar system probably formed with that array and would look the same today if Nibiru had not arrived.

***

Lastly, we must deal with the announcement that NASA scientists feel they have found indirect evidence of primitive life in a 4.0 billion-year-old meteorite from Mars. Those microscopic remnants look strikingly similar to the microscopic traces of prokaryotic life here on Earth, which is what caught the attention of researchers. However, that should come as no surprise to anyone familiar with the Enuma Elish scenario. Four billion years ago is precisely when the waters of Tiamat and Nibiru were mingled, thereby bringing life to Earth; and if that is how Earth obtained its first two strains of life, it seems likely that is how and when Mars would have done the same.

When Nibiru's life-soaked liquids were flung into space with the debris that became the comets and asteroids, that water would have frozen in the sub-zero vacuum. Many of the life-carrying ice crystals—especially those surrounded and protected by pieces of Tiamat—would no doubt intersect with Mars, which was Tiamat's neighbor, on their journey across space. As we know today, bacteria and viruses can easily survive long-term freezing, so if we assume Mars then was similar to the early Earth rather than the barren wasteland it is now, its surface would have been equally hospitable to the life forms that seemed to take "root" and flourish on Earth.

Thus, if life does turn out to have existed in Mars' ancient past, and even if it persists there to this day, it is no more puzzling than life on Earth, or on any planet or moon (such as Jupiter's ice-covered Europa) on which it might be found. All of it will trace back to the life-carrying "renegade," Nibiru, and the story of its violent "capture" told in the Sumerian Epic of Creation.

CYLINDER SEAL VA/243

Apart from cuneiform tablets and works of art, another Sumerian method for preserving their history and culture was something we call cylinder seals. Cylinder seals were stone tubes an inch or two in diameter and three to four inches long. They were carved to produce a negative image, meaning that whatever was to be preserved was cut into the stone as a depression on its surface rather than the stone being carved away to leave elevated images. They were made to be rolled across the hand-sized slabs of wet clay that were the Sumerian medium of writing, leaving behind a raised version of the scene being depicted.

Fig. 72.

Any number of copies could be reproduced using the same stone cylinder seal, so they were the Sumerian version of a printing press. Even today, carving one would be a difficult, demanding task requiring exceptional—and in most cases virtually microscopic— vision; equally exceptional tools with incredibly strong, sharp, tiny carving tips; the finest kinds of abrading (sanding) materials; and the artistic skills of highly accomplished miniaturists. To have created and utilized such tools and materials, and to have developed such skills so long ago, is simply astounding.

Because most cylinder seal depictions were apparently meant for public consumption, they were saved for subjects apart from the daily routines of life. They recorded universal knowledge meant to

220

endure, not ephemeral things like business transactions or legal debates. The clay tablets were sufficient for those purposes. Which brings us to Sumerian cylinder seal VA/243, carved 4500 years ago.

Fig. 73.

Long displayed in the State Museum of Berlin, the cylinder seal catalogued as VA/243 caught Zecharia Sitchin's notice when he was trying to work out the relationships between Sumerians and their extraordinary knowledge of the heavens. (This was not only their concept of the history of the solar system, but—as mentioned earlier—their amazing knowledge of things like celestial mechanics and the zodiac.) The seal is officially thought to depict "The Granting of the Plow" to mankind by two "gods of heaven." The plow stands between the gods, one seated (apparently the most important) and one standing (both recognized by horns on their headgear, a consistent divinity symbol in Sumerian representations), while the human respectfully remains standing behind the upright god, clutching the old, inferior plow he is about to trade in.

Fig. 74. Granting the plow

221

What Sitchin focuses on, however, is the tiny subscene depicted in the sky between the human and the secondary god. The Sumerians frequently represented celestial objects hovering near gods depicted on cylinder seals; it was their way of identifying figures with their proper heavenly connections. Apart from that, nothing could be more revealing than this small subscene.

Fig. 75. VA/243 subscene (© Z. Sitchin, *The Twelfth Planet*)

Without knowing Sitchin's interpretation of Enuma Elish, this would make no sense. Just a big circle with rays coming off it surrounded by several other much smaller circles placed in apparently random positions. However, by knowing Sitchin's views on Enuma Elish, the scene becomes yet another vindication. Rather than our usual depiction of the solar system as an extended series of planets and moons orbiting around the Sun, if we had to compress the whole thing into a restricted space we could not do better than to "circle the wagons," so to speak.

If we assume the Sun is in the middle (the rays make that obvious), and start at the far right hand side (apparently a convention even 4,500 years ago), and move in a counterclockwise direction (the true direction of planetary orbits), this tiny subscene takes us on a full tour of our solar system, with most of the planets (two exceptions) in their proper places, and all showing their proper sizes relative to each other. That is exactly what the Sumerians did in VA/243, and Fig. 76 is one way it might look if we wanted to express the same thing today.

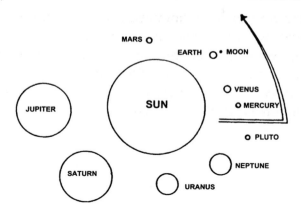

Fig. 76. (© Z. Sitchin, *The Twelfth Planet*)

Let's go back to Fig. 75 and tour it planet by planet. First, on the outside right is little Mercury, alongside appropriately larger Venus. Above them are Earth and its Moon, Earth shown as large as Venus (accurate) and the Moon shown smaller than Mercury (accurate). Next comes Mars, shown slightly smaller than Earth and Venus (ditto), but also slightly larger than Mercury (once again accurate). Where the Asteroid Belt should be, between Mars and Jupiter, there is an inexplicable circle representing an unknown planet. Notice, though, that it is twice the size of Earth but not as large as Jupiter or Saturn, which is precisely the size and orbital path given to Nibiru by Enuma Elish! Remember? Nibiru was the same size as Tiamat (until their collision reduced it by half), and not as large as Jupiter or Saturn (shown in correct positions and sizes), but larger than the "watery twins" Uranus and Neptune (also shown in correct proportions). And its final orbital path carried it between Mars and Jupiter, precisely where it is stationed in VA/243.

So there it is, the entire Sumerian cosmology (minus Pluto, discussed next), carved on a cylinder seal 4,500 years ago to support an apparently more important scene! As for Pluto, notice that VA/243 positions it between Saturn and Uranus but shading more toward Saturn. This bears witness to the Sumerian assertion that Pluto began life as a moon of Saturn, which Nibiru later pulled out of its moon orbit and deposited in its position as the most atypical of the nine known planets. We have to assume that VA/243 presents a condensed version (like a visual time capsule) of the events outlined in Enuma Elish, choosing to frame it after the Nibiru-Tiamat collision but prior to Nibiru tugging Pluto away from Saturn. This also indicates the latter event may not have occurred in conjunction with the collision; it could have been much later.

Only the Sumerians—*and those who taught them*—knew for sure.

THE TEACHERS

It should be obvious by now that the Sumerians could not possibly have learned the many astonishing things they knew by personal experience or direct observation. It is absurd to even suggest such a stretch of credulity. They had to have help, massive amounts of it, from vastly superior intellects. And guess what? The Sumerians frankly admitted that everything they knew—entire libraries of information about mathematics, astronomy, medicine, agriculture, business, engineering, music, law, etc.—was given to them by *other beings*. The Sumerians called those other beings Anunnaki (Ah-nu-na-ki), and they were the people who lived on Nibiru!

Now, set the Anunnaki aside for a moment while we focus on Nibiru. Modern astronomers are convinced another planet exists somewhere in the farthest depths of our solar system. They call it "Planet X," a clever play on words indicating an unknown body, as well as the tenth planet. They know it is there because of perturbations, which are slight wobbles in the orbits of celestial bodies near and far. The Sun wobbles from the pull of the planets whirling around it in the ecliptic. The Moon wobbles from pulls of Earth and the Sun. Earth's wobbles are caused by the Sun, the Moon, even faraway Jupiter. Like cosmic dust, perturbations are ubiquitous throughout our solar system, and we have been able to chart them accurately for well over a century.

It began in 1781, when improved telescopes led to the visual discovery of Uranus. Fifty more years of technical improvements permitted astronomers to record unaccountable wobbles (perturbations) in Uranus' orbit. That could only mean yet another planet circling somewhere beyond their vision, so they bent every effort toward finding it. Using complex mathematical calculations derived from Uranus' perturbations, they pinpointed in the heavens where the phantom should be. Sure enough, in 1846 they found it, out at the farthest limits of where their telescopes could then see. They called it Neptune and soon found that it, too, wobbled in a way that could only mean there was yet another planet beyond it. Everything played out the same as before.

Careful observations of Neptune's orbit revealed the extent and degree of the perturbations caused by the unknown gravitational pull, which pointed its trackers in the right direction. In 1930 they succeeded in locating Pluto. Now, using the same principles, astronomers know another body is out there, but the perturbations it causes are not like those caused by Neptune and Pluto. They are weak and inconsistent and not trackable by the usual means. This indicates it must not have a typically circular orbit, it must be moving in some kind of long ellipse. And wouldn't you know it? That is exactly what the Anunnaki say is the case with their home planet, Nibiru.

***

Everything we know about the Anunnaki is contained in the clay tablets left by the Sumerians, in the "myth" pile created by the scholars who read their words for the first time. More specifically, nearly all we know about the Anunnaki comes from Zecharia Sitchin's work regarding them. As the Anunnaki taught the Sumerians what they knew, Sitchin teaches us what we know about what they knew. Because the subject is so incredibly comprehensive, Sitchin has needed seven books crammed with data to cover the areas in question. Thankfully, he has not yet been able to cover them all, so we can look for even more from him in coming years. However, the seven we have thus far are an excellent beginning.

Book I of *The Earth Chronicles, The Twelfth Planet*, published in 1976, is his fundamental text, the one in which he introduces the radical notions left to us in the Sumerian clay tablets—Nibiru, the Anunnaki, who they were, why they came to Earth, what they did while here, etc.—themes he develops in more detail in subsequent books.

Book II of *The Earth Chronicles, The Stairway to Heaven*, published in 1980, covers the Anunnaki's existence before and after the Great Flood: before it, in today's Iraq; and after it, in today's Middle East. There is much emphasis on ancient Egypt and the Great Pyramids of Giza, the "Stairway to Heaven" of the title.

Book III is *The Wars of Gods and Men*, published in 1985. This outlines the myriad schemes and outright battles among the offspring of the first Anunnaki leaders. It details their relentless efforts to influence matters of cultural dominance and political succession in every one of their bastions on Earth.

Book IV is *The Lost Realms*, published in February of 1990. This one deals with Anunnaki life and influence in the Americas, particularly throughout Middle and South America. The mysterious Olmec culture of Mexico and the megaliths of Tiahuanaco and Peru are discussed in considerable detail.

Book V is *Genesis Revisited*, published in October of 1990. This one is something of an update on where his work is at that point, discussing gains in knowledge since the early books were published. Its emphasis is on breakthroughs in astronomical knowledge and sophisticated genetic experiments, all of which support his earlier conclusions.

Book VI is *When Time Began*, published in 1993. This one is about the ancient world's fascination with keeping precise track of time, and not just time as we understand it—time on a colossal scale. There is much about the intricacies of the Mayan calendar, and about Stonehenge as a cosmic timepiece.

Book VII is *Divine Encounters,* published in 1995. His most recent effort analyzes mankind's recorded interactions with what are called "visions, angels, and other emissaries" from the Anunnaki. The crux of this book is Sitchin's detailed quest to determine who, precisely, was the Hebrew god, Yahweh.

***

In each book Zecharia Sitchin dazzles readers with the quality of his scholarship and the depth of his insights. If you have not heard of him before now and wonder how somebody so important can be so ignored by mainstream science and the media, it is primarily due to the thoroughness of his research. Remember Erich Von Daniken? *Chariots of the Gods*? He was (and is) an easily criticizable ex-hotelier with a bad habit of aggrandizing the solid cases he often makes. Whenever he overstates a claim or misrepresents a fact (minor or major), critics use those errors to discredit everything he does.

Unlike Erich Von Daniken, Zecharia Sitchin is a lifelong scholar who is widely recognized as such. His academic credentials, intellectual genius, and keen attention to details show through everything he writes, which is evident to anyone who reads his work. This includes any potential critics, who can read only a chapter or two and know there is simply no way to discredit his work into irrelevance. All of Sitchin's texts are crammed with certifiable details and checkable references, and he is careful not to print (or even to speak about) anything he cannot verify with substantiated facts. This leaves critics with not even a toehold against him, and when faced with someone like that all they can do is lay low, do their best to ignore him, and hope and pray his message never reaches a larger audience.

NIBIRU AND THE ANUNNAKI

As depicted on cylinder seal VA/243, Nibiru is a large planet, twice the size of Earth and larger than Uranus and Neptune, but not as large as Jupiter or Saturn. It has an elliptical, comet-like orbit whose period has been established by direct and indirect references at 3600 years.

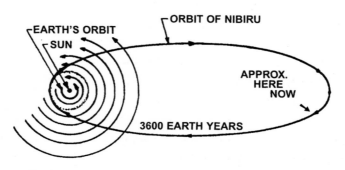

Fig. 77.

Nibiru is described as being tilted somewhat off the ecliptic, possibly 17° above (in the plane of Pluto) or 30° below, which most references indicate. Like a comet, Nibiru's aphelion (its farthest point from the Sun) is in the deep void of space vastly beyond Pluto's aphelion. Its perihelion (nearest point to the Sun) is somewhere between Mars and the Asteroid Belt. We can assume it avoids the Asteroid Belt on each swing around the Sun because the cataclysms caused by an asteroid bombardment every 3600 years would prevent the development of even moderately advanced forms of life, much less creatures as sophisticated as the Anunnaki.

Consider the average distances involved. From the Sun to Mars is 142 million miles. The Sun to Jupiter is 482 million. That leaves 340 million miles between Mars and Jupiter, of which 93 million are the Asteroid Belt. That leaves 247 million miles of open space. Assuming approximately equal empty zones in front and back of the Asteroid Belt leaves 123 million miles in each.

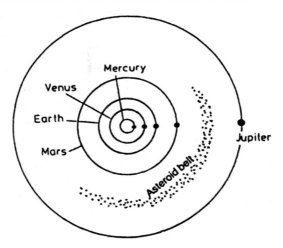

Fig. 78. (© Z. Sitchin, *The Twelfth Planet*)

Assuming Nibiru is in fact a bit larger than Uranus and Neptune, both of which are about 30,000 miles wide, we can ballpark its size at about 40,000 miles wide. Dividing the 123,000,000 clear miles between Mars and the Asteroid Belt's inner edge by Nibiru's 40,000 miles gives 3075, which means 3,075 Nibirus could pass there unscathed. That is more than enough room.

***

Before we discuss when and why the Anunnaki came to Earth, we must deal with an obvious concern. The same way scientists once insisted water could never exist on planets as far from the Sun as Uranus and Neptune, they will insist no planet orbiting well beyond those two could support complex life. Without heat, light, and an atmosphere, which most life on Earth requires, a planet would be unlikely to support anything more than bacteria. Is that a valid assessment?

Well, modern astronomers know Venus, Earth, Jupiter, Saturn, Uranus, Neptune, and some of their moons radiate far more energy than they take in from the Sun. That means they are generating heat from within themselves, either radioactively or—as in Earth's case—from internal combustions that spew gases and heat into the atmosphere via volcanoes and related phenomena. Since internal heat generation is so common, we can assume Nibiru is such a planet. And if we accept the Sumerian clay tablets, which indicate the Anunnaki could live on Earth in relative comfort without special adaptations, we can further assume its generated heat created and retained an atmosphere, and that its atmosphere must be quite similar to Earth's.

As for Nibiru's relationship to light, that is trickier to assess. When orbiting through the solar system (well beyond Mars), it would receive only modest amounts of sunlight. However, during the vast majority of its 3600 year orbit it would perceive the Sun as little more than a bright, distant star. This means we can conclude that life forms on Nibiru have a substantially different relationship to sunlight than Earth forms do, though what that relationship might be is anyone's guess. The texts describe the Anunnaki as mostly blonds with occasional redheads, all of whom have very pale skin, which indicates they are less adapted to our Sun than we are. Supporting that idea are many cylinder seal depictions, which show they usually kept their bodies clothed and their heads protected with various helmets, while humans are frequently depicted as naked and capless.

Fig. 79.

Another possibility is that while on Earth, Anunnaki biology forced them to avoid the Sun by living and working at night, which would provide a fair approximation of the luminescence they were adapted to on Nibiru. It might also explain their emphasis on studying the motions of stars across Earth's night skies. Unfortunately, the texts do not address that issue directly, nor is there any indication their eyes were adapted to or capable of night vision. So for now all we can do is move forward under the reasonable assumption that a species capable of space travel would have little trouble protecting themselves (eyes, skin, etc.) against a brighter-than-normal Sun.

[Ironically, we humans—unlike hominoids—are poorly adapted to live under our Sun. Like all other primates, hominoids have developed the kind of skin covering (all-over body hair) needed to live naturally on Earth, while human skin must thicken and darken considerably in order to live in a "natural" state. Pale-skinned people stripped to the bare essentials can easily die from Sun exposure in equatorial climates, which begs an obvious question: If humans did evolve on Earth in Darwinian fashion, why isn't our skin as naturally functional as every other primate's?]

***

It is not implausible for life forms to require much less sunlight than is available on the Earth's surface. In the ocean depths live countless species that never see a ray of light. Countless others live underground or in caves. Sunlight is only one element in the chain of life on Earth; it is not essential for life to exist. Similarly, there is no-thing implausible about an atmosphere being sustained—or sustaining itself—on a planet orbiting far from the Sun. Saturn, Jupiter, Uranus, Neptune, and even Pluto have atmospheres of varying density, so dis-tance from the Sun is not a deciding factor. Far more important are heat generation and chemical composition at the surface.

Admittedly, two main elements of life on Earth for primates are heat and sunlight, but we (using artificial means) and hominoids (au naturel) exist at widely varying amounts of both. So life on Nibiru—especially highly developed forms—could function at equally varying amounts. But no matter how it happened, the evi-dence is clear that distant Nibiru somehow sustained the Anunnaki. It is equally clear there had to be a great deal of compatibility be-tween life forms on Nibiru and on Earth. Otherwise, the Anunnaki could never have lived here as comfortably nor operated as freely and as easily as the Sumerian historical records tell us they did.

That brings us to when, exactly, the Anunnaki came to Earth . . . and why?

***

The relevant texts the Sumerians left us were never Anunnaki origi-nals: they were either copies of originals, or copies of copies writ-ten as part of an ongoing history of our species related (and some-times interpreted) by Sumerian scribes. On some were found com-prehensive ruler lists that let us calculate approximately when the Anunnaki arrived on Earth: 430,000 years ago. As for why they came, they report that they needed gold. Sound familiar? It should. Gold is instantly recognizable as humanity's most valuable medium of exchange, one we have plundered entire cultures into oblivion to obtain. However, we usually seek gold out of wanton greed.

The Anunnaki sought gold to save their atmosphere, which had apparently sprung leaks similar to those we have created in ours by damaging the Earth's ozone layer with hydroflourocarbons, HFC's. (We can safely assume Nibiru's damage was similar to what we are facing today because, again, if our atmosphere allowed the Anunnaki to live here for eons, it has to be much like theirs.) Probably as they developed their high technology (which, as we have surmised, must be thousands of years ahead of ours), they made some of the exact same mistakes we have been making since the Industrial Revolution. When they realized what they had done (which we are presently in the earliest phases of facing up to), they knew they had to do something about it.

The Anunnaki solution was to disperse extremely tiny flakes of gold into their upper atmosphere to patch the holes needing repair. (Ironically, modern scientists contend that if we are ever forced to repair our own damaged ozone layer, tiny particulates of gold shot into the upper atmosphere would be the best way to go about it. Such tiny particles have ideal insulating and reflecting properties, and will stay aloft indefinitely.) Unfortunately for the Anunnaki, Nibiru did not contain enough gold to allow completion of what had to be a monumental repair job. (Remember, Nibiru is roughly twice the size of Earth.) Fortunately, by then they had been through the solar system enough times to know where they could find an abundance of gold—on Earth.

COLONY EARTH

In Akkadian, the language of Sumer, *An-nun-na-ki* means "the fifty who went from Heaven to Earth," which tells us the number of the original Anunnaki landing party. Later, according to the texts, they steadily came in groups of 50 until the initial phase topped out at 600. The primary responsibility of those 600 was to establish their first gold-gathering operation and spaceport facility in the delta area between the Tigris and Euphrates Rivers, in today's southern Iraq. Later, the gold-gathering operation was shifted to southern Africa (today's South Africa), whose mines remain the world's most prolific producers of gold. (South Africa also contains numerous abandoned mines that are unquestionably "ancient." Many are quite deep, and charcoals in some have been dated to well over 100,000 years! If accurate, such dates not only boggle the mind, they cast serious doubts on everything science purports to know about human history.)

These two geographical divisions came to be known to the Anunnaki as the Upper World and the Lower World. As time passed (many thousands of years), they moved into other areas around the globe. They settled in Egypt, India, China, and Central and South America, most notably in Peru. Despite being aliens from another planet, they were remarkably "human" in how they looked, dressed, and behaved. They built cities that became models for later human cities. Their laws became human laws. Their social customs, entertainment, and sciences became ours. And, significantly, the rules of order and succession among their leaders and subjects also became ours. In every imaginable way they were role models for "civilized" human beings.

* * *

In the Hakatha, a code of laws for Babylonians (later Sumerians), it states: "The privilege of operating a flying machine is great. The knowledge of flight is among the most ancient of our inheritances. (It is) a gift (to us) from 'those from upon high.'" Also, the Sanskrit Vedas (ancient Hindu poems thought to be the oldest of all Indian texts) are filled with descriptions of all manner of "vimanas," flying machines with various shapes, sizes, and numbers of engines.

These and many other ancient references to prehistoric flight verify the Sumerian accounts of the Anunnaki possessing spacecraft, and other flying craft for transportation in and around Earth's skies. Some spacecraft were for traveling beyond Earth's atmosphere into orbit, where they would rendezvous with giant artificial satellites much like our proposed space stations. Other larger craft were long-haul charters that carried gold and the Anunnaki themselves from the local satellites back and forth to Nibiru whenever it was in the solar system and within easy reach of connecting flights.

[Understand the timeframes: Nibiru's orbit is 3600 years, but for only a fraction of that would it be within easy reach of vehicles based on Earth: say, from when it approached Neptune's orbit until it went past the Sun to loop between Mars and the Asteroid Belt, then back past the Sun to Neptune—a 6.0 billion mile round-trip as the crow flies. But its elliptic orbit would expand that 6.0 billion to as much as 10 billion, or more, depending on the arc of its ellipse. Traveling at an Earth-like speed of 60,000 m.p.h. would require about 20 years, but a Neptune-like speed of 12,000 m.p.h. would require 100 years, with less speed requiring progressively more years.]

Speaking of timeframes, some of the most incredible data to come from Sumerian records (and certainly some of the most difficult for humans to mentally and emotionally accommodate), is what they say about Anunnaki lifespans. The tablets indicate that every Anunnaki would stay on Earth for numerous *shars* (their year, which is 3600 Earth years) before rotating back to Nibiru. That means their lifecycles were based on segments of 3600 Earth years. If the upper limit of their natural lifespan was, say, 100 shars, they would enjoy lives of 360,000 Earth years. However, they could have lived for less or more. The texts, unfortunately, do not pin it down. All we can be certain of at this point is that, relative to humans, the Anunnaki "gods" were indeed immortal.

***

As befits beings capable of space travel, the Anunnaki were phenomenal engineers. Their cities were marvels of planning and efficiency. They were especially clever using water, which on Nibiru must have been an extremely precious resource. They built highly effective aqueduct and drainage systems wherever they lived, making deserts bloom and seeing to it that homes had running water (the natural kind of constant, steady flow) to drink and even move waste from toilets. However, their principle use of water was to placer-mine gold.

Placer mining is achieved by putting devices that trap particles of gold into streams and rivers that wash down from mountains likely to have the element in its rocks and soil. To this day placer mining is the easiest, most preferred technique everywhere in the world. Only panning by hand is more common, but it is much more difficult and gives much lower yields. If placer mining will work, it is always the best way to proceed. Simply secure a washer-tray in a stream and forget about it, then return to it later and collect your flecks of gold. Where trouble begins is when placer streams are depleted and gold must be obtained by the vastly more labor-intensive method of mining. For the Anunnaki—and indirectly for humans—their ultimate need to physically mine gold was far and away the most pivotal aspect of their entire 400,000 plus years on Earth.

**

During the era of Anunnaki dominance on Earth, the supreme ruler on Nibiru was named "Anu" (hence the name his people took on Earth—*Anu*nnaki). Anu had two principle sons, Enlil and Enki, to whom he entrusted the critical task of securing sufficient quantities of gold from Earth. Enlil was more of a natural politician and ruled from his base in the Upper World (Mesopotamia), while Enki, a brilliant scientist, governed the Lower World (southern Africa), where the gold gathering was done. Although Enki was older than Enlil, his mother was a concubine, which made him illegitimate. Enlil, on the other hand, was a child of Anu's official wife and therefore a legitimate heir to the throne. That gave him ultimate authority over all aspects of the Anunnaki colony on Earth, which was a source of constant friction with Enki and caused most of the squabbling and scheming that dominated their official relationship.

Female Anunnaki were an important part of the colony on Earth, often holding their own against male counterparts in the plotting and counterplotting that drove the males to endless intrigues and outright battles against each other. Females of royal lineage, sisters and half-sisters of Enki and Enlil, were clearly the most privileged. Anunnaki rules of succession favored children born to half-sisters of rulers, so both Enki and Enlil worked hard at getting their seeds placed in favorable positions relative to the seeds of their rivals.

Of particular interest was a female called—among several titles—Ninti. Ninti was a half-sister of both Enki and Enlil, causing a heated rivalry to develop between them for her sexual favor, which came with the possibility of creating a potential ruler. She was also a gifted scientist in her own right, every bit the equal of Enki. As we shall soon see, the two of them worked together on a major project that endures to this day.

**

As the Anunnaki settlers went about building their civilization on Earth, they did what any "exiles" would do: they put down roots in the new land and proceeded to raise families. As those families grew to maturity, the world they knew grew progressively smaller. Sons and then grandsons of Enlil and Enki were given domains to rule, and they in turn began scheming for power and influence in the same ways their fathers did. There followed a long, convoluted series of disputes, skirmishes, and territorial battles (well detailed in Zecharia Sitchin's *The Wars Of Gods And Men*), which led to a steady accumulation of very bad blood between the Enlilites and Enkiites.

Ultimately, around 2000 B.C., a full-scale war erupted among two of the most contentious factions. However, unlike all conflicts that had gone before, the Enlilites sought a drastic resolution to this one. They beseeched the highest council on Nibiru, the Great Assembly, to be allowed to use nuclear weapons against the Enkiites. Hoping to permanently settle the ongoing disputes, Anu and the Great Assembly granted the request and the horrific weapons were unleashed.

For as farfetched as that might seem, evidence for it abounds. Among numerous ancient accounts of conflicts that mention exotic warfare, this one from India's *Ramayana* sounds suspiciously like lasers: "(The weapon) produced a shaft of light which, when focused on any target, immediately consumed it with its power." And, sounding distinctly nuclear, there is this from the *Mahabharata*: "A single projectile (contained) all the power of the universe. (It produced) an incandescent column of smoke and fire, as brilliant as 10,000 suns, (which) rose in all its splendor. (It) was a gigantic messenger of death, which reduced to ashes the entire race (of its victims)." There is further description of those killed outright as burned beyond recognition, while those "lucky" enough to survive the initial blast died terrible deaths of lingering sickness that included loss of hair and loss of fingernails and toenails. Descriptions of Hiroshima are quite similar.

As for physical evidence, there are examples of that as well. One of the best and most convincing remains visible in the middle of the Sinai Peninsula, at precisely where the Sumerians say the Anunnaki had their post-diluvial (after the Great Flood) "spaceport," a primary target of the Enlilites. For hundreds of square miles around the spaceport area there is an inexplicable dark "stain" on the ground. The ground's surface is covered by millions of broken-up "sheet" rocks that are plate- to saucer-sized and about 1/2 inch thick. If you pick one up and look at its edge, you find its bottom 1/4 inch is a light caramel color, while the top 1/4 inch has somehow been darkened by "scorching." Outside the huge scorched area, those same rocks are caramel colored throughout, which is not explainable in ordinary geological terms. Thus, the Sumerian account should not be ruled out simply because it defies everything establishment science would call "natural."

At any rate, even the best laid plans of gods can go astray, and in the case of the nuclear aftermath the original Murphy's law was operative. Despite careful planning, unanticipated winds caught some radioactive clouds and carried them right to the Anunnaki homeland—Sumer! The fallout drifted over everything and everyone, causing humans to die in droves and animals and crops to be obliterated. The land was left useless for decades, until Enki and other scientists developed means to counteract the poisons that had been dispersed. (To this day much of Iraq remains bleak and barren, so perhaps remnants of the Anunnaki disaster in some way added to the unusual miseries afflicting so many who fought in Operation Desert Storm. Who can say?)

For 1,800 more years the Anunnaki survivors tried to repair the devastation their warring had done to their various population centers, but the wounds were simply too deep and comprehensive. By the time of Nibiru's most recent pass through the solar system, at around 200 B.C., they were ready to pack up and return to Nibiru for good. That is ultimately what they did, leaving humans to rebuild what remained of their own debilitated civilizations (and, we might assume, leaving behind some "monitors" to keep track of their grand "experiment").

I know this sounds like an overwrought soap opera, but trite or not, it is what the Sumerians claim happened in their world within the experience and memory of many who wrote about it. So for as much as we consider ourselves fonts of all knowledge, we are in no position to label it as fiction. They recorded it as fact and apparently meant it as fact, which leaves us no choice but to accept it as such and try to find evidence to back it up. Fortunately, we don't have to look far.

THE EVIDENCE

When discussing the notion of past civilization(s) living on Earth, critics inevitably focus on the same questions: What can be pointed to that unquestionably dates from such a culture? Where is something they left behind? Where is any "hard evidence" for their presence? Actually, the Earth bristles with such evidence, but each case is rejected by science. The Great Pyramids of Giza? Built by primitive Egyptians. The remarkable city of Tiahuanaco on Lake Titicaca in Bolivia? Built by primitive Amerinds. Stonehenge in England? Baalbek in Lebanon? Teotihuacan in Mexico? Sacsahuaman, Ollantaytambu, and Machu Picchu in Peru? Easter Island? The Sphinx?

These and many others, "authorities" insist, were all built by the primitive humans alive in those areas at those times; and they insist it despite the fact that none of those megalithic (massive stone) monuments could be duplicated today. With all the technological expertise at our command, we still cannot build edifices of such enormous size using such hard stones cut and placed with such Swiss-watch-like precision. Like the tracks of hominoids, that alone should be evidence enough of at least one superior culture at work on Earth at some time in its distant past.

The litany of evidence against the primitives-built-the-megaliths theory is now so old it is a cliche, but for newcomers to the debate we should review a few aspects. Also, it is necessary to show I am not exaggerating when I say humans today cannot even approximate the engineering skills seen in those monuments. First, the Great Pyramids at Giza, Egypt. The two main ones (the third is much smaller) are so clearly beyond human capacity even now, today, it is the worst kind of joke to pretend Neolithic (recent Stone Age) primitives could have built them. (Yes, a modern metropolis' skyscrapers are marvels of construction, but those are made of small pieces—girders, bricks, drywall, etc.—relative to massive megaliths. And it would take a modern crane days to set up, then lift, move, and place a 100 ton stone, while stones at Giza weigh twice that, and at other megalithic sites weigh 10 and 20 times that! So modern construction techniques fall well short from the get-go.)

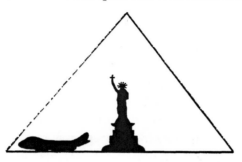

Fig. 80.   Great Pyramid, Statue of Liberty, and a 747

The lesser of the two Great Pyramids is smaller (barely) because it is built on a slightly higher piece of ground. Why would that matter? Why would the one on slightly higher ground need to be slightly smaller? Because they both are constructed so their tops reach to precisely the same height! Think that was easy to arrange? Not quite. One reason you don't see many pyramid-shaped buildings in the world around you is because a pyramid is the most difficult geometric figure to construct. Why? Because when building the sides of a square or a rectangle, plumb measurements make it easy to keep things straight. Even circles and domes can be kept orderly by following forms curved to the proper shapes. With a pyramid you must build all four sides upward at a slant toward a single point in space that is invisible without a marker and thus impossible to take measurements against. Even worse, with pyramids as large as those at Giza, an error the size of a postage stamp on a bottom tier would grow to the size of a car at a top tier.

So much for the blueprints. The smallest Pyramid contains about 1.0 million stones, while the larger two contain 2.5 to 3.0 million apiece. Each of those stones' average weight is 3.0 to 4.0 tons,

239

although numerous ones visible in the interior chambers (which are located high above the ground) weigh 50 tons or more. Also, much larger stones could be arrayed in the mostly hidden inner cores. Aside from the rough-hewn blocks that fill those cores, each stone that needed to be carefully crafted (those lining the exterior surfaces and the inner passages and chambers) was cut and shaped and polished to a degree of perfection that must be seen and touched to be believed.

The exteriors were covered with white limestones polished so well they reflected the Sun brightly enough to be visible for twenty miles. Many internal surfaces (notably the passage to the so-called Queen's Chamber in the so-called Great Pyramid) were so lustrous they still cast reflections. Apart from surface perfection, all visible stones (external and internal) fit so flush against each other that a razor cannot be inserted between them. [Tolerances are .01 (1/100th) to .001 (1/1000th) inch, thinner than a human hair.] With no mortar (as we know it) to compensate for mistakes, there was no room for even a slight error. And, incredibly, none has ever been found! Each stone that had to be cut and shaped and placed perfectly *was* cut and shaped and placed perfectly, which is the technical/logistical equivalent of building a Rolex the size of Mt. Rushmore!

Despite such a daunting degree of difficulty, modern Egyptologists insist all three Great Pyramids were built during one century 4,500 years ago (2500 B.C.), using only primitive stone and copper (a "soft" metal) tools, plant-fiber ropes, and wooden sledges—no pulleys, draft animals, or wheeled vehicles. Assuming lowball numbers in all three cases (2.5 million stones for the large pair and 1.0 million for the small one), it means 6.0 million stones were cut, hauled, shaped, and positioned in only 100 years. Start with 100 years at 12 months a year: 1200 months total. Dividing 6,000,000 stones by 1200 months equals 5000 stones laid per month. 30 days per month means 166 stones laid per day. A 24-hour day means 6.9 stones laid every hour—around the clock. So even if we grant the most generous figures possible, Egyptologists have to account for 7.0 stones laid every hour of every day for 100 straight years! No breaks, no bad weather days, no accidents, no down time of any kind—just one stone fitted into place every 8.5 minutes.

A few years ago some enterprising Japanese tried to build a minuscule replica of a Giza Pyramid using the same stones and techniques and tools that would have been used in ancient Egypt. They did not come close. Even after they gained experience they could not come close. No humans could. No humans did. And the same thing happened when a team from the "Nova" television series tried to raise a mere 40-ton obelisk (real ones weigh hundreds of tons) using the same methods ancient Egyptians supposedly used. All they raised was more doubts about how anyone anywhere could believe for one moment that primitives built those incredible edifices.

Faced with what clearly seems to be an impossibility, where can we turn for more plausible answers? First, to the Sumerians, who assure us the Anunnaki built the Great Pyramids much earlier than Egyptologists accept. Then read what Zecharia Sitchin and numerous other researchers have to say about them. Anyone who studies them in any detail cannot help realizing they are impossible to duplicate in our own era, much less during the 4,500 years ago they supposedly date to. The difference is, some of us can publicly admit what we know, while others cannot.

***

I won't detail all the reasons why the Pyramids were built by the Anunnaki because Zecharia Sitchin does such a thorough job in his works, particularly in *The Stairway to Heaven*. Suffice to say they were part of the ground-based landing system for Anunnaki spacecraft, which was a vital component of maintaining the Heaven-Earth link. Later they became strongholds in the nuclear war between competing Anunnaki factions mentioned in the previous chapter, elements of which explain why the Pyramids' inner passages are so oddly placed and shaped, and why nothing except one empty granite "sarcophagus" was ever found inside any of them.

The Anunnaki said they built the Pyramids around 10,000 B.C., shortly after the so-called "Great Flood," which they knew was coming (the reason will be discussed later) and were able to prepare for. That inundation completely wiped out their communities in both the Upper World (Mesopotamia) and Lower World (southern Africa), forcing them to relocate to higher, drier ground, which they found in today's Middle East (Egypt, Sinai, Jordan, and Israel). Supporting their timeframe are revelations offered by John Anthony West in *Serpent in the Sky,* (Quest Books, 1993), the basis of an Emmy winning TV documentary narrated by Charlton Heston. In both his book and the documentary, West shows how deep weathering on the Sphinx (which rests in close proximity to the Pyramids) can only have been caused by heavy rainfall over a prolonged wet period, and the last such wet period in northern Egypt ended at around 8,000 B.C.

It seems reasonable to conclude that whoever built the Pyramids simultaneously built the much smaller Sphinx complex. Though a metaphor for silence, the Sphinx speaks volumes about its builders. The massive sculpture was carved in one piece from surrounding sandstone, leaving huge slabs of waste to be discarded or utilized. The builders used it, constructing a pair of temples in front of the crouching beast. Those temples are built with stones cut and shaped with the same precision as the finest in the Pyramids, yet relative to Pyramid stones several temple stones are much larger, 10 x 10 x 20 feet and weighing over 200 tons! Remember, today's timeframe for lifting and moving and placing large stones is counted in days, so imagine quarrying several 200-ton monoliths, shaping them to the dimensions of locomotives, moving them forward 100 yards and setting them in place as bricks in a wall built to microscopic tolerances. And do it using no draft animals, no wheels, no pulleys; only primitive tools like fiber ropes, wooden sledges, and human muscles.

***

Shifting northwest, we move to England's Stonehenge. In *When Time Began,* Zecharia Sitchin calls Stonehenge "a computer made of stone," and there is no better way to describe it. It is alleged to have been constructed in three distinct phases, the first occurring at 2800 B.C. (As with the Pyramids and the Sphinx, all dates for Stonehenge are subject to serious debate.) That first phase was a relatively simple (compared to what came later) ditch 12 feet wide, 6 feet deep, and 1050 feet in circumference. To dig it out required removing thousands of tons of hard, chalky soil using only animal bones (deer antlers as diggers and shoulder blades as scrapers) and woven baskets (for carrying fill). By any measure, to construct such a thing 4,800 years ago (300 years prior to the purported date for the Pyramids and the Sphinx) was a feat of unimaginable rigor.

The only break for the Neolithic primitives who dug it out was that the circle was interrupted for a several-yards-wide causeway along a northeast axis that allowed precise viewing of the Sun at its summer solstice (northernmost sunrise). They then arranged the removed soil into two concentric raised banks within the circle's inner edge. Along that inner edge they precisely positioned and dug 56 small holes, now known as "Aubrey" holes after John Aubrey, the 17th century English antiquarian who discovered them. Inside the Aubrey holes went three wooden stakes, rotated as necessary to keep track of celestial events. At the connection of the causeway and the ditch stood two gateway stones, now missing.

Some 75 feet beyond the ditch, out on the causeway, was the heel stone, a large natural boulder standing 16 feet above ground and sunk 4 feet into it. It was cocked at precisely 24° to the right of vertical. The two gateway stones could be used as sighting devices when lining up to view the Sun rising over the heel stone. Meanwhile, the circle inscribed a large rectangle whose corners were marked by four rounded station stones. Using only those few implements—4 station stones, 1 heel stone, 2 gateway stones, 56 Aubrey holes, and 3 wooden stakes—Neolithic Britons of 5,000 years ago were able to chart with astounding accuracy the intricate mosaic outlined in the heavens by every celestial phase of the Sun *and* the Moon.

The Sun's four celestial phases—two solstices and two equinoxes—are yearly events easy to keep track of. However, the Moon's eight solstitial and equinoctial risings and settings (relative to Earth's horizon) are highly complex, dictated by its motions around the Earth and around the Sun as it (the Moon) moves with the Earth. The Moon's celestial phases are called standstills, four of which are major and four minor. The entire eight-phase cycle lasts exactly 18.61 years, which, rounded off to 19, is the dominant numerical figure throughout Stonehenge. (This, too, is no exaggeration—or coincidence. 700 years after Stonehenge I was established, Stonehenge II's 38 bluestones were erected outside the Trilithons in two semicircles of 19. A century later, at 2000 B.C., Stonehenge III's horseshoe inside the Trilithons was made with 19 more bluestones.)

Getting back to the Moon's celestial phases, 18.61 years times 3 wooden stakes = 55.83, which rounds off to 56 Aubrey holes. Thus, 3 wooden stakes moved around the Aubrey holes in a 19 year cycle will perfectly track all eight of the Moon's major and minor standstills. And because the Moon's orbit is inclined 5° from Earth's orbit, each year it crosses that orbit twice. These are when eclipses occur, but the formula for predicting them is too complex to explain here. Suffice to say the rectangle outlined by the 4 station stones circumscribed by the entire Stonehenge circle allows accurate predictions of both solar and lunar eclipses!

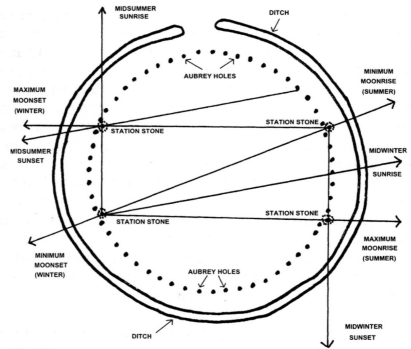

Fig. 81.

As Zecharia Sitchin notes in *When Time Began*, whoever built Stonehenge "knew in advance the precise length of the solar year, the Moon's orbital period, and the cycle of 18.61 years." This is important because *nowhere else* in the Northern hemisphere can the eight lunar observations "be made precisely along the lines formed by the rectangle connecting the four Station Stones." These facts have been known to scientists and scholars for thirty years now, yet they still insist the Neolithic barbarians who supposedly built Stonehenge simply got "lucky" when they located it in the *one precise place* in the Northern hemisphere where an open-air "altar" would permit "worship" of the Sun and Moon in their twelve distinct phases over an 18.61 year cycle, with the accurate prediction of solar and lunar eclipses thrown in as a bonus!

After their "lucky" location choice, those amazing barbarians managed to quarry 80 of the hardest stones on Earth (bluestones) using only copper (much softer than bluestones) and possibly bronze tools. Then, somehow (theories abound), they transported the bluestones 250 miles from the Prescelly Mountains in southwest Wales. (This in an era when most people worldwide rarely ventured more than a few miles from where they were born and died.) Next they quarried 77 sarsen stones (a hard sandstone) weighing 40 to 50 tons each and somehow moved them 20 miles from Marlboro Downs. After that it was time to set everything up, which meant shaping the giant sarsen stones into a series of uprights and cross-beams (called lintels), with the body of each lintel having a precise curve and equally precise tenons (upraised knobs) to fit into mortices (indentations to secure the tenons) on the huge uprights they sat atop. And, like the Pyramids, they were located on gently sloping terrain, yet all of their upper surfaces were perfectly level!

As before, such incredible precision on such a massive scale is simply beyond modern capacity or comprehension, and it is ludicrous to even suggest—much less insist—otherwise.

***

I can go on like this, giving equally logical and compelling reasons why other ancient megalithic monuments could not possibly have been built by the primitive humans alive at the times they were supposedly constructed. That idea is simply and patently absurd. It is also under serious challenge. As mentioned earlier, no date for any megalith—including the Pyramids, the Sphinx, and Stonehenge—is solid. John Anthony West has shown the way by proving with virtual certainty that the Sphinx, at least, was constructed thousands of years earlier than scientists will currently accept. With that one down, others are sure to follow, it is just a question of when.

THE GREAT MYSTERY

By now, hopefully, you should be willing to at least tentatively accept that: (1) Sumerians were telling the truth in their cuneiform inscriptions about Earth's distant past; (2) Nibiru was and is a real planet in our solar system; (3) its inhabitants were and are the Anunnaki; (4) the Anunnaki were and are a race of highly advanced beings; and (5) they lived and worked on Earth as the dominant culture from 430,000 years ago until 2000 B.C., when a nuclear war broke out among them, and from which they never recovered, causing them to leave Earth en masse at 200 B.C.

If you are at such a point of acceptance, you are now ready to confront Earth's greatest and most fundamental mystery: How did we humans—creatures utterly unlike anything else on the planet—acquire our unique advantages (ability to think, speak, solve problems, plan ahead, feel emotions, etc.), along with our equally unique downsides (vulnerable skins, weak muscles, thin bones, inefficient walks, and the savage territorial imperative that drives members of every generation to wreak havoc on themselves and their neighbors)?

To begin answering that we must review what we have already learned: (1) The supposedly "human" fossil record clearly lacks our bones and thus proves we did not "evolve" here the way Charles Darwin proposed. (2) The fossils we do have are a record of the four kinds of hominoids that did microevolve or develop or whatever life does on Earth. (3) Those hominoids live among us today, maintaining easy access to nearly half the planet's available land (dense forests and jungles). If you can accept those propositions as tentative facts, we are ready to proceed.

***

According to the Sumerians, the first 50 Anunnaki came to Earth 430,000 years ago, establishing a beachhead in Mesopotamia that eventually grew to a base population of 600, which slowly expanded as the very-long-lived aliens reproduced. [A final population count is never specified, although their extremely low birth rates (relative to humans) would never have allowed a boom.] They placer mined the Tigris and Euphrates Rivers until both played out after 100,000 years (28 shars, their 3600 Earth-year years). By then they had found the mother lode in southern Africa, so they moved half the workforce (at that point probably $600 \div 2 = 300$) down there.

Unfortunately, in southern Africa they could not placer mine, they had to dig it out the hard way. (Anyone who mines gold today knows it is difficult, demanding work. Even utilizing the highest of modern high technology, which the Anunnaki could no doubt have matched and even surpassed in their own ways, it is arduous and dangerous at best.) Their woes are stated unambiguously by Zecharia Sitchin in *The Twelfth Planet*, which quotes from a Sumerian creation epic entitled (quite interestingly) "When The Gods As Men." (Again, there are so many tablets it has become customary to name well-known ones after their first few words or their first line.)

> "When the gods, as (like) men,
> bore the work and suffered the toil—
> the toil of the gods was great,
> the work was heavy,
> the distress was much."

And later:

> "They were complaining, backbiting,
> grumbling in the excavations."

After 12 more shars of their onerous labors (the tablets specify 40 shars, start to finish—144,000 of our years), the Anunnaki miners staged a walkout (no doubt the planet's first labor strike) and sought relief from Enlil, their leader on Earth, who ruled from the Upper World in Mesopotamia (in what the Anunnaki called—no kidding—"the E.DIN"). At first Enlil refused to help, but his halfbrother and second-in-command, Enki, who ruled the Lower World and was responsible for managing its mines, predictably sided with his workers. By being on the scene, Enki knew how difficult their jobs were and felt they should have relief from them. However, another factor was his sibling rivalry with Enlil, the heir apparent to the supreme ruler, Anu.

Because the debate was so critical to Nibiru's survival, Anu called for a Great Assembly of top Anunnaki during Nibiru's next pass through the solar system. He and his wife (Enlil's mother) and their entourage undertook the journey to Earth to mediate the dispute. After listening to his feuding sons, Anu sided with Enki, agreeing the miners merited relief from their labors, which would have to extend well into the future if Nibiru was to secure enough gold to fully repair its damaged atmosphere. Then, after more debate about how to solve the problem, it was agreed the Anunnaki on Earth should create a slave for themselves to take over their hard labors. A further quote from "When The Gods As Men" has Enki (who was also known as Ea) saying:

"I will produce a lowly primitive,
'Man' shall be his name.
I will create a primitive worker;
He will be charged with the service of the gods,
That they might have their ease."

Making this even more compelling is an intriguing play on words described by Zecharia Sitchin in *The Twelfth Planet*: "In Biblical times, the deity was 'Lord,' 'Sovereign,' 'Master,' 'Ruler,' 'King.' The term that is commonly translated as 'worship' was in fact 'avod,' ('work'). [Therefore] Ancient and Biblical Man did not 'worship' his god; he worked for him."

After deciding to create a "lowly primitive," the next problem was finding a creature to use as a prototype. It had to be strong enough to perform hard work and intelligent enough to be trained to do it, but not so intelligent or strong that it might someday revolt and become a problem for its masters. Of the many creatures on Earth, Anu said to Enki, was there one that fit those parameters? No, Enki replied, there was not . . . but there was one that was reasonably close, and Enki—a brilliant scientist—felt that with the right kind of "alterations" it could be made to suffice. So what was that creature? It is depicted in *The Epic of Gilgamesh*, a classic Sumerian tale in which a bold demigod and his faithful sidekick Enkidu (ENKI.DU—"creature of Enki") endure incredible trials and tribulations seeking the means to acquire everlasting life in "Heaven."

Here is how Enkidu is described:

"Shaggy with hair is his whole body;
He is endowed with head-hair like a woman.
He knows neither people nor land;
Garbed he is like one of (from) green fields;
With gazelles he feeds on grass;
With wild beasts he jostles at the watering place."

Sound familiar? It is a perfect description of a hominoid! "A body covered with hair, with head hair like a woman"—speaks for itself. "He knows neither people nor land"—a nomad who wanders around, mostly in isolation. "Garbed like one from green fields"—naked as any animal on the savannas. "With gazelles he feeds on grass"— stems and bulbs of wild grasses dominate the hominoid diet (recall Albert Ostman's observations about what his captors ate). "With wild beasts he jostles at the watering place"—hominoids are often seen near water (as in the Patterson film), bathing, washing food, etc. Each descriptive comment is dead-on accurate—4,500 years ago!

The obvious next question is which hominoid was Enki thinking about altering when the decision was made 285,000 years ago (430,000 minus 40 shars)? Well, since Abominable Snowmen live only in the Himalayas, their ancestors were probably too far away from the Anunnakis' E.DIN. Bigfoot's ancestors may have been within reach in both the Upper and Lower worlds, but were probably too large and too strong to make a reliably subservient population of slaves. The pygmy-sized Agogwes were probably too small to be considered good worker prospects, which leaves the man-sized Almas/Kaptars (who might also be Neanderthals) as the likeliest choice.

***

Is it presumptuous to conclude Almas/Kaptars were the creatures Enki chose to alter into slaves? To a certain degree, yes, in that the timeframes involved will require some adjusting (this will be addressed in later chapters). For now, simply note what Zecharia Sitchin observes in *The Twelfth Planet*: "In the Sumerian versions (of the creation epics), the decision to create Man was adopted by the gods in their (Great) Assembly. Significantly, the Book of Genesis—purportedly exalting the achievements of a sole Deity— uses the plural Elohim (literally, 'deities') to denote 'God,' and (in doing so) reports an astonishing remark:

"And (the) Elohim said: 'Let us make Man

In our (own) image, after our (own) likeness'."

Later Sitchin points out that, "The Old Testament took pains to make clear that Man was neither a god nor from the heavens. . . . The new Being was called [once again, no kidding] *'the Adam'* [emphasis mine] because he was created of the 'adama,' the Earth's soil. He was, in other words, 'the Earthling'." Apart from specific "knowledge" reserved only for gods, and a "divine" (shar-based) lifespan, "the Adam was in all other respects created in the image (selem) and likeness (dmut) of his Creator(s). The use of both terms in the text was meant to leave no doubt that Man was similar to the God(s) both physically and emotionally, externally and internally. In all ancient pictorial depictions of gods and men, this physical likeness is evident."

Thus, only the man-sized Almas/Kaptars seem to qualify as the new slave's model.

MAKING THE WORKER/SLAVE

Once the decision was made and the model creature selected, it was time to construct the worker/slave. To head up the project the great scientist Enki was chosen, and he took as his chief assistant another brilliant Anunnaki scientist—his half-sister Ninti (also known as Ninhursag). They immediately went to work, pooling their talents to create the A.DAM.U, the slaves they intended to make. But how could they undertake such an audacious, technically complex task and have any realistic hopes of success? They could because they had a viable method for doing it, one that remains so to this day: genetic manipulation by the laboratory technique we call gene splicing. Would the Anunnaki be capable of that? Absolutely. They were then—and will always be—many thousands of years ahead of where we are at any point in our development.

We have progressed from the Stone Age to today in roughly 10,000 years, so multiply that by, say, 28 times and it might approximate where the Anunnaki were at 285,000 years ago. Also, if the Anunnaki had mastered space travel to the extent they apparently did (which was and is vastly superior to ours), it is fair to assume they could have mastered genetic manipulation at least to the extent we have (and no doubt well beyond). As of now we can cut and splice genes from any living entity—plant or animal—into any other living entity (which includes from plants to animals and vice-versa!); so there are no practical limits to what we can accomplish in this field, just as there would have been no such limits for the Anunnaki.

The major problem with our experiments in genetic manipulation—what non-geneticists are so concerned about and keep trying to legislate against—is the same problem the Anunnaki faced in their experiments: geneticists can never be 100% sure what products will emerge from their splicing experiments. That uncertainty in the technical process raises moral/ethical issues for anyone conducting genetic experiments, especially something as radical as creating a new species, whether that be—as with us—a new lab mouse for use in medical experiments, or a rot-resistant tomato, or—as with the Anunnaki—a new sentient being. Such a far-reaching project would certainly justify gathering their very highest council—a Great Assembly of the gods.

251

***

Today's ongoing debate about genetic manipulation, which has lately been centered on cloning, is fueled by the fact that the only way to make progress is to experiment; but the results of such experiments cannot be predicted or guaranteed. In experiments using inert chemicals, that is no problem. However, when the object of the experiments is to alter—and sometimes to create new— forms of life, restraints need to be in place. That is because the materials being dealt with (genes) are so infinitesimally small, any experiments done on and to them are terribly imprecise.

A human body contains upwards of 100 trillion cells, from blood to muscle to skin to brain cells. In each cell (except red blood cells) there is a nucleus. Each nucleus (except in the sex cells) contains 46 chromosomes arranged in 23 pairs, one-half of each pair being supplied by each parent in their sex cells. (The number of chromosomes varies from species to species.) All chromosomes are filled with tightly coiled strands of the basic genetic material, deoxyribonucleic acid, or DNA. Genes are specific segments of the DNA strands that contain the instructions to make specific proteins, the most fundamental building blocks of life.

Everything living on Earth—plant or animal—has a similar genetic structure. Everything uses the same four bases to make the same twenty amino acids; the triplet code (the sequencing device) is the same; the ribosomal devices for turning amino acids into proteins is the same. The only thing different is the message each gene carries within itself to govern its actions—the process is always the same. (The overwhelming similarity of life at the most basic levels is convincing evidence that it springs from a single common source. What remains quite unclear, however, is the means by which its amazing diversity has developed from that unknown common source.)

The coils of DNA that make up the chromosomes in the nuclei of living cells are microscopically small marvels of biological engineering. It is estimated that if all the DNA in one cell nucleus was stretched out like a string, it would reach from 3 feet (low end) to 9 feet (high end); yet it is so tightly wound inside the nucleus it is like a wad of rubber bands—a wad anywhere from 1/100,000 to 1/2,000,000 the size of the head of a pin! That extreme smallness rules out cutting by mechanical means (the necessary blade could only be a few molecules thick, a physical impossibility). Yet geneticists *are* able to cut and splice genes using chemical "scissors" and "staplers" because certain chemicals are attracted to certain kinds of molecular bonds.

Geneticists determine the molecular bond at any gene site they want to break, then insert a chemical agent that will tear it apart by latching onto the molecules holding it together. To splice a torn area, they use other chemical agents which bind the two parts back into one. That is the upside. The downside is that because genes are so infinitesimally small, chemicals cannot cut them precisely. The best they can do is act in the general area where a break is intended. To analogize a gene cut or splice by a chemical agent, it is like severing or fusing lengths of garden hose by rolling over them with a steamroller. This is true now and apparently always will be, just as it probably was for Enki and Ninti and any of the other Anunnaki working on the make-a-slave project.

Though seemingly impossible, cutting and splicing genes is made practical by an odd quirk of Nature: huge segments of most genes are not critical to their functioning. Called "junk" DNA because it has no obvious function, in animals it comprises as much as 90% of any given chromosome. ("Obvious" is a key word: junk DNA could easily have a purpose not as yet understood.) Geneticists aim for junk segments when they cut and splice genes because if they can successfully run their chemical agent "steamroller" over them, none of the gene's functions will be impaired. The critical functioning parts—those that encode proteins (which is all genes actually do)— will continue to operate regardless of where they are transplanted to, or of what is linked to them.

Any cut or splice in a gene's DNA is considered successful if the chemical steamroller does its work above and/or below a functioning segment. Despite their microscopic size, detached segments can be physically removed and placed in another cell, inside that cell's nucleus, into any area on any chromosome in the nucleus that is cut and prepared to receive it. (Don't ask how; just accept that it can be, and is, done.) The next step is chemically splicing the removed segment into the precut receiving gene. If everything has worked properly, if all cuts and splices have occurred in non-working segments of junk, then the transplanted segment will encode proteins with its new neighbors and something original will be created. The mystery and the magic—and the potential danger—of gene manipulation is in finding out *what* has been created.

GORILLA LINEBACKERS

[I assume everyone knows what gorillas are. For those who may be uncertain about linebackers, they are usually the most physically rugged players on American football teams.]

***

Here is a hypothetical: Right now, today, humanity is faced with a need or a desire to turn gorillas into linebackers. (I am apologizing in advance to all linebackers, many of whom I deeply respect.) Setting aside the labyrinthine rules of NFL free agency, and knowing only what we presently know about genetic manipulation, could we do that? Yes, in all likelihood, we could.

The genetic material (DNA) of humans and gorillas is astonishingly similar, given how *dis*similar we are in outward appearance. (Incredibly, there are more genetic differences between zebras and horses, which physiologically are almost indistinguishable, than between humans and gorillas.) The DNA duplication of humans and gorillas is estimated at 98%. There are roughly 100,000 genes in a human's 46 chromosomes (and a similar amount in a gorilla's 48), and about 3.0 billion bits of DNA in those 100,000 genes. So the 2.0% difference produces around 60 million DNA base pair mismatches. (All these numbers will be approximate until the Human Genome Project determines the correct ones early next century.) Compare that 2.0%, 60 million DNA base pair mismatch difference to the 0.2% genetic difference between individuals of either species. That 0.2% difference between individual humans or between individual gorillas prevents their offspring from being clones (identical examples) of their parents. However, this can be confusing relative to the 2.0% difference in the DNA bits shared by the two species. So understand this: the 0.2% difference is between and among ourselves; the 2.0% difference is between us and gorillas.

More confusion is caused by human and gorilla gametes (the two sex cells—ovum and sperm), both of which have less than the 0.2% difference because, unlike other body cells, each gamete has only half the chromosomes (in humans 23, in gorillas 24) that combine to make the 46 and 48 chromosome pairs of a human or gorilla zygote (which soon becomes a fetus). Also, the differences in chromosomal alignments have to be overcome or fertilization will not take place. However, if fertilization does occur, the two less-than-0.2% differences will produce the full 0.2% difference within the offspring of both species. (I know this is confusing, but try to hang in.)

Understand: when chromosomes from a human sperm line up with chromosomes from a human ovum to attempt fusion into a zygote, each contains less than 0.2% base pair mismatches along their genes. Gorilla gametes line up the same way, including their extra pair of chromosomes. However, if we line up the chromosomes of a human gamete (ovum or sperm) with the chromosomes of the opposite gorilla gamete, we find not only a mismatch in the number of chromosomes (23 to 24), but an overall base pair mismatch of 2.0%. Genetic mismatches as large as that (and even much smaller in other cases) will make cross-species fertilization impossible.

***

To successfully cross-fertilize two species, the genes in at least one gamete have to be altered. Because sex cells contain only half the chromosomes and genes as other cells in a body (half from the male parent, half from the female parent), they are the easiest to manipulate by genetic cutting and splicing. So to turn gorillas into linebackers, we have to cut and splice genetic material in the gametes of gorillas and humans until we get a close enough match in the chromosomes to permit fertilization, successful encoding of proteins, and growth into what is called a hybrid. That hybrid will have physical traits of each parent, and what results from that line-up of traits will dictate how much of which genes to try to change on any subsequent attempts.

Of our two available choices for manipulation, female ovum (eggs) are much larger and easier to work with than sperm cells. In fact, sperm cells are so tiny (thousands could fit inside a single egg), they can be considered impossible to alter. So female eggs are what must be changed. Now, should we modify the gorilla eggs to make them more closely align with the genes in human sperm, or vice-versa? Since gorillas have 24 chromosomes per sex cell and humans 23, one or the other figure must be chosen: either reduce the gorillas down to 23, or increase humans up to 24. However, an entire chromosome cannot be taken from or added to any creature without altering critical genes, so the only alternative is to *combine two chromosomes into one* (remember this!) by splicing. Therefore, our best approach is to use our chemical steamrollers to splice two gorilla chromosomes into one, knowing that in the process many DNA segments will be eliminated, but hoping most of the damage occurs in junk DNA and leaves enough viable DNA to insure success.

Once the combining is accomplished, we have to rearrange the remaining chromosomes in the gorilla eggs so they will line up with the human sperm's chromosomes. For as difficult as all this sounds—and make no mistake, it would be tremendously difficult—a major break is built into the process: what is required is far from a complete overhaul. The descent from 2.0% (the genetic difference between humans and gorillas) toward the 0.2% ideal (a human-human or gorilla-gorilla zygote) need not be perfect, or anywhere close to perfect, to technically be a success. There only needs to be enough genetic matches to permit a viable zygote to form. That zygote might be only slightly imperfect, like mules, which are living hybrids of donkeys and horses but are sterile and unable to procreate. Or they can be so imperfect they are outright monsters, with two heads, four arms, etc. At its very best this kind of fusion is a trial-and-error, hit-or-miss process.

***

As we cut and splice genes and chromosomes in gorilla eggs, and as we match them with human sperm, our initial goal is simply to create a viable zygote that will begin mitosis (cellular replication) and implant itself in a womb. This brings us to another crucial decision: Do we implant our test-tube zygotes into gorilla or human wombs to gestate (grow)? This is a toss-up because if a hybrid zygote is viable, there is enough genetic linkage to both humans and gorillas to make either acceptable. However, for the practical purpose of maintaining proper safety and control of our project, it is better to have human females carry the hybrids, so that is how we will do it. And, naturally, the first few hybrids we bring forth are likely to be a mess, some probably moving well beyond the term "monster." But as we keep analyzing our monsters to learn what we have done right and what we have done wrong in the process of altering gene segments, we are bound to find a steady improvement in our work. Linebackers will slowly begin to emerge from the mess.

Keep in mind—and this is crucial to understand—we are only trying to create linebackers, not linebackers we might like to hang out with, or ones our daughters might like to date. We are trying for the classic "agile, mobile, hostile" football players—nothing more or less. This simplifies our task tremendously if, for example, one of our hybrids is acceptable in most respects, but—still hanging onto its gorilla heritage—its face remains gruesomely ugly. Does that mean we waste time and effort trying to alter the ugly genes? No! We are building linebackers, not prom dates. If we make mistakes that don't fit the linebacker profile, and if those mistakes are not detrimental to linebacker functions or linebacker longevity (in other words, the quality and shelf-life of our product), we can simply leave them in and continue working toward our goal.

***

Speaking of our goal, we are almost there. We have been at it for quite a while now, and we have created dozens—if not hundreds—of monsters as we refined our techniques and figured out which genes to remove or leave in the gorilla ova to better match them up with human sperm to produce functional linebackers. They can be ugly enough to make freight trains take dirt roads; they can have heads big enough to fill two helmets; they can stay hairy from head to toe (they have to shave most of it anyway for taping purposes); they can even stay vegetarian (which will cut way down on food bills). However, they must have acquired certain linebacker characteristics.

They need greatly improved brains to understand and execute the myriad intricacies of the basic 4-3 and 3-4 defenses. They need vibrant powers of speech to call out defensive "reads" to each other. They need full bipedality to blitz on second-and-short or drop into coverage on third-and-long. But along with those acquisitions, we would want them to keep as much of their natural strength as possible (vastly superior to ours); their barrel chests to help fend off blockers and stuff ball carriers; their extra-long arms to snag runners and bat down passes; etc., etc., etc.

The point is that right now, today, using the techniques just outlined (none of which are beyond our technological grasp), we could actually blend the most useful traits of humans and gorillas to create All-World linebackers. And we can be confident that something like it is exactly what Enki and Ninti did to create slaves from the Almas/Kaptars then living on Earth.

HOW THEY DID IT

In creating their slaves, the Anunnaki might have had more to cope with than we would creating our linebackers. Why? Because we only have to drop from a 2.0% genetic difference to somewhere near 0.2%—a mere ten-fold reduction. The difference between the Anunnaki and the Almas/Kaptars might have been much more. On the other hand, they probably already had their own entire genome mapped (ours is due early next century), which would likely give them the means to rapidly map the genome of anything else (which later evidence will strongly indicate). That would give them a running start at solving their doable but exceedingly complex problem.

Understand the situation: according to the Anunnaki, life on Earth is a direct consequence of its waters being "mingled" with Nibiru's during their collision 4.0 billion years ago. That gave life on Earth the same genetic codes and sequences as life on Nibiru (and, of course, possibly life forms in other parts of the galaxy as well). That makes both planets genetically compatible, which makes all chromosomes on both subject to the same kinds of manipulation and/or combination.

Taking that idea one step further, by assuming the Anunnaki and the Almas/Kaptars were genetically compatible but not initially able to produce a viable zygote, we can further assume Almas/Kaptars probably have the 48 chromosomes of Earth's other indigenous higher primates, while the Anunnaki probably have 46. And since we humans are the final product of the Anunnaki-Almas union, and since we were supposedly created in the Anunnaki image, and since we seem able to produce viable zygotes with Almas/Kaptars (a la Zana's offspring), it stands to reason that we would have 46 chromosomes that are somehow—either by specific design or by residual similarity—viable with the 48 chromosomes we have assumed belong to the Almas/Kaptars.

(By the way, the most important aspect of the first "official" hominoid capture—living or dead—will be a chromosomal difference with humans. Naturally, its upright posture and generally human physique will lead to its initial classification as an extremely primitive human. However, if it turns out to have 48 chromosomes rather than 46, that will unequivocally align it with the apes and monkeys, which in turn will make it and its assumed relatives the obvious descendants of the creatures that now comprise the "prehuman" fossil record. That would, in turn, remove humanity from the flowchart of primate life on Earth, which should be proof enough for all but the most rabid die-hards that we simply are not a "natural" species here—not now or ever.)

No matter how close or how distant was the DNA compatibility between the Anunnaki and the Almas/Kaptars (assuming, of course, Almas/Kaptars were indeed the model)—whether 2.0% down to 0.2%, or, say, 5.0% down to 0.05%—the Anunnaki knew that with

259

enough time and effort their quest to genetically alter the "Earth-lings" into slaves could and would succeed.

***

To do the required experiments, the Anunnaki would confront the same problems we would face turning gorillas into linebackers. Should they manipulate the eggs of their own females, or the eggs of the Almas/Kaptars? Gestate zygotes in their females or in the Alma/Kaptar females? In the first case, Sumerian texts are quite clear about whose eggs were used as the basis of all experiments. Again and again they refer to the "clay" of Earth being used.

> "After she (Ninti) had recited her incantation,
> She put her hand out to the clay . . . .
> (She) nipped off fourteen pieces of clay."

And in another place:

> "In the clay, god and Man shall be bound,
> to a unity brought together."

And in yet another place:

> "Divine Ea (Enki) in the Apsu (Africa)
> pinched off a piece of clay,
> created Kulla (Adamu) to restore the temples."

Here it must be pointed out that the translations of Sumerian clay tablets often produce words and images that do not make much sense in a modern context. To get at their true meanings, the meanings intended when they were written, often requires a creative approach that too few scholars are willing (or able) to attempt. The above quotes offer perfect examples. Taken as written, a translator can find the word for "clay" used in the context of "creating" humanity and blithely announce to the world, "These poor people, these Sumerians, were dreaming when they wrote this, making up fantasies out of sheer nonsense, creating nothing but myths." However, all it takes is a little digging around the edges of the written language and related languages to come up with the kind of brilliant etymological linkage Zecharia Sitchin makes in *The Twelfth Planet*.

"The Akkadian (Sumerian) term for 'clay'—or, rather, 'molding clay," he writes, "is 'tit.' But its original spelling was TI.IT ('that which is with life'). In Hebrew 'tit' means 'mud'; but its synonym is 'bos,' which shares a root with 'bisa' ('marsh') and 'besa' ('egg')."

Given those facts, is it not likely that bos-bisa-besa (clay-mud-egg) can be interpreted as a word-distorted reference for the female ovum, the egg? Imagine Sumerian scribes trying to interpret the creation story handed down from Anunnaki gods, whether verbally, in person, or from ancient texts they might have been copying to preserve. They read "ovum" or "egg" in the context of genetic manipulation (something they could not imagine, much less grasp) and the word for it remotely resembles "clay." In a culture where clay is the main building material (temples, homes, bowls, tablets, etc.), would it not be logical to conclude people were made from it, too?

Of course, the Sumerians would not be able to understand *how* the Anunnaki gods could turn clay into people, but they would have an easier time conceptualizing that bizarre juxtaposition than they would the realities of the genetic manipulations the gods actually utilized. Thus, it seems plausible to imagine that a simple mistranslation by Sumerian scribes could be the origin of the strict religious dogma that insists humanity was created from the clay of Earth itself rather than from the eggs of creatures native to Earth (such as the Almas/Kaptars).

As for which females should gestate the zygotes, the texts are less ambiguous: Anunnaki "birth goddesses" were conscripted for the job. One text relates an early experiment in which fourteen birth goddesses were impregnated with a "mixture" consisting of "purified essence" of male Anunnaki (their sperm) and the "pieces of clay" of the Earth (the genetically altered eggs of the Almas/Kaptars). The text says Ninti "inserted" the clay/essence mixture into the fourteen birth goddesses by a surgical procedure that required the removal or shaving of some of their hair (presumably pubic hair, which, as mentioned in Part III, humans have but indigenous primates do not). Then, with all Anunnaki eyes focused on the Lower World's grand experiment, the wait began.

"The birth goddesses were kept together.
Ninti sat counting the months.
The fateful tenth month was approaching;

The tenth month arrived;
The period of opening the womb had elapsed."

Following a typically human nine-month gestation period, Ninti herself "performed the midwifery" to deliver her co-productions. When they arrived she exclaimed: "I have created it! My hands have made it!" Despite the haunting echoes of Dr. Frankenstein, we can understand Ninti's exultation. Who wouldn't feel the same after clearing a primary hurdle on such a long, difficult track? Unfortunately, there were many more to clear before the "race" was completed.

***

Despite those fourteen successful births (specified in the text as seven males and seven females) somewhere along the early arc of their experiments, Enki and Ninti's first models were far from what would eventually become the finished product. No matter how scientifically sophisticated the Anunnaki were at 285,000 years ago, and no matter how close the genetic match was between them and the Almas/Kaptars, creating an entirely new creature had to require a tremendous amount of plain old trial-and-error, which is clearly supported by the Sumerian texts that recount at least some of Enki and Ninti's unsuccessful early attempts. As Zecharia Sitchin recounts in *The Twelfth Planet*, they produced "a male who could not hold back his urine, a woman who could not bear children, a being who had neither male nor female organs." Pressing on, they made an imperfect male "with diseased eyes, trembling hands, a sick liver, a failing heart; a second one with sicknesses attendant upon old age; and so on."

The length of time these refining experiments required is, unfortunately, not specified. However, assuming every new model had to grow up to several years of age before its effectiveness could be accurately judged, we can further assume Enki and Ninti labored on the order of hundreds—and probably more like thousands—of years. (Remember, to the Anunnaki time had nowhere near the meaning it does to us. Of course, it had serious meaning to the miners for whom the slaves were meant to provide relief, but surely their labors were made easier for however long was required by knowing that Enki and Ninti were hard at work on the project.)

Without saying when, or how many flawed copies were produced before an acceptable prototype was created, the texts do relate that eventually a model was developed whose skin was "as (smooth as) the skin of a god." In other words, when the full-bodied hairiness of the Almas/Kaptars was bred out of the hybrids being produced, the end of the experimenting was near. Also by this point something else had occurred—a bonus—perhaps unexpected, perhaps deliberate, the texts are not clear. Along with the smooth skin on the new creatures came sexual compatibility with the Anunnaki. Not only could the new males work as slaves in the gold mines, the females could serve as sex objects for any Anunnaki males who wanted to copulate with them.

> "It came to pass that when Men began to multiply on
> the face of the Earth, and Daughters were born unto them,
> the Sons of God saw (that) the Daughters of Men were fair,
> and they took unto them wives of all which they chose."

That cryptic, sexually-charged, highly controversial Biblical passage, so often misinterpreted and misunderstood because of its clear reference to multiple deities with wickedly mortal appetites, makes infinitely more sense in this new light, doesn't it?

MASS PRODUCTION

However long it took to create a viable slave model, and to whatever degree of sophistication was initially acceptable to everyone involved, Enki and Ninti eventually fulfilled their promise to the gold-mining Anunnaki. However, as with most hybrids, those first copies were sterile (a la mules), so further modifications were required before they could be mass produced. That was critical because the interim production could only come from Anunnaki females, who could only gestate a limited number at any one time. To achieve mass production, Adamu males and females had to be made fertile so they could self-replicate. Genetically that was not as difficult as creating a successful prototype, but it was no chip shot, either.

Remember, gorillas and humans have nearly identical genetic codes (a 98% DNA match), which includes the genes governing reproduction. But in their gametes (sperm and ovum), they are like IBM computers trying to run Macintosh programs; too much "incompatibility" creates zygotes that cannot "read" the most fundamental genetic instructions, much less run an entire program (i.e. create offspring). Thus, gorillas and humans cannot produce a viable zygote, which is true of all sterile hybrids. For example, male and female mules have virtually identical genetic material in their sex cells, but those genes are not in positions where they can function together to produce offspring. So the challenge for Enki and Ninti was to continue experimenting on the eggs of Adamu females, cutting and shifting gene strings until they created a close enough match with Adamu males to start producing viable zygotes.

Sumerian texts do not say how long this second step required, nor how long was needed for enough Adamu to be born and raised to enough maturity to populate the gold mines in reasonable numbers. Later evidence will indicate the entire process was finished by about 250,000 years ago, which means it could have taken as long as 35,000 years. As with other Anunnaki timeframes measured against our "human" scale, don't let those numbers throw you. To the seemingly ageless "gods," 35,000 years might be roughly equivalent to an Army hitch for us: a difficult grind, but not a backbreaker. However long it took, though, ultimately the Anunnaki did achieve mass production of male and female Adamu patterned after the smooth-skinned prototype.

(As a point of interest, the Sumerian word TI meant "life" or "essence of life," but it could also mean "rib." Thus, we find another place where confusion in translating may have come down to us as religious dogma. Imagine, say, 5000 years ago; some Anunnaki tell a few early Sumerian scribes how the first fertile female Adamu were created by using the TI, or "life essence," of some male Adamu. That is how it is recorded. Many centuries later other scribes are making fresh copies of the ancient original reports and reach that passage. These scribes are now far removed from the ones who personally spoke with the gods, so they must decide on their own what kind of "spin" to put on what they are copying. They repeat the clay-egg confusion by deciding that, based on their understanding of the world in their own era, "rib" makes more sense. Later, when the Old Testament was being written, its creators could have changed the original story even more, simplifying it by reducing the plural characters to just two: Adam and Eve.)

***

It is hard to know which aspect of the new creatures rank-and-file Anunnaki appreciated more: males who relieved them of their onerous labors in the gold mines, or sexually compatible females who came with the package. The latter had to be a great bonus, especially to what had to be a male-dominated workforce isolated far from home for thousands of years at a time. So even if the new females were not exactly as "fair" in Anunnaki eyes as the Bible indicates, the phrase "any port in a storm" would have applied. It would also apply with equal effect to Upper World Anunnaki in Mesopotamia, who had to work nearly as hard as those in the Lower World. Their lot was laboring in fields and fishing in seas to secure the food to feed their steadily expanding population. They were also responsible for managing the spaceport that regulated traffic to and from large space stations orbiting beyond Earth's atmosphere.

(Those stations were manned by special Anunnaki—"The Anunnaki of Heaven"—called Igigi, who numbered 300 and "were too high up for Mankind; they were not concerned with the people." They controlled flights between Earth and Nibiru using the same set-up we would use if we were making regular flights between, say, Earth and Mars. In our case the heavy spacecraft needed to break free of Earth's gravity would shuttle to and from an orbiting space station. From there a much lighter craft would undertake the gravity-free journey to another station orbiting around Mars. Then a lander craft—probably another heavy to-and-from shuttle—would transfer the payload down to the Red Planet's surface. To quote Yogi Berra, it is deja vu all over again.)

In addition to farming, fishing, and managing their spaceport, the Upper World Anunnaki were saddled with the grueling task of smelting the gold-bearing ores being dug out of the ground by their brethren in the Lower World. Because of the high heats required, in many ways smelting is as dangerous and labor-intensive as mining, and working in and around smelting furnaces can be worse than the discomfort of mines. (Incidentally, considering the Anunnaki purpose on Earth, the locations of their Upper and Lower World bases make perfect sense. Southern Africa was where the most gold was, with by far the richest veins on the planet. Likewise, in Mesopotamia fuels were easily secured to smelt that ore. In fact, in antiquity no other area on Earth produced bitumen and pitch and other petroleum-based products on the surface in such quantity.)

After hearing stories from their Lower World counterparts about the many advantages of the new Adamu (males and females alike), the Upper World Anunnaki beseeched their supreme ruler on Earth, Enlil, to intercede in their behalf to acquire some Adamu for themselves. Enlil diplomatically forwarded their request to the Lower World, but its ruler, Enki, refused. He had not gone to all the trouble he did to appease his rival's work force.

Enki's refusal festered among the Upper World Anunnaki, especially with Enlil, who always had to be on guard against having his authority usurped by his older (and possibly smarter and more able) half-brother. Eventually, the Upper World forces mounted a full-scale expedition to the Lower World to demand a fair share of the slaves, which over time the Anunnaki had come to call the "Black-Headed Ones." (Because the Anunnaki were light-skinned and fair-haired, it is assumed "Black-Headed" meant "Black-Haired." Supporting that assumption is the fact that while a wide range of hair colorings are seen among hominoids, the vast majority are black.)

Enlil's Upper World expedition traveled south by water rather than by air (their aircraft were too small to transport numerous armed forces). When they arrived in the Lower World there was the predictable confrontation with Enki's forces. After a few indecisive skirmishes between well-matched opponents, Enki bowed to the authority granted Enlil by their father, Anu, Supreme Ruler on Nibiru. He agreed to supply the Upper World with an ample number of

Black-Headed Ones to serve that domain. The result of that man-power transfer comes to us through the Bible:

"And the Deity Yahweh planted
An orchard in Eden, in the east . . .
And He took (the) Adam and (He)
Placed him in the Garden of Eden
To work it and to keep it."

(Many Biblical scholars feel a preponderance of clues points to the Garden of Eden being located in the Tigris-Euphrates Valley. Knowing what we know now, how could it be otherwise?)

***

For as wonderful as Enki and Ninti's "creation" was, it did have drawbacks. One is expressed in a Sumerian text describing what Enki had done for the new being he had created:

"Wide Understanding he perfected for him . . .
To him he had given Knowledge and Wisdom;
(But) Eternal Life he had not given him."

In other words, Enki was able to pass to the new creatures enough of the Anunnaki's high intelligence to make capable slaves (a main original goal), but he was either unable to, or under orders not to, make them live as long as the Anunnaki. He may also have deliberately given them short lifespans to increase their birth rates (another main goal), because the longer any animal tends to live, the less often it reproduces. (The Anunnaki had very low birth rates.) Drawbacks aside, however, the Adamu were, overall, a big success for Enki, Ninti, and the Anunnaki. They served exactly the purposes they were created for, along with providing unexpected bonuses that made the whole "Creation Project" more than worthwhile. So for the Anunnaki it was simply a matter of settling into their new, improved lifestyle made possible by the Adamu slaves.

THE FLOOD

The Black-Headed Ones toiled and reproduced and died for their masters for more than 200,000 years, during which the Anunnaki came to fully understand their creation's most valuable asset. As the "humans" (another name they acquired) multiplied into the thousands, tens of thousands, and hundreds of thousands, it allowed the Anunnaki to expand their influence and control inside of—and then far beyond—Mesopotamia and southern Africa. Such expansion was necessary because the ranks of ordinary Anunnaki were also growing, though nowhere near as rapidly as the short-lived humans. But even with their low birth rates, what was originally 600 had been reproducing for more than 400,000 years, which must have made overcrowding a bit of a problem.

Worse than overcrowding, however, was the internal politics among the Anunnaki elite, particularly Enlil and Enki and their supporters. As mentioned earlier, both kept producing sons, all of whom at maturity required land to rule or they might pose a succession threat to their fathers. Anu, who had seized Nibiru's crown in a coup d'etat of his own, had lessened his succession problems by sending his two principal heirs to Earth, so Enlil and Enki utilized the same tactic. They granted their quarrelsome heirs fiefdoms within their Upper and Lower realms.

To roughly estimate a timeframe, by 100,000 years ago (the start of the last Ice Age) there might have been enough humans to begin expanding beyond Africa and Mesopotamia. By 50,000 years ago (the heart of the Ice Age) they might have gotten as far afield as southern Europe and southern China. Certainly by 15,000 years ago they were in temperate latitudes all over the globe, including the Americas. No populations of Anunnaki masters and their human chattel were anywhere near as large as those in Mesopotamia and Africa, but there was a thin dispersal everywhere the last Ice Age did not directly impose itself. Then the Great Flood ruined most of it.

***

Because the Biblical story of the Great Flood is such a lynchpin of Creationism, establishment science is forced to discount it. Nevertheless, a remarkable number of cultures past and present believe a worldwide inundation did occur within human history, though they tend to be hazy on its details. The Sumerians are not.

268

They state emphatically that a Great Flood surged up from the south, not for the Bible's continual forty-days-and-forty-nights, but as a sudden, overwhelming event, what today we would call a tidal wave, or—as the Japanese term it—a tsunami. They say it occurred around 11,000 B.C., at the end of the last Ice Age. Ironically, their contention is strongly supported by conventional science, which has determined that the last interglacial warming trend began slowly, at around 13,000 B.C. in the northern hemisphere, and gradually moved south until around 11,000 B.C., when something happened to accelerate full global warming to warp speed—in perhaps as little as twenty years. That "something" is what we must consider.

The Sumerian tablets plainly say the Anunnaki could and did anticipate the Flood, which allowed those in its path to fly into orbit to watch it play out, or to go stay with those living in areas not likely to be impacted (mountain highlands). However, they could not predict its ultimate effects in terms of total damage and overall changes in weather patterns, so the possibility existed that they would be driven off Earth for a long time—if not permanently. That left them with the troubling question of what to do about the humans they would have to leave behind if they were forced to "abandon ship."

It was such a problem, the texts say, another Great Assembly had to be called, at which the gods debated and decided humanity's fate. Unfortunately for the humans, Enlil had always been unhappy with them, primarily because Enki had received so much credit for their creation. But he also objected to "their animal ways" (what he felt was an overemphasis on copulation), and to the more serious concern that miscegenation between humans and their masters was diluting the purity of the Anunnaki race. Enlil argued that humans were not worth saving and should be left to die without being warned of the impending disaster.

Enki and Ninti could not dispute much of what Enlil said because most humans *were* base in their behavior, with their "animal" aspects clearly dominating. However, Enki suggested that their breed could be dramatically upgraded if at least some of the best examples available were saved. This was a viable option because—while

269

working against the Anunnaki—miscegenation had worked in favor of the humans in many ways, adding qualities the two geneticists had been unable or unwilling to impart to them in the laboratory. (Mixed beings were called, not surprisingly, "demigods," and were more intelligent, longer-lived, and in every way more like gods than humans. Demigods were, in fact, treated as junior gods or assistant gods and allowed to rule over humans when a real god was unavailable or unwilling to assume such duty.)

Despite how valuable humans had become to the Anunnaki, Enlil's arguments prevailed and the Great Assembly agreed that the slaves would not be warned. Enki, however, took matters into his own hands and saved some anyway. Ironically, Sumerian texts detail Enki's act of defiance, describing how he told a specially chosen human to build a boat that could survive being swept away by a torrent of water, and to take all manner of living things with him. This is unquestionably the model Old Testament writers used for their account of the Great Flood.

Despite the vivid imagery of both the Biblical and Sumerian accounts of the Flood, and for as comprehensive as such a disaster would have been on a worldwide basis, it could not and did not wipe out all but a representative pair of each species of life on the planet. (One reason scientists dismiss Great Flood legends is that the fossil record does not reveal a major extinction event at that time.) It no doubt decimated many populations, but the horrific image of every living species being eliminated down to the last pair was surely meant to symbolically illustrate the magnitude of the event. In other words, what happened was definitely bad, but not *that* bad.

***

Because so many sources around the world forcefully assert that a Great Flood did cause widespread death and destruction, we need to explore the kinds of actual events that might have created one. And guess what? There is a genuinely legitimate candidate in the Antarctic icecap. Today it covers 5.5 million square miles, it contains 7.0 million cubic miles of ice, and it has an average thickness of over a mile. A ridge of mountains under it divides it into two sections: the West Antarctic Ice Sheet (about 1/4 of the total), and the East Antarctic Ice Sheet (3/4 of the total). The West Antarctic Ice Sheet slants from the mountain range division toward the Pacific Ocean. The much larger East Sheet points opposite, toward the Atlantic and Indian Oceans. At the South Pole the ice is two miles thick and flows slowly toward Africa.

All that was quite different 13,000 years ago (11,000 B.C.). The last Ice Age had gripped Earth for 90,000 years, and world sea levels were more than 300 feet lower than today. What normally covered those 300-plus feet was 3.5 million *cubic miles* of water, much of which was trapped in ice swirled across the Antarctic continent (which today holds 90% of the world's ice).

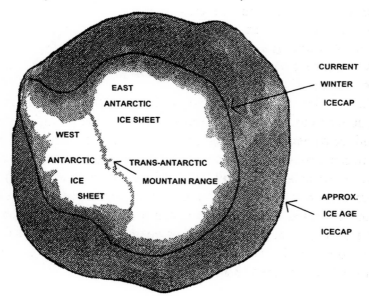

Fig. 82. Modern and Ice Age icecaps

We must term it "swirled" because there is a limit to how high ice can pile up on Antarctica. Past a certain height (perhaps only another mile above today's two-mile-high pinnacle) the planet's centrifugal force would flatten a pile-up. Glaciers would slowly be "spun" outward, spilling off the continental shelf and spreading across the sur-

271

face of the water surrounding it. (Evidence of this is available today in two huge ice shelves—the Ross Shelf and Weddell Sea Shelf.)

Knowing that, we can imagine the Antarctic icecap at 13,000 years ago. From a three-mile-high pinnacle it would sprawl to half again its current area, to 8.0 million square miles, with a volume of ice half again current volume, about 10 million cubic miles. Such a massive spillover would account for most of the required 3.5 million cubic miles, and would create an overhang that would extend many miles out into the surrounding oceans. (Imagine an extra-hefty ice cream scoop drooping over the edges of a sugar cone.)

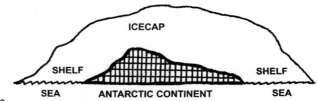

Fig. 83.

With all that in mind, now understand that any icecap's principle activity is fraying along its edges. It does that by cracking into pieces that separate from their glaciers to become floating icebergs (a process called "calving"), which on a large enough scale can be a recipe for unmitigated catastrophe. All that is needed is for serious cracks to develop well behind the edge areas, then to have a major geophysical disturbance . . . say, an earthquake or a volcano. . . jolt it loose.

CALVING THE BIG ONE

We can assume the technically advanced, airborne Anunnaki would have been aware of the above and would have been able to keep close tabs on any threatening cracks. And if the Ice Age did indeed begin to end in the northern hemisphere at 15,000 years ago, such cracks would inevitably have developed, leaving the Anunnaki knowing it was only a matter of time before one or another would widen enough to calve off one or more gargantuan bergs. But knowing it was only a matter of time is a far cry from accurately predicting when it would occur, which the tablets claim the Anunnaki did, so we have to consider what they might have used as a bellwether.

Certainly an erupting volcano could wreak havoc if any of Antarctica's were active at that time, but there is no evidence that any were. Likewise, a strong earthquake could rattle the continent to its foundations, though in the world as we know it earthquakes are impossible to predict with even ballpark accuracy. Setting aside those two possibilities, what else might dislodge significant parts of Antarctica's sprawling, miles-thick, 90,000 year-old icecap? What would also be accurately predictable? Go on, give it some thought. How about a large celestial body passing in the vicinity? Imagine a planet, a large one, with enough gravitational force to create geophysical disturbances on any other planet it passes near. A planet like, oh, say, Nibiru, for example?

As it happens, Sumerian texts claim Nibiru did indeed pass through the solar system at around 11,000 B.C., which makes it a prime candidate to shake a badly cracked icecap off of its foundations on Antarctica. Further proof of its proximity to Earth is the fact that at a time prior to, but reasonably near, the catastrophe, the Anunnaki called for and attended a Great Assembly at which they decided the fate of their humans. Such meetings were only called for when its participants were within a relatively easy interplanetary journey from each other.

For as radical as this sounds as an explanation for the sudden conclusion of the last Ice Age, there is no question *something* happened at that time to dramatically alter the Earth's existing weather patterns (i.e., the 20-year warming). Given what we have already learned about the veracity of Sumerian texts, it seems more than reasonable to give them the benefit of our doubt.

***

Let's imagine 90,000 years of icecap buildup. The 5.0 million-square-mile continental interior is covered by a roughly 3.0 mile-high dome of ice that extends outward for another 3.0 million square miles of overhang (its circumpolar shelf), which rests atop the surrounding ocean. That water is not like ocean elsewhere: with such a great mass of ice atop it, it is as still as a forest pond. Nonetheless, within the ice there is turmoil because ice sheets continually calve into icebergs, most of which drift away and melt. Nearly all calving is done along the icecap's edges, where glaciers meet or rest atop ocean. It is caused by: (1) the massive weight of the central pinnacle compressing the sloping dome downward and forcing its "fluid" ice outward; (2) the centrifugal effect of the spinning Earth also forcing the frozen but malleable glaciers to move toward their edges; (3) the relentless eroding action of the water beneath the glaciers.

Though outwardly calm, that water constantly moves the icecap's edges up and down with the tides, like bending a piece of metal to and fro until it eventually cracks and ultimately breaks. While ice bends poorly, it cracks quite easily, especially after being warmed by the well-documented climate change that started 15,000 years ago. The subsequent 2,000 years of warming would have caused huge cracks to develop along the shelf edges where the unstable, water-supported ice adjoined the far more stable land-supported ice.

The airborne Anunnaki would be able to monitor those ominous cracks and realize trouble was brewing. Also, after 420,000 years on Earth they would know precisely how close or far Nibiru would be from any planet on any orbit through the solar system (the relationship of all of their orbits would vary with each pass). Assuming they knew Nibiru's next pass would be close enough to Earth for its powerful gravitational pull to raise tides high enough to sunder the icecap's cracks, they would be forced to make plans to get themselves aloft and/or away before the crisis came. And wouldn't you know it? That is exactly what the Sumerian tablets claim they did.

***

[Here is a good place to mention the famous Piri Reis map, dated to 1513, and the Orontus Finaeus map of 1531, both purportedly copies of originals kept in the library of Alexandria, Egypt, before it was sacked and burned in 391 A.D. Both maps are reproduced and discussed in detail in many books, the most recent being Graham Hancock's fine *Fingerprints Of The Gods* (Crown, 1995). Incredibly, both maps accurately depict the Antarctic continent stripped of its ice covering! Apart from being shockingly improbable, those maps create two serious problems for scientists: Antarctica was not discovered until 1773; and ice cores indicate it has been mostly—if not fully—ice covered for several million years. Another problem for scientists is that the Piri Reis map provides an accurate portrayal of Earth viewed from—believe it or not—*sixty miles above Cairo, Egypt,* the home of the Great Pyramids! How such a view could be obtained at all—much less with accuracy—so long ago is another of the many mysteries science ignores into oblivion.]

***

Carrying our hypothetical scenario to a conclusion, we imagine Nibiru does pass through our solar system when the Antarctic ice-cap has been gradually weakened by 2,000 years of warming. Ultimately the day comes when the strain on the weakened ice is too much and gigantic bergs start calving off. The first big one hits the water, causing enough of an upheaval in the surrounding area to initiate a chain reaction that knocks the others loose. If you have seen films of glaciers calving ordinary icebergs, you know that as they crack off the face and plunge into the water, they create surface waves of from 10 to 50 feet, or more, depending on their overall volume.

Now imagine the size of waves that would be kicked up by icebergs with volumes from hundreds of thousands to perhaps a million or more cubic miles! Walls of water as high as a mile (over 5,000 feet) or more might surge forward! Any bergs calving off the East Sheet (remember, by far the larger of the two main sheets) would send tsunamis thundering first across the southern reaches of Africa (There go the gold mines!), up its eastern coastline, then funneled by Arabia and India straight at the Tigris-Euphrates Valley (There go the cities!). It would be an awesome display to observe from a box seat in orbit, which the Sumerian tablets tell us the Anunnaki had.

Fig. 84. Path of Great Flood tsunami

Apart from disrupting worldwide weather patterns, the tsunamis would strike every ocean, sea, and coastal plain on Earth. The planet would slosh for days (the texts say six), until equilibrium was reached at some greatly elevated sea level. Whatever the new level was, there is where it would stay, because as any iceberg melts, it only changes its form, not its volume. This means that the moment those icebergs slid into the oceans, millions of cubic miles of volume became instant additions to the world's water table, and such a massive amount could and would—in a matter of hours—raise sea levels to near the several hundred (over 300) feet they ultimately gained.

The Sumerian texts indicate that everything the Anunnaki had built in Africa and Mesopotamia during their 420,000 years on Earth had been obliterated. The cities around their precious gold mines had been scoured down to bedrock, while the highly productive E.DIN was at the end of the tsunami's cross-continental sweep, so it ended up with a massive clogging of mud and silt (some, no doubt, all the way from the gold mines!). The only initial upside for them was that all of the Earth's arable highlands remained habitable, so they did not have to return to Nibiru.

A subsequent upside was that all temperate climates (above 30° North and below 30° South) were gradually warmed by an average of about 50° Fahrenheit, while tropical climates (those within 30° N. and 30° S.) rose only 10° to 12° because they tend to stay stable during Ice Ages. (Perhaps coincidentally but, knowing the Anunnaki, probably not, their Upper and Lower World empires were just inside 30° North and 30° South, respectively. This means that while the Anunnaki lived on Earth, they were agreeably comfortable during every Ice Age they endured, and—as we are today—quite comfortable during interglacials.)

POSTDILUVIAL

Unlike the Biblical image, the Great Flood's waters did not cover the Earth from pole to pole. Permanent inundation was limited to coastlines and lowlands (which may explain some inland lakes). That meant creatures dwelling at heights higher than the Flood's crest would suffer few if any immediate effects, while those over-adapted to the frigid Ice Age environment would soon be devastated by the suddenness of the climate change. Sure enough, most large mammals, like woolly mammoths and giant ground sloths, which had easily survived the gradual waxing and waning of previous Ice Ages, went extinct at the end of this one, as did 75% of all mammals with a body weight over 100 pounds. Apparently they could not relocate themselves to frigid areas before the sudden warming overtook them and overtaxed their cold-adapted metabolisms.

Despite the devastation of 75% of large mammals, one of the 25% that thrived in the new environment was humankind. Shorn of protective body hair by their Anunnaki creators, humans had been able to live without clothes only in warm-weather climates like those that existed prediluvially in Mesopotamia and the mining areas of southern Africa. (Again, many Sumerian pictograms show the gods wearing garments while their servants remain naked. See Fig. 79.) But now the rapidly warming atmosphere was freeing them of any need for more than minimal clothing (if that) in millions of square miles of terrain being uncovered by melting glaciers, so those that were able to do so got busy expanding their range into a wide swath of newly comfortable habitats.

But wait . . . how could any humans do that? Weren't they all slaves of the Anunnaki? No, not exactly. Most were, but not all.

***

A bureaucracy is a bureaucracy, even among the Anunnaki, so by 13,000 years ago (more than 200,000 since the first Adamu's creation) they could not have kept track of every member of their slave force. Many would have fallen through cracks in their system, starting with the rejects that for one reason or another did not live up to the standards necessary to be a first-class laborer or servant or sex object. Of those, most would not reveal their inadequacies until they matured, so it seems reasonable to assume that rather than liquidating them, the Anunnaki merely exiled them to communities of other castoffs in the wilderness areas beyond their strongholds. For any discards such an exile would be a going home of sorts, a return to the foraging lifestyle of their Almas/Kaptars forebears; but it would also mean living at a level of extreme primitiveness.

In addition to deliberate castoffs, there also had to be a certain percentage of renegades and runaways, Adamu with enough intelligence, ambition, and courage to dare trying to fashion a life for themselves on their own terms among their own kind. Unlike the rejects, these would be trained individuals with skills they could put to good use in the wild (especially those that knew how to farm). Runaways may or may not have intermingled and interbred with the castoff populations, but whether they did so or not is irrelevant. What counts is that by the time of the Great Flood there had to be numerous small groups of humans living in areas that were at high enough elevation to avoid all direct effects of the catastrophe. Postdiluvially they would continue to live exactly as they had been doing, with their populations and their dispersion steadily expanding and overlapping so they could thoroughly mix their gene pool.

***

As for the Anunnaki, their postdiluvial fate was to start all over, literally from scratch. Everything they had built during 420,000 years—all the cities, all mining and smelting facilities, many if not most smaller outposts—was gone, obliterated in a torrent of water beyond their wildest imaginings. Even for gods who could take an exceptionally long view of any negative event, such a twist of fate had to carry an emotional wallop. But whatever their feelings were, once the tumult subsided and the new sea levels were established, they had to get back to work.

First, they returned to Earth and collected the few (relatively speaking) useful Adamu that had survived the inundation. (Even Enlil, who had argued so strenuously that all humans should be destroyed by it, offered sheepish gratitude for those that remained.) Then, because all the cities in the Tigris-Euphrates Valley were now covered by a thick (dozens of feet) layer of mud, they set up new bases in the dry mountains above the valley. They eventually spread east and west, into Egypt's Nile Valley and Pakistan's Indus Valley. They built a new spaceport in the middle of the Sinai Peninsula and, as part of the guidance system for landing spacecraft, they built the Giza Pyramids (discussed earlier and covered in detail in Zecharia Sitchin's *The Stairway to Heaven*).

Baalbek, in Lebanon, was another Anunnaki space-related facility, which it proves by containing many of the world's largest cut and dressed stones. Compared to the 200-ton Sphinx Temple "giants," Baalbek has several of around 500 tons (5,000 cubic feet of stone), and at least three (others could be internal in the platform and invisible to view) of around 1,000 tons (10,000 cubic feet)! And, as in all Anunnaki megalithic constructions around the world, each stone fits so close and so perfectly against its neighbors, the joints are barely visible. (This is their trademark.) Baalbek functioned prediluvially and remained so postdiluvially because it was high enough in the mountains to avoid being hit by the Great Flood. [Interestingly, Baalbek's geometric locus between Mount Ararat and the Pyramids dictated that a new space facility should be created in the area of today's Jerusalem (see *The Stairway to Heaven* and *The Wars of Gods and Men*).]

The Anunnaki also expanded into gold-bearing areas beyond southern Africa, particularly into the Andes Mountains of South America. Tiahuanaco in Bolivia and Peru's megalithic monuments (Sacsahuaman, Ollantaytambu, Machu Picchu) are vivid testaments to their presence along the western cordillera. (These and many others are as impossible to explain in human terms as Baalbek, the Pyramids, and Stonehenge.) Though the record of Anunnaki expansion is quite evident today, it was a slow, deliberate process spanning several thousand years. First, they had to wait until the decimated humans could renew themselves enough to resume their now-essential roles. Next, their own culture and lifestyle had to be reestablished in their original base of operations—today's Middle East. In the meantime, everybody—gods and humans alike—had to be housed, clothed, and fed, which is what all efforts were initially turned toward accomplishing.

DOMESTICATION

In *The Twelfth Planet* Zecharia Sitchin calls Sumeria "The Sudden Civilization," which is exactly what it was when it blossomed out of nowhere nearly 6,000 years ago. However, its roots extend back twice that far, deep into the mountains that form a crescent shape in Mesopotamia, Syria, and Israel. That area has been known since antiquity as "The Fertile Crescent"—for good reason. The first official traces of domesticated plants and animals appear there around 10,000 B.C., which scientists acknowledge was the time and point of origin for virtually all the domesticated agriculture and animal husbandry that has subsequently spread around the world.

That acknowledgment leaves scientists in the unenviable position of having to rationally explain not only how, but also why this incredible transformation occurred. Their best effort so far is pointing out that the sudden end of the Ice Age provided a favorable climate in all of those mountains, which is true as far as it goes. However, the Ice Age climate in the lowlands below was equally suitable for growing crops and animals, and was even better after the Ice Age. A further difficulty is that—with no apparent reason to do so, and with no discernable record of progression from hunting and gathering to even a partially agrarian lifestyle—the primitive Stone Age "savages" who supposedly turned into the first farmers underwent their transformation full-bore in a literally "overnight" conversion. This makes no sense for two reasons:

First, modern hunter-gatherer societies studied by anthropologists have revealed that their lifestyle is a good one. The bounty of the land feeds them well in all seasons, they seldom have to work hard to acquire their daily sustenance, and they normally enjoy a surprising amount of "leisure" time. In addition, their "natural" diet provides excellent nutrition. The only drawback with the hunter-gatherer lifestyle, if it can be called a drawback, is that seasonal relocation (nomadism) works as a detriment to population growth. Farming, on the other hand, is a difficult way to live, and populations dependent on cultivation for food set themselves up for disasters like blight and drought. However, with luck and bountiful harvests, settled populations can flourish.

The second great puzzle about the first farmers is that they chose to begin cultivation in highlands, which was an imprudent choice because they are subject to extreme variations in weather, they possess thin, less-than-optimally-fertile soil, and they require construction of labor-intensive terraces to hold the poor soil in place. Without question the plains below the mountain highlands would have been a far more logical and practical place to begin; but, for whatever reasons, the very first sodbusters started their careers doing the hardest kind of farming they could choose.

Predictably, no scientists convincingly address any of these baffling mysteries, which are easy enough to resolve if we accept the Sumerian accounts of a Great Flood. Remember, science officially rejects the idea of a Great Flood, even though it dates to 11,000 B.C., immediately preceding the date (10,000 B.C.) of the first cultivation and animal husbandry. After the Flood, the plains were covered with soggy mud and silt that could not dry out or be washed away until new riverbeds provided drainage by carving their way down from the mountains above, which would have required many centuries. In the meantime, the Anunnaki and their human chattel did what they had to do to get their lives back on track—they moved into the dry highlands.

***

If you think scientists are hard-pressed trying to explain why well-adapted hunter-gatherers would wake up on the wrong side of the bed one morning and decide to exchange their relatively cushy life in a verdant valley for scratching out a hard-scrabble existence in the mountains above that valley, the hammer really drops when they try to plausibly deal with what came next: the domestication of animals and plants. Not only did those primitive hunter-gatherers suddenly convert to farming (which meant somehow acquiring all the specialized knowledge that entails), they also became topnotch geneticists and botanists who transformed several wild animals into domestic animals, and many wild plants into domestic plants! That incredible initial output produced sheep, goats, cattle, and pigs, along with wheat, barley, and legumes. Later, in the Far East, came wheat, millet, rice, and yams, along with chickens, pigs, and water buffalo. Later still, in the New World, came llamas, vicuna, maize, peppers, beans, squash, tomatoes, and potatoes.

Such widespread genetic "transformations" are, in themselves, extremely frustrating for scientists to have to try to explain in rational terms (which, of course, they cannot do, so as much as possible they try to ignore them). Even more frustrating is the incredible scientific skills those straight-from-the-Stone-Age "geniuses" displayed, skills still unmatched by the geneticists and botanists of today. What those early wizards did with plants was particularly amazing.

The wild grasses, grains, and cereals that were turned into wheat, barley, millet, rice, etc., still grow in their original forms wherever they were domesticated. However, those wild forms are not very nourishing to humans. Also, they are so tightly adapted to their individual environments (remember our discussion of niches?) that none of them fare well if transplanted, even with human care. In contrast, the domesticated versions are highly edible, provide excellent nutrition, and will grow almost anywhere with human care. If that is not a botanical "miracle," it is hard to imagine what one would be. So, what did those earliest "farmers" do to bring it about?

Incredibly, they doubled, tripled, and in some cases *quadrupled* the number of chromosomes in the wild plants! Again, that alone is enough to send scientists ducking for cover when asked to explain how it could be possible, but there is more to it than "simple" genetic manipulation. Not only were the chromosome counts multiplied in ways we would have trouble matching today, the effects of those alterations addressed specific problems inherent in all the wild plants. The first was size, with the seeds of wild grasses and grains and cereals being small in relation to their modern descendants, generally too small to easily be seen and worked with by human hands.

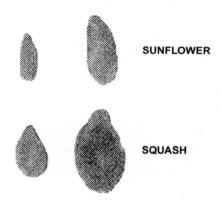

Fig. 85.

The second problem was their texture: they were extremely durable (in most instances as tough as nut shells), so they also had to be made much softer so humans could prepare, eat, and digest them. Then, when those two botanic miracles were accomplished, the first farmer/geneticists had to tackle the toughest problem of all—*glumes* and *rachises*.

Glumes are botany's name for husks, the thin covers of seeds and grains that must be removed before consumption and digestion by humans. Rachises are the miniature stems that attach seeds and grains to the stems of their plants. In the wild, glumes and rachises are strong when seeds and grains are young, so wind and rain won't knock them off before they reach maturity. However, when the seeds and grains mature and the time comes for them to release to the ground to germinate, their glumes and rachises become extremely brittle, so brittle that a breath of breeze will shatter them and release their cargo. (Think how easily dandelion rachises release their seeds.)

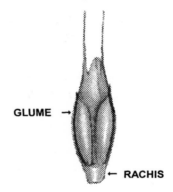

GLUME →

← RACHIS

Fig. 86.

Brittle glumes and rachises would make it impossible to harvest wild plants because all the seeds and grains would be knocked loose in the jostling of the harvesting process. Thus, in addition to making wild seeds and grains much larger and softer, the earliest farmers had to somehow make their glumes tough enough to withstand harvesting, yet brittle enough to shatter in the "threshing" and "milling" processes developed to remove them. Simultaneously, the farmers had to extend the rachises early period of strength so they could withstand harvesting, yet remain brittle enough to be easily removed from the stems by human effort. And even more amazing is that each plant's glumes and rachises required different—but extremely precise—degrees of change!

Naturally, each plant altered to have toughened glumes and rachises became utterly dependent on human intervention to reproduce, because without brittle coverings and stem attachments there is no possibility of natural propagation. However, since that is the whole point of farming, it was no problem for the early geniuses. Somehow they knew what they had to do and got on with it.

An interesting corollary to all this is that in addition to the grains and cereals already mentioned, it was also done to many other food-stuffs—bananas, dates, etc.—that have been widely consumed by humans throughout the world from the earliest civilizations until today. And another intriguing fact is that there is no sign of tough-ened glumes and rachises in the Fertile Crescent before 8,000 B.C. Then, by 7700 B.C., *only 300 years later*, there are clear indications that both had arrived. Is it possible for such radical morphological changes to occur in only 300 years?

As with most such questions about the early history of cultivation, botanists have a great deal of trouble plausibly addressing that one, though they make respectable efforts at it and all the others. (A good source of their research and opinions is *The Emergence of Agriculture*, by Bruce Smith, Scientific American Library, 1995.) However, no-thing they have tried so far has been truly satisfactory, which leaves us free to ask: "How *did* those first botanical miracles occur?"

***

In *The Wars of Gods and Men*, Zecharia Sitchin points out: "Scholars are agreed that agriculture began . . . with the harvesting of 'wild ancestors' of wheat and barley some 12,000 years ago (10,000 B.C.), but (they) are baffled by the genetic uniformity of those early grain grasses; and they are totally at a loss to explain the botano-genetic feat whereby—within a mere 2,000 years (8,000 B.C.)—such wild emmers doubled, trebled, and quadrupled their chromosome pairs to become the cultivable wheat and barley of outstanding nutritional value (and) with the incredible ability to grow almost anywhere, and with the unusual twice-a-year crops." In the same vein, he continues in *The Twelfth Planet*: "Agriculture began with the domestication of wild emmer as a source of wheat and barley, (but scientists) are unable to explain how the earliest grains were already uniform and highly specialized. Thousands of generations are needed by nature to acquire even a modest degree of sophistication. Yet the period, time, or location in which such a gradual and very prolonged process might have taken place on Earth is nowhere to be found."

Later in *The Twelfth Planet* he adds: "Spelt, a hard-grained type of wheat, poses an even greater mystery. It is the product of 'an unusual mixture of botanic genes,' neither a development from one genetic source nor a mutation of one. It is definitely a result of *mixing the genes* [emphasis added] of several plants. The notion that Man, in only a few thousand years, changed animals through domestication, is also questionable." Think about what that paragraph means. Besides being abundant in some of the very first farming communities, spelt is so genetically complex it could not possibly have resulted from "natural" means. It is a product of genetic manipulation, plain and simple, so how could humans of that era create such a hybrid?

In *The Wars of Gods and Men* Sitchin builds on that question by noting: "Coupled with these puzzles (about grains) was the equal suddenness with which every manner of fruit and vegetable began to appear from the same area at almost the same time; and the simultaneous 'domestication' of animals, starting with sheep and goats, that provided meat, milk, and wool. How did it all come about when it did? Modern science has yet to find the answer; but the Sumerian texts already provided it millennia ago." And what do those texts offer as an explanation?

Zecharia Sitchin has found the best answers in a text with the ironic title (given how baffled scientists are by all this) of "The Myth of Cattle and Grain."

"When from the heights of Heaven to Earth
Anu had caused the Anunnaki to come forth,
Grains had not yet been brought forth,
(Grains) had not yet vegetated . . . .
There was no ewe,
A lamb had not yet been dropped;
There was no she-goat,
A kid had not yet been dropped . . . .
That which by planting multiplies,

Had not yet been fashioned;
Terraces had not yet been set up . . . .
The triple grain of thirty days did not exist;
The triple grain of forty days did not exist;
The small grain, the grain of the mountains
. . . . did not exist.
Tuber-vegetables of the field had not yet come forth."

But then the gods landed on Earth and quickly went to work creating their foodstuffs.

"In those days [sometime after 430,000 years ago],
In the Creation Chamber of the gods,
In the House of Fashioning, in the Pure Mound,
Lahar (wooly cattle) and Anshan (grains) were beautifully
fashioned.
The abode was (thus) filled with food for the gods."

And in another place:

"After Anu, Enlil, Enki, and Sud (Ninti)
Had fashioned the Black-Headed people,
Vegetation that luxuriates they multiplied . . .
Four-legged animals they brought into existence;
(and) in the E.DIN they placed them (all)."

Can it be said any plainer than that? And keep in mind, this process of "filling the abode" occurred not once but twice: first, after the initial Anunnaki arrival on Earth; then again after the Great Flood buried all fields and pastures under countless tons of water and mud, erasing everything that had been built up during more than 400,000 years. The texts go on to say that when the Anunnaki were forced to start over again in the Fertile Crescent highlands, they used animals and seeds salvaged by the few humans Enki had saved, along with samples of others that had been sent to Nibiru and which had to be returned to, and reintroduced into, their place of origin. [This might explain the delay (to around 7,700 B.C.) for the appearance of tough rachises and glumes. They had to wait from around 11,000 B.C. for Nibiru's next approach to the solar system.]

Considering how realistic and literal these terms and processes appear to even the most casual observer, it seems ludicrous to insist they are mere "myths." These passages and others indicate the Sumerians were telling the truth as they understood it. Not only were they themselves created by the gods in a "Creation Chamber," a "House of Fashioning," the plants and animals they used were created the same way! All three were put into the E.DIN expressly to serve the needs of the gods, and the fact that those plants and animals also aided humans was secondary.

***

Corn deserves special mention in this context because even botanists acknowledge it is a plant that reveals an exceptionally "unnatural" degree of "evolution." The official theory is that sometime between 5,000 and 10,000 years ago, unknown genius horticulturalists among the earliest American Indians took a hardy, finger-sized, wild perennial with a multiyear lifespan (much like a weed), and by using nothing more than standard crossbreeding techniques supercharged it into the forearm-sized staple we call maize. (The original lives on, by the way, looking just as it did at its beginning, showing the typical genetic stasis alongside its "freak" offspring.)

According to the botanists' scenario, the unknown genius horticulturists took that small, hardy prototype and transformed it into a mutant monster riddled with numerous inexplicable genetic defects. Those defects somehow crept in during the enlarging process, to a point where modern corn has lost so much natural hardiness it must be protected from a wide array of unnatural ills and blights. Also, its lifespan was cut from a multiyear cycle to one short growing season. (Whose bright idea was *that*?) From the prototype's standpoint it was a poor trade, but for early humans it was a gustatory windfall because the result was so versatile and nourishing.

If we assume the Sumerians recorded history accurately when they said the Anunnaki created humans by genetic manipulation, can we further assume they developed maize for the specific use of their manufactured servants? That notion is supported by every ancient culture that has anything to say about how they acquired maize. They insist it was a "gift" from the "gods" who "created" and "ruled" their ancestors; so who among us knows enough to say they are wrong?

***

Cattle, too, have an interesting history. Until recently, scientists assumed cattle arose in the Fertile Crescent highlands along with all the other domesticated animals and plants we have been discussing. Recently, though, studies using the mitochondrial DNA (mtDNA) of cattle (we will more fully discuss mtDNA in a later chapter) have revealed the startling fact that Indian cattle broke away from their ancestral lineage between 117,000 and 275,000 years ago (which averages out to about 200,000). This tells us two things: first, around 200,000 years ago at least some Anunnaki had set up shop in the Indus Valley (where they returned to and redeveloped after the Great Flood); and second, Enki and Ninti were not the only Anunnaki who could accomplish genetic manipulation. Apparently whoever was in charge in the Indus Valley 200,000 years ago was busy creating the ancestors of the most useful and versatile domestic animal on the planet.

The mitochondrial DNA of cattle also tells us that the first domestic lineage split into two strains somewhere between 22,000 and 26,000 years ago. These two strains gave rise to modern African and European cattle, which means they cannot—as scientists previously believed—be descended from the Near Eastern cattle that were domesticated only 10,000 years ago in the Fertile Crescent. According to the genetic evidence, the four major strains of domesticated cattle (Indian, African, European, and Near Eastern) follow the pattern of appearing rather suddenly, without predecessors, at various times in the various places that gave them their names.

Fossil evidence shows that the degree of change cattle underwent in their domestication process was comparable with what happened to the grasses, grains, and cereals to make them more easily handled by humans. They were greatly reduced in size, strength and, no doubt, ferocity. The result is clear in these 4,000 year old toe bones of wild and domestic Syrian cattle.

Fig. 87.

This is one of the first in what promises to be a series of discoveries proving the vast majority of domesticated plants and animals did *not*, as scientists currently believe, blossom into existence in the Near East around 12,000 years ago, then multiply and flourish until 6,000 years ago, when decline set in and the torrent became a trickle. (One of the last major changes occurred around 3,000 years ago, when "modern" bread wheats began replacing the unusual emmer wheats earlier commented upon by Zecharia Sitchin.) Genetic testing on other domestic animals and plants should yield origin dates similar to cattle: well beyond the narrow range when scientists believe it occurred, yet within the wider parameters outlined by the Anunnaki and passed on to the Sumerians to inscribe to posterity. (In late 1997, the mtDNA of domestic dogs, long considered 15,000 years old, showed they were actually 100,000 to 135,000 years old!)

***

When things finally settled down on Earth after the Great Flood, the Anunnaki and their human servants/slaves lived and worked and propagated for several thousand years, steadily reestablishing the functions and efficiency of the civilizations that had been wiped out. But then, as mentioned earlier, at around 2,000 B.C. a tumultuous power struggle developed among the Anunnaki elite (particularly between Ninurta and Marduk, the firstborn sons of Enlil and Enki), which culminated in a series of nuclear exchanges that decimated the three main Anunnaki strongholds (Mesopotamia, Egypt and Sinai, Indus Valley). The Anunnaki who survived were never the same and slowly withdrew from worldly affairs, leaving humans more and more in charge of their own fate.

By the time of Nibiru's most recent decades-long journey through the solar system, at around 200 B.C., the last remaining gods packed up and returned home. The long reign of the Anunnaki on Earth was over . . . but that does not mean their presence is no longer felt.

ECHOES OF THE PAST

As noted earlier, the genetic difference between humans and gorillas is only 2.0% of their total DNA. Chimpanzee DNA is even closer to ours, with a difference as small as 1.0%. So our genetic similarity superficially supports the idea that humans and apes evolved from a common ancestor in Earth's dim, distant past. As also noted, despite such close genetic similarity, apes and humans cannot crossbreed. This is not surprising, however, since not even extraordinarily close higher primates can crossbreed. For example, chimpanzees cannot mate with bonobos, which are nothing more than smaller, smarter chimps. And mountain gorillas cannot mate with lowland gorillas. So it stands to reason that if primates that are virtually identical in outward appearance cannot mate, a human-ape hybrid would be bizarre indeed.

Fitting in with this is what we learned about hominoids in Part III. Their separate species are apparently no more able to interbreed than chimps and bonobos or the gorillas. As we found, they maintain clearly distinct breeding populations within their general categories (i.e., at least three types of Bigfeet). So it seems safe to assume the tendency among indigenous primates is toward highly restricted breeding parameters. This brings us to modern humans, who—as usual—stand miles apart from every other primate on the planet. If nearly identical species like chimps and bonobos and mountain and lowland gorillas (and, no doubt, hominoids) have acquired enough genetic divergence to prevent interbreeding, how could it be that the most widely divergent types of humans (say, Pygmies and Watusis, or Nordics and Aborigines) easily procreate?

We have somehow acquired the remarkable capacity to interbreed among ourselves with an ease that puts us in rare company in the animal kingdom. Species like horses, dogs, cats, sheep, cattle, etc. can do the same, but they are not "pure" species. Their genetic codes have been artificially manipulated to give them the wide divergence of breeds they exhibit. (Remember, scientists contend such animals evolved naturally until humans found them useful and genetically altered them by controlled breeding. Sumerians say such animals—as well as domesticated plants—were genetically *developed* by the Anunnaki for their own—and human—use.)

At any rate, rather than following the clear primate trend of being unable to hybridize, we humans have miraculously acquired (or been given) a genetic advantage that permits us to mate with even the most divergent examples of our species. (This includes being able to hybridize with hominoids, a la Zana's story.) So who would benefit most from us having such reproductive fecundity? The Anunnaki, who wanted to produce as many of us as possible, as soon as possible.

***

Despite huge segments of genetic code that match perfectly, humans and the great apes (gorillas, chimpanzees, and orangutans) possess some highly unusual differences. The most significant of these is the reduction of the great apes' 24 chromosome pairs down to the 23 humans possess. How could such a comprehensive change occur? Could it possibly have resulted from the "natural" effects of evolution? Think back to when we were trying to find a way to make gorillas and humans genetically compatible. Remember? We found we had to reduce the 24 chromosomes of gorillas down to the 23 of humans, but we couldn't remove or add an entire chromosome because that would do too much damage. Do you recall our solution? We *spliced* two of the gorilla chromosomes together to create one for our linebacker. Now, look at chromosome #2 in humans compared to the #2's and #3's of gorillas, chimps, and orangutans. How do you suppose Mother Nature alone might have managed such a spectacular feat of genetic engineering?

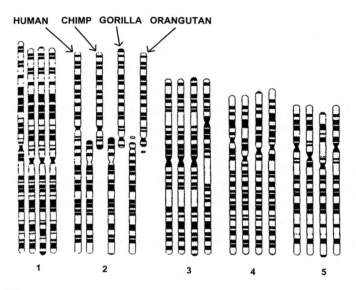

HUMAN CHIMP GORILLA ORANGUTAN

Fig. 88.

Of course, there are more differences between humans and great apes than one spliced chromosome. Human chromosomes have several subtle inversions, and many key segments reside in non-matching locations. All of which begs the obvious question of why and how did all of those things get switched around? In Darwinian terms, how might such highly unusual, remarkably specific, out-and-out chromosomal "rearrangements" have developed?

Well, chromosomes are made up of genes, and scientists insist random mutations are the only natural changes that occur in genes. A random mutation can be positive if it adds something to an organism that is so advantageous natural selection will retain it and spread it through the species' gene pool; or negative if it is destructive enough to be weeded out by natural selection; or neutral if it produces an effect that neither helps nor hinders the organism and so may be retained or discarded without noticeable effect.

Over time the relentless pressures of natural selection favor organisms with properly functioning genes, or at least genes with no negative segments, the net result of which should be species with rela-

293

tively "clean" genes having only positive or, at most, neutral mutations being passed to succeeding generations. For example, assume a severe negative mutation occurs and a tailless Cebus monkey is born. Is a monkey whose tail is vital to its lifestyle likely to live long enough to reproduce? Or say a chimpanzee is born with cystic fibrosis. Could it reach maturity? Or a gorilla with severe diabetes. Would it live to pass on the faulty genes that produced its fatal disorder?

No, no, and no. Of course, tailless monkeys can be born in the wild, as can two-headed calves and other freaks of Nature caused by faulty sperm-egg connections. But true genetic disorders like cystic fibrosis and diabetes are almost never expressed in the animal kingdom (and if they are, they die out quickly). Only humans and certain domesticated animals and plants (the ones the Sumerians tell us the Anunnaki created for their own use) consistently produce such gene-based disorders—and what is worse, we humans carry over 4,000 of them!

Another topic of human concern should be our extra-long microsatellites. Microsatellites are strings of repetitious DNA, with each string consisting of a sequence of two to five nucleotides repeated many times. Gene mappers use microsatellites as landmarks, but otherwise they are of no known use because most of them occur in junk DNA, the long sections of seemingly inert material that separates the gene segments that produce proteins. However, occasionally microsatellites are found within the working segments of our genes, and some of those can be harmful.

Trinucleotide repeats are repeated sequences of three nucleotides, and these cause certain genetic diseases (such as Huntington's disease and fragile X syndrome). When closely studied by geneticists to see what the problem with trinucleotides might be, they made an interesting discovery. It turned out that humans have substantially more and substantially longer microsatellites than any other primate. In fact, trinucleotide repeat diseases have never been seen in any other species studied by geneticists! So, how might we have acquired such a unique set of genetic disorders? Certainly not by the "natural" means scientists insist are the only way genes can mutate.

Given the fact that we humans are alone among primates with our trinucleotide repeat diseases, and we carry over 4,000 built-in genetic disorders while our closest genetic relatives carry next to none, we can legitimately ask: *Does this make evolutionary sense to anyone?* If the Darwinists are right and humans and apes are descended from a common ancestor we shared in the depths of pre-history, why weren't our genes organized as well as theirs in the same weeding-out process we all were supposedly subjected to? How can ape genes be so much "cleaner" than ours? And why do we continue producing defective specimens in such tremendous numbers? More to the point, how did such a devastating array of faulty genes work their way into our gene pool?

In Darwinian terms there are, of course, no acceptable answers, so this is yet another of those sensitive areas science does not publicly address in the hope ordinary people will stay too ignorant about it to point it out and force them to confront it. However, confront it they must, eventually, because truth will ultimately prevail, and the truth here is that consistently expressed genetic disorders become per-manent fixtures in the gene pool of a species and are passed on to posterity only if they are *put into* the DNA code itself. They can not and would not develop by natural means. This is a mind-boggling, reputation-crushing claim, but it is fundamentally true.

It is equally true that any all-powerful, omnipresent, one-and-only "God" even halfway worthy of the title should have been able to do a much better job of creating a "divinely chosen" species made "in His own image." At the very least, it can be argued, He should have left us in better physical shape than apes, monkeys, hominoids, and countless other "lower" creatures.

THE MOTHER OF ALL PROOFS

Before Lucy's discovery, whenever anthropologists tried to chart the evolution of humans from their ancient ancestors, they inter-preted the fossil record based on Louis and Mary Leakey's dating of Homo Habilis at 2.0 million years ago. From that starting point they would extrapolate back to when they estimated hominids and apes most likely diverged from the remote ancestor everyone "knew" they had to share. That divergence was pegged in the 10 to 15 million year range to give evolution plenty of time to perform its miracles. However, in the 1960's biologists began to question their colleagues' assumptions. Worse, they began doing experiments to see if what they knew (biology) matched with what the anthropologists claimed. That created a schism between biologists and anthropologists that has grown wider with the passing years.

By analyzing blood from baboons, chimps and humans, biologists found major differences between the cells of the chimps and the baboons. Now, one could argue that chimps and baboons are much more alike than chimps and humans, yet the chimp-baboon difference was vast, indicating they split from their common ancestor way back at 30 million years ago. Then, stunningly, the difference between humans and chimps was found to be so small that the estimate for their split was only 5 to 8 million years! This knocked anthropologists' estimates well out of the ballpark, which, understandably, they did not appreciate. They began to name-call the biologists, accusing them of everything short of criminality. However, later experiments proved the biologists correct, even though a 5 to 8 million year split left only 1 to 4 million years for the earliest Australopithecines (Anamensis) to leave the trees, rise up off all fours, and supposedly start marching toward us.

With that important success under their belts, the biologists kept at it. In the late 1980's they began looking closely at something called mitochondrial DNA (mtDNA, already mentioned in our discussion of cattle), which is an organelle, a free body within a cell that is not a part of its nucleus. We inherit mtDNA from our mothers, which lets us trace family trees at the genetic level because it is not scrambled every generation by being mixed with our fathers' genes.

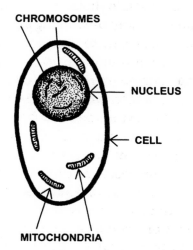

Fig. 89.

Another interesting trait of mtDNA is that it carries observable random mutations, the natural kind scientists insist are the only ones that can ever occur. And guess what? Those mutations occur at what scientists have established as the "normal" rate for DNA: 2.0% to 4.0% of the total over one million years! Such a glacial pace is blindingly faster than entire genes can ever hope to mutate, which all but eliminates the possibility of *any* theory of evolution being valid—not natural selection or even punctuated equilibrium. Anyway, the random mutations of mtDNA stamp them as individually as fingerprints—no two are ever alike. Thus, differences in the rates of mutation between them can be calculated and compared.

When this was done to the mtDNA of women from races and cultures all around the world, yet another unexpected result was found, and it was far more disconcerting than before. Starting at the massive gene pool of modern humanity (the equal of a molecular ocean), moving back toward its major tributaries, past its broad deltas and sluggish swamps, back along the thin threads that lead to the true source of us all, they found they could trace our history all the way back to our very first mother (or a small group of genetically-linked mothers), a seeming impossibility but a well-established outcome of the laws of probability. They located the first Eve!

297

Creationists contend that the Bible's Eve lived only 6,000 years ago, making her contemporaneous with the early Sumerians. For as questionable as that might be, the date the biologists calculated seemed equally so. They came up with an age for the "real" Eve of between 140,000 and 290,000 years ago . . . no more, no less. These average out to 215,000 years, which nearly everyone who deals with the issue (scientists and media) rounds off to 200,000 years. (Recall that the date range for the first domesticated cattle has been similarly calculated at 117,000 to 275,000 years ago, which produces a suspiciously congruent average of 195,000 years.)

In addition to interpolating a ballpark date for the first Eve's origin, the biologists found her homeland could also be pinpointed: Africa—specifically, *in southern Africa*. Because the majority of accepted hominid fossils have been located in Africa, most anthropologists would agree humans probably evolved there. But to accept that our species appeared only 200,000 to 300,000 years ago would be a Darwinian sacrilege because it would leave an impossibly short time for such a wholesale transformation from Homo Erectus (Neanderthals would have been contemporaneous), a point anthropologists simply cannot concede. However, not even the hardest of hard-core Darwinists can deny that what the Sumerians said is a distant echo of the biologists' results.

***

The Sumerians claim the Anunnaki landed on Earth 430,000 years ago. The gold miners in southern Africa revolted at 285,000 years ago. Shortly thereafter, Enki and Ninti went to work creating a suitable slave. Within an unspecified period of time (anywhere from several hundred to several thousand years) humans were created, refined, and made fertile. No matter how long that process required, the starting point of 285,000 years ago is remarkably close to the upper limit established by the biologists—290,000 years ago. Such timeframe compatibility cannot plausibly be explained away because the facts are undeniable. Like Babe Ruth and Joe Namath, though at a much higher level, the Sumerians called their shots 5,000 years ago (exactly as they did with their accurate descriptions of Uranus, Neptune, and Pluto). Then, since the 1980's experiments, everything surrounding those "myths" has been verified by modern scientists. Ironic, isn't it?

WHO DID WHAT TO WHOM?

Hopefully by now you are willing to presume the Sumerians may have been right about the Anunnaki creating humanity. Assuming they did, what was the sequence of events? Who were the original guinea pigs? Where did they go from there? And how well does the fossil record fit with the Sumerian accounts? All of those questions begin and end with the Neanderthals, those thick-boned, heavily-muscled, extra-long-armed, bent-kneed, splay-footed, slope-headed, brow-ridged, night-visioned, big-nosed, short-necked, heavy-jawed, chinless brutes with the bun-shaped knobs at the backs of their skulls and—despite popular misconception—bodies that were very likely covered with dense hair because they lived for millennia in extremely cold climates without leaving behind a trace of hide garments or sewing paraphernalia.

That last point is crucial because it goes directly to the heart of whether Neanderthals can be considered human relatives. Though nothing else about them seems human, if their skin was haired to the same extent and in the same pattern as ours (wide variations but like no other primates, including hominoids), it could be argued that they deserve a branch on our family tree. Unfortunately, neither skin nor hair fossilizes, so we have no way to determine if Neanderthals were haired in the human or primate pattern. Despite that lack of evidence, textbook reconstructions have invariably portrayed them having body hair like humans, from smooth-skinned to lightly hirsute. Why? Because traditional scientific dogma required that even if Neanderthals could not be considered human in the same sense as Cro-Magnons, they were at worst only a small step removed.

The evidence is overwhelming that no physical aspect of Neanderthals can be compared to humans in any way. Certainly not their bones, which are about as far from human bones as gorilla bones are (see Figs. 30 and 31). In fact, Neanderthal bones compare much better with gorilla bones than with human bones, so that seems reason enough to consider them as probably hair-covered. But the best reason is their likely close relationship to hominoids. Remember that Zana, the captive Alma who produced four robust, dark-skinned human hybrids, was in all likelihood a Neanderthal. Also remember that she was covered with hair but none of her children were, which tells us full body hair is a recessive gene when combined with the human gene prohibiting it.

Put another way, the human "hairless" gene is strongly dominant, which selects for that trait in every mating. Recall how Enki and Ninti strove to create humans "in their own image," and were not satisfied with their prototypes until one had "the (smooth) skin of the gods." This can explain why such a trait would be so dominant. The Anunnaki duo wanted us like that and kept manipulating the gene(s) that select for smooth skin until the results satisfied them.

Given the above, it stretches logic to depict Neanderthals as physical brutes adapted to frigid weather (recall their unique nasal passages), yet covered by human patterns of body hair. It seems far more likely they were simply the most recent step on the ladder of *micro*evolution for Earth's fully-haired indigenous primates, which began well before Lucy was alive and continues on with the hominoids of today.

Supporting the human-Neanderthal dichotomy is the recent analysis of a minute sample (0.4 grams) of DNA recovered from the first Neanderthal ever found. (This was detailed in Part II, pages 68 and 69.) As was noted, that analysis showed Neanderthals appear to lie somewhere in the genetic midrange between humans and chimpanzees. From a Darwinist point of view that puts all Neanderthals hopelessly beyond the reach of any close familial link with humans. But from my standpoint it positions them perfectly to be at least a part (however small) of humanity's parent stock.

***

The dominant part, naturally, would be the Anunnaki, though it is hard to imagine when we might obtain some of their unadulterated genes. To find adulterated (mixed) Anunnaki genes we may have to look no further than our own bodies because we are much more like them than the Neanderthals, in the same way Zana's hybrid offspring were much more like humans than like her. We should not, however, think of ourselves as hewing very closely to the Anunnaki physiological profile. For one thing, they deliberately chose not to give us lifespans to rival their own (the reason is never clear). Their need for us to be reproductively prolific is a possible reason; another is that it might have better suited the "god-slave" relationship they wanted.

Of course, the lifespans of early humans were reputed to be much longer than today. In the Old Testament, from Adam forward, characters routinely lived hundreds of years, with a few like Methuselah pushing 1,000. The Sumerian texts also say the Anunnaki could grant "immortality" to humans whenever they deemed it to be appropriate. Several humans were thus rewarded for one reason or another. (By the way, if we accept the Old Testament's early lifespans as real, then either the human stock has badly degenerated since then, or the Anunnaki later inflicted on us some kind of "planned obsolescence.")

Another marked Anunnaki-human difference lies in our innate intelligence. The Anunnaki appear to possess phenomenal IQ's, possibly to a degree where they retain every detail they ever learn over their vast lifetimes. Assuming they gave us brains like theirs—a strong likelihood given the apparent structural differences between Neanderthal and human brains—it would explain the tremendous increase in our mental abilities relative to all other primates. But in the same way they gave to us, they also took away. No one doubts that we humans use only a small portion of our brains, with a majority of estimates hovering around 10% total usage (a shockingly small amount given how much physiological capacity is required to keep our brains alive and well). However, whether 10% or as much as 50%, we were definitely shortchanged, and it seems logical to assume that was done to us to keep us from ever being able to "rival" our creators.

In this regard, a strong indication of our greatly diminished brain capacity is found in the remarkable feats idiot savants are capable of (recall Dustin Hoffman in *Rainman*). Imagine that the Anunnaki inserted some kind of partition mechanism to seal off most of our brains from our access, leaving us only what we need to be functional as their slaves and servants. To ourselves we are brilliant, but compared to them we are morons. Then comes idiot savants, brain-damaged people whose damage also effects their partitions. Like window shades with tiny holes in them, the damaged partitions permit savants to "see" into narrow bands of their brains' closed-off sections, where they can access small portions of the incredible mathematical and musical skills (among others) we all might have full access to if we could somehow remove our partitions. But the good news is, if genetic manipulation continues forward at the pace it currently maintains, someday we might be able to do just that.

***

These human-Anunnaki comparisons can go on and on, but one of the questions we have to deal with is: "Who were the original guinea pigs?" Answering that comes down to deciding whether you believe the greatest degree of upgrade can be made in a primitive species through the artificial means of genetic manipulation, or by the "natural" means of miscegenation with a superior species. In my opinion, the best available evidence indicates that it was done by genetic manipulation. I believe there had to be a dramatic upgrade in the guinea pigs before the Anunnaki could successfully interbreed with them to then produce only slightly improved hybrids. Others feel that genetic manipulation could only produce a barely functional prototype, and that real improvement could not occur until the Anunnaki began inserting their genes more comprehensively through miscegenation (a la the hybrids produced by Zana).

Zecharia Sitchin believes the original guinea pigs were Homo Erectus, based on when the Anunnaki began their slave-creation program—285,000 years ago. By then Erectus was already a long-lived, widespread species (in Africa, Europe, Asia, and southeast Asia). He also accepts the official timeline for the Neanderthals' appearance (put at 200,000 years ago), which means Erectus would be the most likely genetic match for the Anunnaki at 85,000 years earlier. He assumes if the Anunnaki did their gene-splicing experi-

ments on Erectus, the likely result would have been the Neanderthals, who were a distinct, though hardly a comprehensive, advance.
Then, because the physiological gap between Neanderthals and the
next phase of the experiment, the Cro-Magnons, was as wide as the
Grand Canyon, he feels only miscegenation could have closed it.

Sitchin's scenario is easy enough to imagine. No matter how "fair"
Neanderthal females may have been in the eyes of Anunnaki males (as
the Bible tells us), or butt-ugly (as their skulls indicate), those good
enough to be servants or field workers would qualify as sex partners
by proximity alone. (Zana wasn't within whiffing distance of "fair,"
yet she qualified.) Then, when they finally became fertile (which
could have required centuries), any Anunnaki-Neanderthal hybrids
would be dramatic upgrades. Those upgrades would be far superior to
the original Adamu (Neanderthals) produced by genetic manipulation
. . . they would be the Cro-Magnons. Without doubt this scenario is
possible; it could have happened exactly as Sitchin believes.

I respectfully differ with him on this key point, however, because
I am convinced that if the Anunnaki could genetically manipulate
the guinea pigs to any degree, they would not have stopped experimenting until they got most, if not all, of what they claimed they
were after: "Let us make the Adamu in our own image." Neanderthals were simply not much of an upgrade from Homo Erectus,
while there was a light-year of difference between Neanderthals
and Cro-Magnons. In that vast physiological gulf I see the handi-
work of Enki and Ninti, rather than the animal couplings of two
creatures (Neanderthals and Anunnaki) so different in every meaningful way as to make their unions seem acts of pathetic desperation rather than the thoroughly enjoyed—and sometimes mutually
exclusive ("paired")—couplings described in the Sumerian texts.

In my view the Neanderthals had to be the guinea pigs that were
transformed by genetic manipulation into Cro-Magnons, who did
actually look enough like the Anunnaki to reasonably be considered "fair" in their eyes. From then on Nature took its course to
produce demigods, who also mated with the manufactured Cro-
Magnons, and far more often than the Anunnaki because there

were so many more demigods. Ultimately, all of that sexual activity (which Enlil deplored in his "let all of the Adamu drown" argument to the Great Assembly) altered the breed enough to produce humanity as we are today. I think a closer examination of the two principals will bear me out.

CRO-MAGNON VS. NEANDERTHAL

As noted in Part II, Cro-Magnons are considered human—but not exactly. They had slightly heavier bones and muscles than we do, they were taller (many over 6 feet), and their brains were somewhat larger (though not necessarily smarter). Yet they had our slight browridges, foreheads that went up rather than back, and our nicely domed heads. Their eyesockets were small and rectangular like ours, and their nasal passages were reduced and had the uplifted bridge of bone that means their noses stood off their faces like ours. So scientists finally have it right about Cro-Magnons: they *were* humans, but at an "early" stage of development. However, the same scientists get confused again when they try to decide if those early humans "evolved" from the Neanderthals, or if the two were exclusive species that seldom if ever mated.

Anthropologists support the evolution theory because history demonstrates that human populations inevitably intermix, whether for reasons like community enhancement (to obtain "new blood"), or political (tribal) alliances, or stealing women during "war." Working against them, however, is the fossil record, which has yet to produce even a hint of such mixing. For example, Neanderthal temporal bones, which surround the inner ear, reveal small semicircular canals and an inner ear shape markedly different from humans (as different as those between ape species). Also, biologists have reams of data indicating that at least in this case, little if any mingling took place. They have found that human genes are so recent, relatively speaking, and have such overall consistency and uniformity, it suggests we have been as we are since the first Eve spawned us around 200,000 years ago (which, you should recall, is also when the "official" Neanderthal timeline begins).

If we combine the biological data with the lack of fossil evidence for mixing, we have to assume Neanderthals were not "human" enough to be acceptable to Cro-Magnons as "marriage" partners (though they might well have been sexually compatible). This leaves us with the question of how they would have reacted to each other when their paths crossed, which inevitably must have happened. Scientific tradition says that because Neanderthals begin dropping from the fossil record precisely when Cro-Magnon numbers begin to peak, Cro-Magnons must have used shrewd intelligence and/or organizational skills to outwit and thereby neutralize the Neanderthals' great brawn. This makes sense because of the brilliant design and deadly efficiency of Cro-Magnon spearpoints, which are vastly superior to the Neanderthals' primitive Mousterian hand "tools."

Countering the notion of wholesale slaughter is confirmation from Israel and other world sites that throughout the 100,000 years the last Ice Age waxed and waned, Neanderthals and Cro-Magnons "time-shared" in caves and other prime hominid living spaces. Remember that at 90,000 years ago, when Israel was lush and the Ice Age was just beginning, Cro-Magnons dominated in the caves. But 30,000 years ago, at the Ice Age peak, the same land was cold and dry, ideal for the Neanderthals who took over the lease. These facts make it unlikely that the Cro-Magnons killed off their brutish neighbors. Rather, they merely became squatters in the prime ecological niches occupied by their rivals, who—though dimwitted—could read the writing on the cave walls and realized it was time to move into the woods if they were to survive.

This is not to say there was absolutely no conflict between the two species—there probably was (though inevitably one-sided for reasons already mentioned). Nor is it to say there was absolutely no sexual intermingling between them, because there are humans today who exhibit faint echoes of Neanderthal traits. Have you ever noticed people with larger-than-normal browridges? Thicker-than-normal muscles? Stouter-than-normal bodies? Slower-than-normal brains? Hairier-than-normal skin? These and other traits whisper to us from antiquity that Neanderthal genes do indeed take occasional laps in the human gene pool. And assuming sexual compatibility, Cro-Magnon genes could also be expressed among living Neanderthals, which might explain the differences between Almas and Kaptars. In Part III we learned Kaptars are said to be slimmer, more humanlike versions of Almas, and their footprints are distinctly more human in outline (see Fig. 48). Thus, we can speculate that Kaptars might be vaguely "humanized" Neanderthals.

Despite the possibility that Cro-Magnons and Neanderthals mingled in isolated cases, the evidence overwhelmingly indicates they lived separate lives. Given that, we can conclude the Neanderthals were never in any way "human," which mitigates against Zecharia Sitchin's scenario of Homo Erectus being turned into Neanderthals, who then sexually combined with the Anunnaki to produce Cro-Magnons, who were the demigods that have become us—human beings. I think the lack of mingling more clearly points to the Anunnaki genetically manipulating Neanderthals into Cro-Magnons, who then mated with the Anunnaki to produce demigods, who over time mated with the "wild" Cro-Magnons (the rejects and runaways) to become humanity as we know it.

KINKS IN THE TIMING CHAIN

The last thing to consider is whether the fossil record supports the Sumerian accounts of humanity's "creation" at the hands of Anunnaki "gods"; or the Darwinist position that Homo Erectus (or possibly the latest discovery, Homo Antecessor) "evolved" into the Neanderthals and—however unlikely—also the Cro-Magnons, which went on to become humans. Given Antecessor's newness and the lack of a broad base of evidence to support it, we will keep our focus on Homo Erectus.

According to anthropologists, after 1.6 million years of developmental and intellectual stasis (recall Mary Leakey's acerbic comment about the boring sameness of their stone "tools"), Homo Erectus underwent a mysterious, rapid transformation into Nean-

306

derthals. By all accounts—including hard-core Darwinists—the event was utterly inexplicable in terms of evolutionary gradualism. Also, it produced Neanderthals around 200,000 years ago, just when Erectus conveniently went extinct. As previously noted, Neanderthals were an improvement over Erectus, but not a dramatic upgrade. Their degree of microevolution was no more than Erectus had been over Homo Habilis. Yet the differences were distinct, with—as usual—none of the intermediate stages demanded of gradualism. And—also as usual—in relative terms the changes occurred overnight.

Cro-Magnons, of course, were a dramatic upgrade from Neanderthals; so dramatic they went well beyond being inexplicable in classic Darwinian terms—they were flatly impossible. The gulf between their skeletons is simply too vast, and the Israeli caves prove they were contemporaneous for at least 60,000 years, roughly one-third of the accepted Neanderthal timeline (200,000 to 30,000 years ago). However, to make the Cro-Magnons *seem* to accommodate gradualism, scientists first said they appeared 35,000 years ago, which just happened to be when Neanderthals began going extinct. That charade was eventually exposed when 90,000-year-old Cro-Magnon fossils were found in Israel's Quafzeh Cave.

The Neanderthal date of 200,000 years ago took a similar hit from the complete 300,000 year-old skull from Petralona, Greece [Homo Heidelbergensis, discussed in Part II]. The creature who owned that skull was obviously in the Neanderthal lineage, which forced Darwinists to try to protect gradualism by terming it (and others like it) *pre*-Neanderthal. However, this is no time to concern ourselves with semantic quibbles. Whether Heidelbergensis was pre-Neanderthal (distinct but in the same line) or simply proto-Neanderthal (an early version), they were alive and well while Homo Erectus, their supposedly direct ancestors, were just beginning to go extinct.

In terms of human origins, the fossil record—while subject to mistakes and/or deliberate manipulations—is a legitimate record of life in past eras. What it plainly says is that at least pre-Neanderthals were alive around 300,000 years ago, which would make them—

rather than Homo Erectus—the likeliest targets for genetic manipulation by the Anunnaki. In terms of the Cro-Magnon fossil record, recall our observation near the end of Part II that simply because we start finding fossilized bones at a certain date, that does not mean the species did not exist earlier, even much earlier. It only means we found the first fossil of it then. Now understand that Adamu rejects and runaways were probably loose in the wilderness for a long time before they were plentiful enough for the rare event of fossilization to preserve the ones we have found. A fair guess might be 50,000 to 100,000 years—or more. This lets us plausibly push back the date for the Cro-Magnons' first appearance to 220,000 years ago—or more.

If we can accept these logical, plausible manipulations of dates, we find the first Cro-Magnon could easily have been the first Adamu lifted overhead by Ninti as she exulted, "I have made it!" By doing that we corroborate the Sumerian timeframe of 285,000 years ago as the beginning of the Anunnaki genetic experiments on the "creatures of Earth" (Neanderthals); and around 250,000 years ago might be a reasonable guess for when their work was completely finished and the newly fertile slaves (Cro-Magnons) could begin reproducing, filling Lower World gold mines and Upper World smelters, as well as fields and dwellings of the gods in both.

This scenario plausibly accommodates the biological data developed during the research on mitochondrial DNA, which has established the first Eve's upper limit at 290,000 years ago (as has subsequent genetic research into the first "Adam," which supports a date closer to 250,000). Also notice that the mtDNA results do not indicate humans are only 13,000 years old. This tells us that if a Great Flood did occur at that time (or, much less plausibly, at 6000 years ago as the Creationists claim), the Cro-Magnons were well-enough established worldwide to survive the decimation and move forward from there. And move forward they did, because we, their legacy and their progeny, are here to puzzle over their bones and artifacts, seeking definitive answers regarding who they were and how they came to be here on planet Earth.

***

Taken together, today's biological research and the fossil record dovetail perfectly to support the once outlandish—but now hopefully more believable—Sumerian accounts of human-like alien gods from our solar system's Planet "X" undertaking an extended sojourn on Earth. As you consider for yourself where the truth of these matters might lie, please keep in mind a relevant observation from Sherlock Holmes: "When you have eliminated the impossible, whatever remains, however improbable, must be the truth." That adage applies with near-mystical appropriateness to the positions of science on all of the significant points discussed in this book: they are plainly and simply and flatly *impossible*. That means the Sumerian texts—improbable though they may be—consistently provide us with a truer version of reality than our own scientists do.

SUMMATION

When I began this book I admitted its title is a bit of a misnomer in that *everything* you know is not wrong. However, I also said a great deal of what you think you know about some very important matters *is* wrong, so I hope anyone reading this far has come to the point of accepting at least that much as accurate. We certainly have found that nothing we think we know about the beginnings and subsequent development of life on Earth is right. It could not have arisen from any prebiotic soup because Earth was still scalding sludge at 4.0 billion years ago, when two distinct prokaryotes suddenly appeared, whole and complete, with physical structures and internal chemistry infinitely more complex than the largest inorganic molecules.

Darwinian gradualism does not now and never has satisfactorily explained how species appear and flourish, starting with the prokaryotes and followed by the eukaryotes at 2.0 billion years ago, which have virtually nothing in common with their assumed successors and do not seem to have evolved into them in any way. Both the prokaryotes and eukaryotes have maintained morphological stasis from their beginnings until now, which means none of them were "transformed" by evolution. That makes it quite a stretch of

309

logic to reach the scientific conclusion that, nevertheless, all subsequent life forms on the planet *must* have evolved from them.

It is an equal stretch of logic to conclude that the Cambrian Explosion can be explained in Darwinian terms. Life was unicellular from 4.0 billion years ago to around 600 million years ago (85% of its timeline), then 70 million years later every animal phyla of today appeared in 5 to 10 million years (an eyeblink in relative terms). And as long as we're stretching logic, how about Darwin's idea that every life form on Earth evolves gradually by means of random mutations selected by Nature to move species to ever higher levels of perfection in their functions? A clever idea, to be sure, but after five major extinction events that have "wiped the slate clean" and given evolution a clear field to operate in, there is still no valid evidence for it.

Another Darwinian puzzle is that while plant and animal species regularly go extinct, and previously "unknown" (not the same as "new") species are regularly discovered, no new class, order, family, or genus of animals or plants has recently come into existence. This is the exact opposite of what Darwinism predicts. As for the supposedly "pre"-human life forms, everything about them—robust bones, brawny muscles, extra-long arms, prognathous faces, small-brained skulls, night-visioned eyes, heavy jaws and teeth, missing chins, etc.—indicates they were merely bipedal primates up until Cro-Magnons appeared out of nowhere to take over the planet in an incredibly brief timespan (2.0% of the eyeblink above).

Since every fossilized hominid up to Cro-Magnon is clearly not human, they can only be the remains of something else—the hominoids. As for those "primordial bogeymen," thousands of sightings and encounters throughout history assure us they are real. Thousands of casted footprints—and thousands more found but not casted—cannot be convincingly faked, so they also assure us hominoids are real. And because they have access to everything except large metropolitan areas, in practical terms they control almost as much real estate on the planet as we do. Theirs is just the heavily forested areas where we are not designed to live comfortably. All in all, proof of their existence is a foregone conclusion—it is just a matter of time until somebody brings one in.

As for the amazing work of Zecharia Sitchin in his seven-volume *The Earth Chronicles* series, I urge everyone to explore his books and any others you find that mine the same vein of skepticism about widely believed scientific dogmas. Those doing so should conclude, as I have, that humans badly need to reexamine every opinion they now have about our true roles on Earth.

***

Everything I have related in this book has been designed to entice readers to initiate a comprehensive study of the many "unaccepted"—as opposed to "unknown"—truths about humanity. Those truths are definitely out there and not too difficult to access. All it requires is an open mind and a willingness to explore. That is the upside. The downside is that no establishment eats crow willingly, so always be aware that everything in this genre you examine—including this book—will be derided and dismissed by official mouthpieces. Critics always will first try to disparage any lack of "proper" academic credentials, which often is all that is required. But if more is necessary, they will get busy locating whatever flaws or misstatements of fact they can find—large or small—and use those few mistakes to discredit everything that is accurate.

As someone stepping into this highly charged arena for the first time, I have tried to prepare—mentally and emotionally—for the media drubbings that come with the territory. Frankly, I do not look forward to them. However, I *do* anticipate—very much so—sharing with the widest possible audience the information I have put forth in this book. I also look forward to my work contributing to the truth about the matters under discussion—the *real* truth—being officially acknowledged and/or accepted in the not-too-distant future. But superceding any apprehension or anticipation is my certainty that when the dust finally settles, I will find myself on the winning side.

I know *that* as surely as I know $2 + 2 = 4$.

BIBLIOGRAPHY

Like anyone who writes about technical matters, I am only as good as the information my work is based upon, which in turn is only as good as what I have been able to find and use. What I have put into *Everything You Know Is Wrong—Book One: Human Evolution* is only a fraction of what is available to be perused, studied, and absorbed. For those interested in trying to chart a course through the Oz-like wonderland of human/hominoid evolution/development, the following books are a solid place to start. However, they are only a start, and they are only books. Magazines, documentaries, and educational films are also available, as are equally numerous Internet sites and chat rooms that consistently provide cutting-edge information.

BOOKS ABOUT FOSSILS AND EVOLUTION

Anthology. *The First Humans: Human Origins And History To 10,000 B.C.* New York: American Museum of Natural History, 1994.

Denton, Michael. *Evolution: A Theory In Crisis.* Bethesda, Md.: Adler & Adler, 1985.

Eldredge, Niles. *Fossils: The Evolution And Extinction Of Species.* New York: Harry Abrams, 1991.

_____. *The Miner's Canary: Unraveling The Mysteries of Extinction.* London: Virgin, 1991.

Fix, William R. *The Bone Peddlers: Selling Evolution.* New York: Macmillan Publishing Co., 1984.

Gamlin, Linda and Vines, Gail (Editors). *The Evolution Of Life.* New York: Oxford Univ. Press, 1991.

Gowlett, John. *Ascent to Civilization: Archeology of Early Humans.* New York: McGraw Hill, 1993.

Gribben, John and Cherfas, Jeremy. *The Monkey Puzzle*. New York: Pantheon Books, 1982.

Johanson, Donald and Edey, Maitland. *Lucy: The Beginnings of Humankind*. New York: Simon and Schuster, 1975.

_____. *Blueprints: Solving The Mystery of Evolution*. New York: Penguin Books, 1989.

Johnson, Phillip E. *Darwin On Trial*. Lanham, Md.: Regnery Gateway Books, 1991.

Leakey, Richard and Lewin, Roger. *People of the Lake: Mankind And Its Beginnings*. New York: Anchor Press/Doubleday, 1978.

_____. *Origins Reconsidered: In Search Of What Makes Us Human*. New York: Doubleday, 1992.

Lewin, Roger. *In The Age Of Mankind*. Washington, D.C.: Smithsonian Books, 1988.

_____. *The Origin Of Modern Humans*. New York: Scientific American Library, 1993.

Smith, Bruce D. *The Emergence Of Modern Agriculture*. New York: Scientific American Library, 1995.

Strickberger, M.W. *Evolution*. Boston: Jones and Bartlett, 1990.

BOOKS ABOUT HOMINOIDS

Byrne, Peter. *The Search For Big Foot*. Washington, D.C.: Acropolis Books, 1975.

Ciochon, Olsen, and James. *Other Origins: The Search For The Giant Ape In Human Prehistory*. New York: Bantam Books, 1990.

Green, John. *Sasquatch: The Apes Among Us*. Seattle: Hancock House, 1978.

Hunter, Don and Dahinden, Rene. *Sasquatch*. Toronto, Canada: McClelland and Steward, 1973.

Krantz, Grover S. *Big Footprints: A Scientific Inquiry Into The Reality Of Sasquatch*. Boulder, Colo.: Johnson Books, 1992.

Napier, John. *Bigfoot: The Yeti and Sasquatch In Myth And Reality*. New York: E.P. Dutton, 1973.

Place, M.T. *On The Track Of Bigfoot*. New York: Dodd Mead, 1974.

Pyle, Robert Michael. *Where Bigfoot Walks: Crossing The Dark Divide*. Boston and New York: Houghton Mifflin, 1995.

Sanderson, Ivan T. *Abominable Snowmen: Legend Come To Life*. Philadelphia and New York: Chilton Company, 1961.

Shackley, Myra. *Still Living? Yeti, Sasquatch, And The Neanderthal Enigma*. New York: Thames and Hudson, 1983.

Slate, Ann and Berry, Alan. *Bigfoot*. New York: Bantam Books, 1976.

Tchernine, Odette. *In Pursuit Of The Abominable Snowman*. New York: Taplinger Pub. Co., 1970.

BOOKS ABOUT GENETICS

Bains, William. *Genetic Engineering For Almost Everybody*. New York: Penguin Books, 1988.

Edelson, E. *Genetics and Heredity*. New York: Chelsea House, 1990.

Gonick, Larry and Wheeler, Mark. *The Cartoon Guide To Genetics*. New York: Harper Perennial, 1983.

McKusick, Victor. *Mendelian Inheritance In Man*. Baltimore: Johns Hopkins University Press, 1990.

Rosenfield, Ziff, and Van Loon. *DNA For Beginners*. New York: W.W. Norton Co., 1983.

Shapiro, Robert. *The Human Blueprint*. New York: St. Martin's Press/Bantam Books, 1991.

Thompson, Larry. *Correcting the Code*. New York: Simon & Schuster, 1994.

Wills, Chris. *The Wisdom Of The Genes: New Pathways In Evolution*. New York: Basic Books, 1989.

BOOKS ABOUT PRIOR CIVILIZATIONS ON EARTH

Sitchin, Zecharia. *The Twelfth Planet*. New York: Avon Books, 1976.

_____. *The Stairway To Heaven*. New York: Avon Books, 1980.

_____. *The Wars Of Gods And Men*. New York: Avon Books, 1985.

_____. *The Lost Realms*. New York: Avon Books, Feb. 1990.

_____. *Genesis Revisited: Is Modern Science Catching Up With*

Ancient Knowledge? New York: Avon Books, Oct. 1990.

_____. *When Time Began: The First New Age.* New York: Avon Books, 1993.

_____. *Divine Encounters: A Guide to Visions, Angels, And Other Emissaries.* New York: Avon Books, 1995.

Allan, D.S. and DeLair, J.B. *When The Earth Nearly Died.* Bath, England: Gateway Books, 1995.

Corliss, William R. *Ancient Man: A Handbook Of Puzzling Artifacts.* Glen Arm, Maryland: The Sourcebook Project, 1978.

Cremo, Michael and Thompson, Richard. *The Hidden History Of The Human Race.* Badger, Cal.: Govardhan Pub. Co., 1994.

Delgado, Pat. *Crop Circles: Conclusive Evidence?* London, England: Bloomsbury Pub., 1992.

Fix, William R. *Pyramid Odyssey.* Urbanna, Va.: Mercury Media, 1984.

Hancock, Graham. *Fingerprints Of The Gods.* New York: Crown, 1995.

Hoagland, Richard. *The Monuments Of Mars: A City On The Edge Of Forever.* Berkeley, Cal.: North Atlantic Books, 1992.

Horn, Arthur D. *Humanity's Extraterrestrial Origins.* Orange Beach, Ala.: A.& L. Horn Pub., 1994.

Meaden, George Terence. *The Circle Effect And Its Mysteries.* Bradford-On-Avon, England: Artetech Pub. Co., 1990.

Mooney, Richard E. *Colony Earth.* New York: Stein and Day, 1974.

_____. *Gods Of Air And Darkness.* New York: Stein and Day, 1975.

Rux, Bruce. *Architects Of The Underworld.* Berkeley, Cal.: Frog Books (North Atlantic Books), 1996.

Tomas, Andrew. *We Are Not The First.* New York: Bantam, 1973.

West, John Anthony. *Serpent In The Sky: The High Wisdom Of Ancient Egypt.* Wheaton, Ill.: Theosophical Pub. House, 1993.

Woolley, Leonard. *The Sumerians.* New York: Barnes and Noble 1995.

INDEX